The Resilient Entrepreneur

The Methods and Mindset to Help You Succeed on Your Entrepreneurial Journey

Hardcover ISBN: 978-0-578-53977-5

Lance McNeill, MBA, MPAff

General Disclaimer

The reader is ultimately responsible for the success or failure of their business. All decisions pertaining to the planning, execution and fundraising obligations related to your business endeavors are solely your responsibility. This publication is based on compiled best practices, research and personal experience. The author makes no guarantee that any business will be successful but hopes that you will utilize this information to aid in your own success.

Disclaimer of any Responsibility for Links to Websites

This book contains links to websites which are not maintained by Lance McNeill. While we try to include only links that are in good taste and safe for our readers, we are not responsible for the content of those sites and cannot guarantee that sites will not change without our knowledge, and inclusion of such links does not imply endorsement of the linked or framed sites or their content.

Table of Contents

Introduction: The Story of Self

"There is no greater agony than bearing an untold story inside you."

- Maya Angelou

The entrepreneur's journey is filled with uplifting milestones and troughs of tribulation. The stories that inspire them to embark on their entrepreneurial journey begin long before they ever make their first sale. Their stories are unique, multifaceted and demanding. Through their experiences, they are given the opportunity to become resilient, and it's that resiliency that continues to push them closer and closer toward achieving their entrepreneurial dreams.

To demonstrate this, I want to share a bit of my own story. Before understanding how to tell my own story, I had to first understand my father's. My father was only a few years old when he and his five siblings were taken in by the Child Welfare Division of the Tennessee Department of Public Welfare. Imagine a kind of home environment where a first-grader, my eldest uncle, misses school to babysit his five younger siblings – the youngest of whom were still in diapers.

My dad's father was in jail at the time, a destination he arrived at by way of alcoholism, drug addiction and thievery; my dad's mother was aloof, absent and negligent. That led to Child Welfare intervening, collecting my dad and his siblings. Sadly, they were then separated into different children's homes.

When my dad entered the sixth grade, he and a friend began walking around neighborhoods with a push mower, earning a few dollars for each lawn they mowed. In an informal sense, they had self-employed themselves. Where did this entrepreneurial drive come from? Perhaps it was circumstance. Significant life events and adversity, such as growing up in a children's home, can often trigger a desire to act on one's own behalf to create a better path – in essence, to become an entrepreneur.[1]

Entrepreneurs benefit from a high degree of independence and autonomy, but those traits are often incompatible when you grow up a ward of the state, and your life is continuously disrupted by changes in policy, funding, etc. Consequently, in the seventh grade, my father was transferred from the children's home in Memphis to Monroe Harding Children's Home in Nashville.

When I asked my dad how he coped he said, "I didn't know any other type of upbringing outside the children's homes. If I were a child raised in Michael and Susan Dell's home, for example, and then sent to Monroe Harding, it would have been a devastating transition, but I never had those expectations.[A]

In high school my dad played football and during his senior year his team won the state championship. He was offered a full scholarship to play offensive guard at Mississippi State University, where he studied social work. After graduating, he moved to Austin, Texas, but soon realized that there were few opportunities for social workers with only a bachelor's degree

---

[A] An interesting side note: my father actually spent quite a bit of time at the Michael and Susan Dell home, where he worked for several years as part of their weekend security detail.

education. When applying for jobs, he found himself losing out to other applicants with a master's degree. When advised to go back to school and pursue a masters, he responded that he would like to use the first degree he had earned before going back for another.

So, again, in the face of adversity and rejection, he started offering landscaping and lawn maintenance services to businesses and apartment complexes. When few options exist, entrepreneurship often offers a path forward. Again, he began with just a single push-mower, mowing 15-acre apartment complexes by himself. His hard work was reflected in the quality of the jobs he completed, and his customers began referring new clients to him.

Although his business grew, he still had the dream of helping others by using his social work degree. A tangential opportunity emerged when a friend suggested he apply to become a police officer, which he did. In 1979, he started full-time with the Austin Police Department. He also kept the landscaping business going at the same time – working a combined 100+ hours each week for the first six years of his police career.

Without knowing my dad, you might think I'm exaggerating, but my father, like so many other resilient entrepreneurs, is an outlier when it comes to self-discipline and work ethic. There was never such a thing as 'not having enough hours in a day.' He would sometimes mow his customers' commercial properties at one in the morning. He received a lot of funny stares and wisecracks from people leaving the bars after they had closed, but if you've ever spent a scorching summer day in Central Texas, mowing at night had its perks.

His police work never came second or suffered because of his side business' success. Over his 28-year career with the Austin Police Department, he would move up several ranks to become a Commander, managing multi-million-dollar budgets and several hundred peace officers and support staff. When asked about balancing a growing business with a career in policing, here's what he had to say:

"The landscaping work was more of a hobby to me than a job because I genuinely enjoyed the work. I took great satisfaction driving around Austin and seeing businesses and homes that I had landscaped. It also turned out to be a good outlet from police work.

As my business grew to about 19 large customers, I couldn't keep up with the work by myself. I eventually had three employees working for me because the business was growing so rapidly. Although I worked in the business, I never took any money out for myself; the money I made, I reinvested back into buying new equipment and paying my employees.

Over the years, the business experience I gained was invaluable; putting in bids for new jobs, writing up contracts, negotiating prices with customers, paying business taxes, maintaining insurance, etc. One of the most edifying lessons I learned was when I subcontracted for a larger landscaping company that had a portfolio of high-end condominiums.

I took great pride in my business, so when the contractor told me that their customers were complaining that they didn't feel like they were getting their money's worth, I took it to heart and questioned the quality of my work. Then I found out that the contractor was charging the condos four times what they were paying me, even though I was doing all the work! It's no wonder the customers were complaining – they must have expected a Victorian garden terrace for the money they were dishing out.

Although the business did well most of the time, there were a couple of recessions over the years where I took my police salary and put it back into the business to keep it afloat and make payroll. A few of my customers went bankrupt and most of my other customers were months behind in paying us.

Over the years, having had the experience of owning my own business made me understand and appreciate small business owners and the amount of work that goes into running a successful business. You haven't known the real world until you know the business world."

Eventually, my dad sold his landscaping business to his brother, Michael. After he retired from police work, he kept a few landscaping jobs on the side to stay active and healthy. There's a lot that I learned from my father's journey that contributed to the foundation of my own entrepreneurial *story of self*, but I didn't always see it that way.

My mother, Arlene, passed away from ovarian cancer when I was ten. My parents had divorced before my second birthday and I lived with my mother full-time after their separation. My mom wasn't an entrepreneur, but she worked hard and gave me everything she could. When she got sick, she and my father agreed that if she didn't get well that I would go to live with him after she passed.

I didn't know my father like most ten-year-old boys know their father – from the time I started kindergarten until my mother became terminally ill, me and my dad never spent a full day together. My parents didn't get along at all after their divorce.

My dad would always pay child support and drop off Christmas and birthday presents on the doorstep, but we never visited face-to-face. Instead, my dad chose to focus his time and energy on his business and police career.

After my mother succumbed to the cancer, I went to live with my dad and stepmother. My mother's passing and the transition to live with my father was probably the most difficult time of my life. We buried my mother in the morning and the very same evening I spent the night at my dad and stepmother's house. That was the first night I had spent at my dad's house since I began grade school – some five years before. I felt like I was being sent to live at a stranger's house. I'm not sure many people can point to the exact day that their childhood ended and adulthood began, but for me, this was it.

A year or two after moving in with my dad, I had an opportunity to follow in my father's entrepreneurial footsteps. We lived in Bastrop, Texas, a rural county just outside of Austin. Our neighborhood was nearby the Colorado River and it seemed like just about every home in the neighborhood was surrounded by enormous pecan trees. Our next-door neighbors, the Onsteads, also had a lot of trees, but they produced more leaves than nuts.

One autumn day, I was playing outside when Mr. Onstead, a retired man in his late seventies, asked if me if I wanted to earn some extra money. He offered me $25 to rake all the leaves in his yard. That was a lot of money to a ten-year-old, so I eagerly accepted the offer without much thought about the amount of effort or time that would be needed to complete the job.

Filled with naïve enthusiasm, I grabbed one of my dad's rakes and a box of large black trash bags from Mr. Onstead. I raked up pile after pile of leaves into small mounds that rose beyond my knees. I filled bag after bag and lined them up along the fence. It only took about half an hour to realize the true depth of foliage that I had gotten myself into. I felt stranded in a never-ending sea of crackling dry leaves. Yet, on I raked, and raked some more. Every time the breeze blew, my spirits were crushed, as I watched a new batch of leaves fall from their branches and cover the freshly raked ground. I was like Sisyphus with a rake.

Dejected, I left the rake against a tree and went home. I told my dad about my unfortunate predicament, hoping he might help me negotiate more money, or at the very least some mercy, from Mr. Onstead. It was obvious that I had accepted a much larger job than I had anticipated. Gary was a little frustrated with Mr. Onstead's unfair terms, but he told me that he had made an agreement and needed to uphold his end of the deal.

The next day, I returned and continued raking, adding another row of bulging black bags along the fence line. When I depleted the entire box of trash bags, Mr. Onstead finally showed some clemency and said I had done enough. There were still plenty of leaves left to rake, but the effective hourly rate Mr. Onstead was paying was starting to dip below the minimum wage of his own working days of yesteryear, and he started to feel a little guilty. That was the first of many valuable lessons I would learn business over the years.

A few years later, when I was in the seventh grade, my dad bought an expensive new Dell desktop computer, and for the first time, there was an option to upgrade it with a CD burner. I convinced my dad to pay close to $500 dollars extra for that CD burner.

Around the same time, the pirates of the internet began seeding stolen music through peer-to-peer file-sharing networks like Kazaa and Napster. I started downloading the most popular songs, almost as soon as they were released, burned them onto a hit compilation CD and then sold them for ten dollars a pop at school. I had a first-mover advantage on the CD burning technology, and since the music was pirated, my only real cost of goods sold were the physical CDs, which cost a couple bucks each at the time. I had the creativity of an entrepreneur, but I hadn't yet developed a guiding set of values to go along with it, and I wouldn't for years to come.

When I was seventeen, in the middle of my senior year in high school, I left home and spent the rest of the school term living with friends. My father and I weren't on speaking terms and wouldn't be for another year. The last few months of school, I became consistently truant and almost didn't graduate because of my absences. Still, I somehow managed to pass my classes and walk across the stage with diploma in-hand.

After graduation, I signed a one-year lease on a two-bedroom apartment with a friend I'd known since middle school. My roommate and I both enrolled in the local community college full time while working full time at the same sandwich restaurant chain. Being financially responsible for rent, utilities, car insurance, groceries and tuition on the budget of a low-wage sandwich artisan was difficult, and some months unmanageable.

I noticed that my roommate struggled less though. Ever since high school, he made extra income by selling marijuana on the side. A lot of the side business happened at the sandwich shop we worked at. I wouldn't be surprised if every sandwich shop in

Austin, unbeknownst to the restaurant owners, has had ounces of something other than meat and cheese sold from behind the counter.

Seeing my roommate's illicit side business grow alongside my own financial struggles, I asked if we could partner. My roommate agreed. My new business partner and I pooled our funds and invested in larger quantities of product. We divided and grew our customer base. I created spreadsheets to help manage inventory, analyze sales and ensure profit margins. At a small scale, we had become the supplier to suppliers, and eventually, paying rent got a whole lot easier. Out of circumstance, I had become an entrepreneur, albeit a lawless one.

As the months went by though, I found himself being immersed in a lifestyle that didn't align with who I wanted to be. There were no posted hours on our black-market business, so "customers" would show up at our apartment anytime they wanted, often unannounced, often in the middle of the night. Some of these "patrons" showed up and expected to hang out well beyond the amount of time it took to complete a transaction.

As I sat there with them, I realized that these weren't the people I wanted to be friends with. I wanted to do something more with my life. I wanted to make my own way. I enjoyed the liberty of making my own way and becoming financially independent by selling, but I slowly recognized that it wasn't the path I wanted to continue down.

One transaction in particular went very badly. Afterward, I spent the next several weeks worrying that someone was going to surprise me in a dark parking lot after work. That's when I decided I was finished living the type of life I was living. I wasn't writing the story I wanted to for himself and I surely wasn't living a life that my mother or father would have been proud of.

Milestones of Clarity

I want to pause here because this isn't an autobiography. I'm going to share more about my work with entrepreneurs throughout this book, but this book isn't about me. I shared my *story of self*, not because I think I'm that interesting, but rather to illustrate an important lesson and to demonstrate a useful technique that I hope you will adopt for yourself.

What's the lesson in entrepreneurship? For me, telling my story, helps me trace a line through the journey that leads to writing this book. By better understanding my origin, I can shape my business goals and entrepreneurial path to align with who I am and the entrepreneur I aspire to become. Being able to do that helps keep me motivated and focused.

Research has shown that those who are more apt to self-reflection are better able to build a reservoir of knowledge about themselves, and from their experiences they are more motivated toward a sense of significance and purpose for their life.[2] In short, you can't move forward until you understand where you've been.

I also grappled with *how* to tell my *story of self*. I could have written my story in a way that focused on establishing my credibility as a subject matter expert, but there's nothing vulnerable or courageous about advertising your accomplishments. It's much more difficult to expose your own blemishes and reflect on the mistakes you've made.

Brené Brown is an expert on vulnerability, trust and living courageously. In her bestselling book, *Rising Strong*, she shares some thoughtful words of wisdom about telling our story of self: "We attempt to disown our difficult stories to appear more whole or more acceptable, but our wholeness – even our wholeheartedness – actually depends on the integration of all our experiences, including the falls [and fails]."[6] Our story of self shouldn't just be a prideful highlight reel. It should be honest about both the successes and the difficult lessons learned.

A vulnerable and authentic *story of self* also helps us recognize the important milestones of clarity. If you listen closely to the stories of successful entrepreneurs, you'll recognize when these milestones happened in their journeys.

Take Sara Blakey, for example. Sara is the founder of SPANX shapewear and undergarments. She founded the company in 2000, and twelve years later, she became the youngest female entrepreneur in the United States to become a billionaire.[3] Before she started her own business, Sara was selling fax machines. In an interview with Guy Raz on NPR's popular podcast, *How I Built This*, she recounts her moment of clarity: "When I was selling fax machines door to door, I kept feeling like I'm in the wrong movie. Where's the director? Where's the producer? This is not my movie and I was really determined to create a better life for myself."[4]

I had the exact same realization in the movie I saw myself in. So, I did what every desperate person should do when they feel that they're out of options - I reached out for help. The most consistently reliable person in my life that I knew I could call on for unconditional support was my grandmother. The next week I moved into her home. I lived with my grandmother for the next five years and finished my undergraduate degree. I never sold marijuana or any other illegal substances ever again, and a few months after moving in with my grandmother, my father and I began to mend our relationship.

I finished my graduate degree during the Great Recession. After graduating, I submitted close to four hundred job applications including an application to become a volunteer with the U.S Peace Corps. I was invited to be part of a pilot group of volunteers going to Namibia to teach entrepreneurship to secondary school students and advise micro-enterprises in rural communities.

The school I taught at was in "the bush," meaning it was very rural. We didn't have electricity in the classrooms, so we taught with the windows open and hoped for a breeze to bring relief on 100+ degree days. During my first semester of teaching, two other teachers who taught entrepreneurship resigned without a replacement. There is no substitute system in Namibia and it's very difficult to recruit teachers to move from the more urban areas into the bush. So, I picked up their classes and began teaching ten classes a week with more than 125 students spread across three grade levels. The work was fulfilling, and the days went by quickly.

I also taught an evening class each week for aspiring entrepreneurs in the community. I had to be mindful about how to connect and build trust with both the students and the adults. Many of the community entrepreneurs were older and had lived through the oppressive apartheid system. They hadn't had many positive experiences with white people throughout their lives. Many spoke only Oshiwambo, the local tribal language, while others were bilingual in both Oshiwambo and

Afrikaans. I don't know any Afrikaans and I was only proficient enough in Oshiwambo for greetings, small talk and emergency situations – not enough to teach a business class.

My secondary school students, on the other hand, had studied English since early grade school and understood English well enough to engage with the material. So, I started an entrepreneurship club where I matched one or two secondary school students with an aspiring entrepreneur from the community. My hope was that the students would serve as translators and co-teachers of the material.

What I noticed, as a byproduct of the matchmaking, was a very valuable mentoring relationship form between the secondary school students and community members. The entrepreneurs in the community were much older than the students and thus had more life experience, and the students were learning the fundamentals of starting a business. The complement of these two perspectives was enriching for everyone involved. The students in the entrepreneurship club become some of my best, most engaged students and the entrepreneurs in the community learned how to better manage their costs and strategically set their prices for better margins and competitiveness.

I was inspired by their learning and fulfilled by the small role I played in helping them form their mentoring relationship. Recalling Sara Blakely's metaphor, I finally felt like I was starring in the movie role I was supposed to be featured in. This was the *story of self* that I wanted to tell – a story I could share proudly. My time in the Peace Corps helped mark the trailhead along the path that I'm still on today.

1: With my fellow teachers at Pendukeni Iivula Ithana High School in Namibia during the Peace Corps

As you may have noticed, I started my entrepreneurial *story of self* with my father's story. Yes, his story is his own, but my story isn't possible without understanding his journey and his father's journey before him. I can learn important lessons from their mistakes and hardships, and how they managed to overcome them.

In many ways I admire my father's ability to rise above the adversity he faced. I also recognize there was a huge chunk of my childhood when he was mostly absent. Reflecting on your own story, you might reveal certain paradoxes like this. Life's story doesn't always tie up neatly – there's dissonance and incongruence. That's okay. Loose ends are part of everyone's story.

Yet, we all have an important choice when it comes to the parts of our story that we focus on. When you see yourself in your story, are you the victim or the victor? Do you dwell on what was missing, the hardships and what might have been? Or, do you seek out the positive lessons learned to take forward with you? When you look back at the adversity in your *story of self,* do you only see things falling apart, or do you see things falling into place? This frame of mind is our first lesson in becoming a more resilient entrepreneur.

In later chapters, we'll look at practical ways to cultivate the mindset and methods that help us learn from and overcome adversity. You will learn how to see yourself as a victor of a setback, rather than a victim. It's not easy and it will take practice, but you can do it. Your ability to adapt and become more resilient is part of who you are. Literally, it's in your DNA.

In fact, emerging genetic research suggests that it might be possible to inherit the resiliency that our ancestors developed through their adversarial experiences. Dr. Sharon Moalem, bestselling author of *Inheritance: How Our Genes Change Our Lives – and Our Lives Change Our Genes*, says, "We are the culmination of our life experience, as well as the life experiences of our parents and ancestors. Because our genes don't easily forget. War, peace, feast, famine, diaspora, disease – if our ancestors went through it and survived, we've inherited it. And once we got it, we're that much more likely to pass it on to the next generation in one way or another."[5]

Who among your parents and grandparents might have helped you become more resilient through their story? It's an interesting question, and one that might encourage us to wonder how we might also help future generations become more resilient.

Over the past decade, I've coached and taught entrepreneurship to thousands of aspiring entrepreneurs and small business owners. I've worked with entrepreneurs of all ages, from middle school students to retirees. Through one-on-one coaching alone, I've logged more than 3,000 hours of consultation with businesses spanning just about every industry you can imagine. I've met amazing people from across the globe, from Namibia to Russia, Chile to the United Arab Emirates. I've listened to and walked alongside entrepreneurs as they've faced a variety of challenges along their journey. Throughout this book, I'm going to share some stories and lessons learned from these experiences, but first I'm going to ask you to share your own *story of self*.

Share Your Story

Brené Brown says, "If we can learn how to feel our way through [our] experiences and our own stories of struggle, we can write our own brave endings. When we own our stories, we avoid being trapped as characters in stories that someone else is telling."[6] This is why I'm starting this book with my own *story of self*. I believe it to be an essential part of developing into an entrepreneur, and I strongly encourage you to start your entrepreneurial journey by uncovering your story.

There is tremendous value in telling our own story – both for ourselves and for others - but it oftentimes doesn't come naturally. It requires that we engage in a process that psychologists refer to as "autobiographical remembering and reasoning." Autobiographical remembering, also referred to as autobiographical recall, happens when we recount the details of past events: *where was I? What did I do? Where did I go? How did I get there? Who else was there with me?* These questions help answer the details of the story. It's like reciting your resume.

Autobiographical reasoning, on the other hand, happens when we reflect on the meaning and significance of past events, not just a description of what happened.[7] Autobiographical reasoning helps us shape our personal identity. It allows us to reflect on how past experiences helped shape who we are in the present moment. It forces us to examine our emotions. *How did we feel when that event happened? How did that significant event help you establish the values that are important to you? Did that event set you on a different trajectory?* Autobiographical reasoning helps us establish a foundation of continuity in our identity, so that when times are most challenging, and we feel unsure about our ability to persevere, we have anchors of support that we can rely on.

Studies have shown that autobiographical reasoning is an integral part of developing and maturing our self-identity.[8] We learn from the experience of others, as well as ourselves. Certain key events in our *story of self* are drivers of our decision to embark on the entrepreneur's journey and as we will see, it's also an important step toward becoming a more resilient entrepreneur.

A mentor of mine, Rosa Rios Valdez, was the first person to encourage me to share my *story of self*. In return, I handed her a brief, superficial bio. She pushed back and encouraged me to dig deeper. "What led you to the path you're on today?" she asked. "What were the hardships and adversities you experienced and how were you made stronger by overcoming them?"

I revisited my short little bio. It stared at me, as I reflected on the more substantive journey that took me from school to work and from one job to the next. A lot of thoughts popped into my mind, but I found it challenging to put those thoughts into words. Initially, it was awkward writing about myself in such reflective, almost eulogistic prose. Compared to people I've read or heard about on the news, my own journey seemed inadequately short-lived. I wasn't even 30 years old at the time. I didn't feel like I had enough knowledge, experience or success to justify my own story – at least not yet. I mean, what did I know, really? I feel the same way today, years after writing my *story of self* for the first time.

In his book, *Hit Refresh*, Microsoft CEO, Satya Nadella admits that he "was excited to write [his] book, but also a little reluctant. Who really cares about my journey? With only a few years under my belt as Microsoft's CEO, it felt premature to write about how we've succeeded or failed…"[9]

Even the most successful CEOs and entrepreneurs feel the same reluctance about sharing their story as the rest of us. Yet, 95 percent of entrepreneurs say that learning from experience influences their professional development and growth.[10] As you'll learn throughout this book, establishing our self-identity is foundational to becoming a more resilient entrepreneur.

Looking back on my own entrepreneurial *story of self*, there's nothing particularly harrowing compared to a lot of other peoples' stories. It's true that not every child loses a parent at a young age like I did, and not every child grows up as a ward of the child welfare system like my father. We both certainly faced bouts of adversity growing up, but we could also recite stories ad nauseam about people whose struggle with adversity would be more compelling and inspiring than ours. We could find more gripping and rousing stories of the entrepreneur's journey, but I didn't tell my story to compete with others. I told my *story of self* to illustrate, through example, that any and every *story of self* contains trials, tribulations and lessons learned.

The purpose of recounting our *story of self* is not to create a gauge we use to evaluate ourselves compared to someone else. In fact, according to Dr. Meg Jay, author of *Supernormal: The Untold Story of Adversity and Resilience*, "the most recent research tells us there is no hierarchy of trauma. When something bad happens—whether it be sexual assault or physical abuse or a family splits apart or any other adversity—how much this event affects us depends on many different variables: how old we are when it happens, how long it lasts, how much it changes our lives, how we cope at the time, how others react when we tell them, what sources of support we have, what other stressors we are managing, what other successes we can point to, as well as the genetic material we bring to the situation. Comparing adversities leads nowhere."[95]

Recounting our *story of self* is an opportunity to deeply reflect, introspectively, on our ability to learn from failure and stand steadfast and be resilient in the face of misfortune. Wherever we're at along the path of entrepreneurship, our story has value. We don't have to have a typical "success story' defined by popular standards. We don't need to have had deeply traumatic experiences to have faced and overcome adversity in our life. Our stories cannot be zero sum tales of either triumph or tribulation – our journeys are too unique and multifaceted for such oversimplification.

When we acknowledge and appreciate the adversity of our own story, we build the self-confidence and resiliency needed to face and overcome future hardships. Self-focused reflection helps us process emotions and fosters stress-related growth.[11] The ability to do this has been found to be a significant driver of entrepreneurship – even the seemingly small feats we've overcome, the interim victories along our nascent entrepreneurial journey, can lead to increased assurance in our ability to meet future challenges.[12]

With an increased sense of confidence comes the belief that our sustained efforts will eventually get us past the difficulty of the moment, so we persevere and persist longer than we might have otherwise. Reflecting on your story of self resurfaces the times when you faced hardship, overcame obstacles, processed feedback in a constructive way and emerged on the other side better, stronger and more resilient.

If you're still not sure or completely confident about your own *story of self*, that's okay. It takes courage to own and share your story. You must put yourself out there. Yet, doing so is necessary because when adversity strikes, you'll need to call back to it to remember where you've been, who you are and where you're going. Let's look at one last example.

Whitney Wolfe Herd is the co-founder of Bumble, a female-first dating app where the woman always makes the first move. Her story of resilience illustrates how the *story of self* can become lost and manipulated when we allow other people to hijack it. Before Bumble, Herd was the co-founder of Tinder, another popular dating app. She and another Tinder co-founder, Justin Mateen, were involved romantically, but the relationship ended bitterly after about a year. The events that ensued after the break-up resulted in Mateen bombarding Herd with viciously insulting text messages, calling her a "whore" and "gold digger." Herd responded with a law suit against Tinder, which settled outside of court for around $1 million.[13]

As the story became public knowledge, people weighed in with their opinions on message boards and social media. Herd became victim to internet-led hostility and bullying that made her question herself. "I was being told the ugliest things by complete strangers," she said in an interview with Forbes.[14] The online bullying escalated into rape and death threats via social media. Herd became depressed and couldn't sleep.[15] "I really felt completely lost and scared," she told CNN Money in 2017. "I felt like I had lost a piece of my identity. I didn't know who I was anymore, and I was letting these strangers on the internet define that."[16]

It's when we are most vulnerable that we need our *story of self* to anchor us. When the bullying led Herd to lose a piece of her identity, she forgot who she was – she forgot her story. Despite the barrage of hate and negativity, Herd's entrepreneurial spirit could not be diminished. She began planning a social network exclusively for women – a place for women to support one another through positivity. As we will see throughout this book, surrounding ourselves with positive social networks is key to becoming a more resilient entrepreneur.

Herd's social media idea evolved into Bumble. As it evolved, so did Herd. She redefined her *story of self* and in the process, the world and roles of online dating. Bumble differentiates itself with its female-first model, but more than a dating app, Bumble is an online platform designed to help people learn how to "establish and maintain healthier connections."[17] The pieces of

Herd's career and personal life fell apart, but she managed to piece them back together and create a foundation for something much stronger – and much more profitable as well. Bumble has amassed more than 22 million users with approximately 2.2 million users paying up to $9.99 a month in subscription fees. In its first 15 months of sales, revenue surpassed $100 million and is expected to increase two-fold in the next fiscal year.[14]

In an interview with Entrepreneur.com, Wolfe shared that "No matter who you are in life, where you come from or where you live, everyone is fighting their own battle and everyone's battle is equally important as the next. To each person, those are their problems and they are more important than everyone else's."[18]

Wolfe's story is a testament to the value of telling your *story of self* as you continue along your own entrepreneurial journey. I hope as you read through and practice the techniques in the Resilient Entrepreneur, you'll find the strength and courage to write, re-write, and fully live your *story of self*.

In the chapters that follow, I will share what I've learned firsthand about resilient entrepreneurs and supplement my own experience with a deep dive into the cutting-edge research on resiliency. After finishing this book, I'm confident that you will be better prepared to face and overcome the obstacles along your entrepreneurial journey. The knowledge, skills and abilities you will gain will make you a more resilient, more successful entrepreneur.

"Adversity without triumph is not inspiring; it's depressing. Adversity without growth is not encouraging; it's discouraging. The great potential story in adversity is one of hope and success. Adversity is everyone's, but the story you write with your life is yours alone. Everyone gets a chance to be the hero in a potentially great story. Some step up to that role and some don't. The choice is yours."

- John C. Maxwell

Leadership guru and bestselling author of more than 70 books

Take Action! Share your story of self:

Most people start reflecting on the events that made a big impact on them between the ages of 15 and 25, but wherever you are in life, take a moment to find your entrepreneurial origin story. As you write your *story of self*, get started by asking yourself some of the following questions:[39]

1. When was your first exposure to the idea of entrepreneurship? It doesn't have to be a business endeavor in the traditional sense, it could have been that time you participated in fundraising for a school activity or sport. What did you learn from that experience? How does that experience relate to the entrepreneurial journey you're on today?
2. Think of a difficult situation you encountered when you were younger. How did you deal with that challenge? What did you learn from it?
3. Was there a special person in your life that taught you something new (A parent, a grandparent, an aunt, an uncle, a coach, a teacher a friend, etc.)? Was that person there for you during a challenging time? How did they help you? What did you learn?
4. Reflect on a time when you were given a new responsibility that you might not have felt ready for at the time. How did you respond? Did it make you more self-reliant?
5. Remember a time when you worked hard for something. How was it that you were able to persevere when you might have wanted to quit instead? Did the hard work pay off?

My Story of Self:

Chapter 1: Entrepreneurship and Resilience

It's not that I'm so smart, it's just that I stay with problems longer."

\- Albert Einstein

What factors help a burgeoning entrepreneur move forward and persevere through the hardships of the startup phase? Why do some entrepreneurs get stuck in the idea stage, while others are able to successfully implement their idea and grow their business? Why do serial entrepreneurs continue to start new businesses even after experiencing one failure after another? What helps existing small business owners weather the storms and bounce back from setbacks? These are some of the questions I hope to answer in the following chapters.

The nascent entrepreneur may have nothing more than an idea, they might have already started the planning process, or they might already be operating something on the side. Nascent, as defined by the Global Entrepreneurship Monitor (GEM), refers to business owners who are so new that they have not paid salaries, wages or dividends for longer than three months. To put it another way, nascent entrepreneurs are those with a seed in their hand, but haven't decided if, how or where they're going to plant it. They might start building their garden bed and filling it with dirt, but they haven't yet planted that seed.

If this sounds like you, you're not alone. According to GEM, approximately 9 percent of the U.S population can be described as nascent entrepreneurs - people who are actively working toward starting a new business that they will either own or co-own.[19] That means that there are tens of millions of budding entrepreneurs in the United States at any given time.

Of these, some will never do anything besides hold and admire the seedling of their idea. Some might start building and preparing the garden bed, but never plant that seed, and still some may plant the seed, but never water it, reinforce its frail stem or dive out invasive weeds.

Plenty of aspiring entrepreneurs never get past the idea stage. When the entrepreneurial journey starts to get a little bumpy, they take the first exit ramp they see. Later they'll come up with another idea that they will fall in and out of love with all over again. I call the aspiring entrepreneurs stuck in this loop, *serial ideators*. They're the window shoppers of entrepreneurship. They adopt and abandon one idea after another without ever moving beyond the idea phase.

Entrepreneurship is hard and can be intimidating. The idea of entrepreneurship can be enticing, but starting a business is a huge investment of time, energy and resources, and the investment is a risky one. It's estimated that at least 50 percent of all new businesses fail within five years of their inception.[274] Other studies estimate that six years after discovering an entrepreneurial idea, approximately 66 percent of aspiring entrepreneurs either give up on entrepreneurship altogether or are still stuck spinning their wheels in the idea or startup stage.[20] Kellogg School of Management Professor, Steven Rogers, says that the average entrepreneur fails about four times before succeeding.[21] If we measured entrepreneurial success using the traditional return on investment (ROI) calculation used by large corporations, 95 percent of all startups would fail to produce an acceptable financial return in a reasonable timeframe.[22]

What does that mean though – that their business failed? A failure in business often means that you gave up and quit or you were unable or unwilling to learn and pivot in a new direction. In fact, not pivoting quickly enough away from a suboptimal decision (misaligned product-market fit, poor hiring, etc.) was cited as one of the top reasons why startups dissolve.[23]

Yet, despite the high *failure* rate, the path of entrepreneurship can be exciting and liberating, and for many, a journey worth pursuing. Entrepreneurs get the unique opportunity to blaze their own path – to write their *story of self* with a sense of control and ownership that few other professional endeavors allow. Despite the high failure rates, there are still millions of entrepreneurs who have found a path to success.

The first thing we should understand and accept about entrepreneurship is that it isn't for everyone. I don't purport the ideas in this book to be a panacea for new business creation. Some people don't want to be entrepreneurs and others probably shouldn't be entrepreneurs. Yet, many of us will benefit by gaining a better understanding of how we can help the willing and passionate entrepreneur become a more resilient one. The ideas presented in this book can be applied to almost any entrepreneurial path or endeavor, whether you're involved in professional services, retail, education, non-profits, etc.

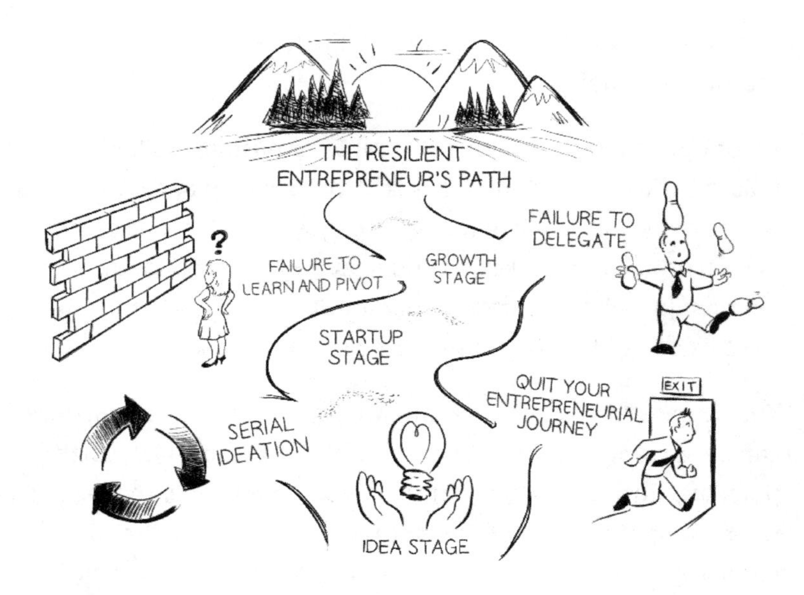

Figure 2: The Resilient Entrepreneur's Path
From the initial idea stage, we move into the startup stage. The startup stage is where we work to turn our idea into reality. During this transition, many entrepreneurs will decide that entrepreneurship isn't right for them and they will cease pursuing their business endeavor. Others will seek to stay in the more comforting realm of ideation. Instead of acting on their idea, these serial ideators prefer to conduct business as a thought experiment.

In the startup stage, entrepreneurs are learning a lot about how to start and grow a business. Those that fail to learn and pivot toward the most promising direction will hit a brick wall. The resilient entrepreneur's path is paved with new knowledge, skills and abilities acquired through experimenting and learning.

As our business grows, we must learn to delegate. We can no longer do everything ourselves. Those that fail to delegate will eventually buckle under the weight of the growing business. The resilient entrepreneur's path is curvy and bumpy, but the methods and mindset outlined in this book will help you reach your destination.

A lack of persistence has been cited as a leading reason for the high percentage of entrepreneurial failures.[24] Iconic entrepreneur Steve Jobs once said, "I'm convinced that about half of what separates the successful entrepreneurs from the non-successful ones is pure perseverance."[25] Yet, a lack of persistence is too simplistic of an explanation. Persistence is really the act of persevering, but what is it that inspires, motivates, and sustains our persistence and perseverance? Why do some believe they have control over the adversity they face while others feel helpless?[51] The answer is *entrepreneurial resilience,* a term we'll revisit throughout this book.

So, what exactly is a resilient entrepreneur? We know that resilience is a key factor for entrepreneurial success, but we don't yet have a good understanding of how entrepreneurs build resilience.[26] To better understand entrepreneurial resilience, let's look at each concept separately.

Entrepreneurship

"Entrepreneurship isn't for the faint of heart, and it's impossible to tell how your story will turn out. All you have is your conviction, your ability to work hard, and your determination to never give up."

- Daniel Lubetzky
Founder and CEO of Kind Snacks

What does it mean to be an entrepreneur? Let's briefly explore the concept. The Merriam-Webster Dictionary defines an entrepreneur as someone who organizes and manages any enterprise, especially a business, usually with considerable risk and initiative. The origin comes from the French word *entreprendre* which literally means to do something, or to undertake a task. Entrepreneurship, according to Babson College Professor William D. Bygrave, "is a process of becoming rather than a state of being."[27]

As expected, initiative is one of the most important characteristics of an entrepreneur. Initiative is about acting and happens after you've accepted the potential risks involved with your start-up. That initiative or intent is a prerequisite to taking the first steps to start your own business[28]. Learning how to foster and ignite that intention is key to catalyzing your entrepreneurial spirit.

The inspiration to embark on an entrepreneurial journey comes from both internal and external motivators.[44] Many will wish to gain financial independence or wealth through entrepreneurship. It would be misleading to say that entrepreneurship is a guaranteed path to wealth, but approximately two out of three millionaires in the United States are self-employed entrepreneurs. This is significant because the self-employed population makes up only about 20 percent of the entire U.S. workforce.[29]

So, although accumulating substantial wealth isn't guaranteed for any entrepreneur, many have attained a level of prosperity that will benefit themselves and their family for generations. In the world of economic development, this concept is referred to as *upward economic mobility* – the idea that one has access to opportunities and can accumulate financial independence to increase his or her standard of living. In short, it's realizing the American Dream.

Some people embark on the entrepreneurial path for reasons other than money. Social entrepreneurship, for example, has emerged to include the desire for social, civic, or environmental impact. We will talk about these social motivators and how to leverage them to make yourself, your business, and your community more resilient.

Awareness is an important underlying trait for entrepreneurs. The most successful use their awareness to scan their environment and continually seek out new information. For example, if you actively seek out information on new or emerging technologies, then you're more likely to spot a potential opportunity to make your business more efficient or penetrate a new market. This type of awareness is outward-facing, looking externally to see what's up ahead. According to Peter Drucker, one of the greatest minds on the subject, "The entrepreneur always searches for change, responds to it, and exploits it as an opportunity."[30] As you'll learn throughout this book, an entrepreneur's internal self-awareness is perhaps even more important.

Another commonly-cited characteristic of an entrepreneur is perseverance. When we think about untiring, persistent entrepreneurs, who comes to mind? We might typically think of the all-stars of entrepreneurship: Elon Musk, Sara Blakely, Steve Jobs, Lori Greiner, Mark Zuckerberg, Bill Gates, Michael Dell, Sir Richard Branson, Jeff Bezos, etc.

Jeff Bezos built Amazon.com on the idea of persistence and perseverance. In fact, when he was trying to decide on a name for Amazon, he had initially decided on Relentless. You can still type Relentless.com into your browser and it will take you to Amazon.com.[31]

Like Bezos and many other all-star entrepreneurs, the ability to adapt positively to change is a key ingredient to success. The business environment that exists today isn't the same environment that will exist tomorrow. New competition will emerge, rivals will innovate and take advantage of new technologies, laws and regulations will change, and of course, consumer trends will evolve. To keep on pace with these changes, successful entrepreneurs must be open-minded and receptive to new ideas and innovations.

These concepts of what it means to be entrepreneurial aren't new. They've been regurgitated in countless business publications and have become colloquial in startup circles. What's new is the evolution and understanding of these entrepreneurial characteristics as they relate to resiliency.

When Inc. Magazine asked the CEO's behind the 500 fastest growing companies in the U.S. which qualities they attributed to their success, grit and resilience most often topped the list (alongside risk-taking and thinking big).[32] Whether an aspiring entrepreneur, existing small business owner, or the CEO behind one of the fastest-growing companies in the nation, those who adjust better to change are more likely to create and sustain a successful company through the many challenges of owning and operating a business.

Successful businesses are sustained by those with the abilities, resources and motivation to persevere.[33] This ability to adapt positively and effectively to adversity is resilience.

"The entrepreneurial journey is not for everyone. Yes, the highs are high, and the rewards can be thrilling. But the lows can break your heart. Entrepreneurs must love what they do to such a degree that doing it is worth sacrifice and, at times, pain. But doing anything else, we think, would be unimaginable."

- Howard Schultz
Former CEO and Chairman of Starbucks

Resilience

The word *resilience* derives from the Latin word *resilire*, meaning to rebound or recoil.[34] Resiliency is the process by which we emerge from hardships, strengthened and more resourceful than we were before. Resilience has been defined as the "ability to maintain relatively stable, healthy levels of psychological and emotional functioning over time after experiencing a trauma or serious loss."[35]

Our capacity to be resilient depends on how we mentally and emotionally respond to adversity, as well as how we mobilize external supportive resources that might help to minimize the negative impacts of trying times.[36] Resiliency is about increasing our wherewithal and endurance so that we're less likely to experience entrepreneurial burnout. We will look at the mindset and methods to help us become more resilient entrepreneurs.

The concept of resiliency arose in the 1980s when researchers studied the impact that schizophrenic mothers had on their children.[37] They investigated why some children with schizophrenic mothers did better than others. More recently, resiliency has been studied in those who have experienced a trauma or catastrophe like war, natural disaster, the loss of a loved one, or a chronic illness. In these contexts, those who've experienced acute tragedies and were able to re-emerge and carry on were seemingly inoculated against many adversities later in life. This posttraumatic growth is the fabric of resiliency. Yet, we don't need to experience a life-altering catastrophe to become more resilient.

Recent studies have shown that resiliency is also an important mechanism in less extraordinary traumas such as getting through the "ordinary" struggles of life and business. For example, the typical day-to-day hardships that every entrepreneur will face include a lack of structure, inadequate information, ambiguous possibilities, self-doubt, threat from intense competition, and an overall risky decision-making environment. Studies have shown that perceived failure on any project that's new to you with an uncertain outcome necessitates resiliency to bounce back and carry onward.[38] Resiliency can be applied to organizations, cities, regions and societies at large.[39] For our purpose, we will look at resiliency as it relates to the individual entrepreneur, a team of entrepreneurs, or co-founders and small businesses.

If you're skeptical and believe that resiliency is just a new *kumbaya* buzz word in business management, then you'd be mistaken. Scientific research has shown that entrepreneurs who demonstrate higher levels of resiliency enjoy up to 37 percent greater earnings compared to those in the bottom quintile of resiliency.[40] Furthermore, resilient entrepreneurs have been shown to learn at an accelerated pace after failure, and they're able to pick themselves up faster to start again.[35] The bottom line is that resilience is a predictor of entrepreneurial success.[41]

Entrepreneurship and Resilience

Entrepreneurship and resiliency go hand in hand. I once coached an entrepreneur named Anthony, a self-employed fitness trainer, who had already worked for himself for over 15 years when we met. Anthony was interested in opening his own vitamin and smoothie shop. He knew that as he got older, it would become more and more difficult to meet the physical demands and expectations common in his line of work.

Anthony had a good business idea, but not enough money to pay for the startup expenses without some outside capital. So, he began putting together a written business plan – standard procedure for anyone applying for a loan or trying to attract an investor. The challenge for Anthony, though, is that he suffers from dyslexia. If you've ever put together a business plan before, you know it can be extremely intimidating; imagine how much harder it is for someone who struggles with reading and writing.

Dyslexia affects about 20 percent of the general population. Many students with dyslexia struggle academically. Much greater, however, is the prevalence of dyslexia in entrepreneurs, which is closer to 35 percent.[42] Despite having a learning disability, people with dyslexia are often quick, creative thinkers who demonstrate strong reasoning skills.[43] Anthony struggled in school, but as he grew older, he found that his strengths were well-suited for entrepreneurship where he had the flexibility and autonomy to be creative.

Anthony and I went over his business plan draft during our first meeting together. Before coming to me, he had taken a business planning class and worked one-on-one with a different business coach for over 15 hours. I told him the plan was off to a good start, but still had a long way to go before presenting it to a lender or investor. He wasn't thrilled to hear that, but he took my feedback and revised his business plan.

When he sent it to me for another review, I sent it back with another round of critiques. Undeterred, he dutifully incorporated my edits and changes each time. For every hour that we met, he would leave our meeting with more hours' worth of research and writing to do. It wasn't easy for him, but he kept making progress and he never thought about quitting. After 15 hours of coaching, he sent me a fundable business plan.

How are entrepreneurs like Anthony able to overcome their challenges, and in his case, a disability, to move their business dreams forward? Like Anthony, resilient entrepreneurs display several key characteristics: hardiness, resourcefulness, patience, a tolerance for ambiguity or uncertainty, optimism and sometimes faith. [166] Do any of those characteristics jump out as a way you might describe yourself? If not, that's okay. It turns out that our ability to be resilient is something that we can cultivate and improve over time. It's not a fixed trait.

Resiliency, like entrepreneurship, is a learnable process.[44] It is comprised of three main phases:

1. The adverse experience and absorption of its resulting effects
2. A period of rehabilitation and regeneration
3. Reflection on the meaning of the adversity and lessons learned.[45]

Looking at how people navigate these phases, research by Professor Mathew Hayward helped construct a three-part framework for better understanding entrepreneurial resilience built on emotional, cognitive, and social resilience.[56]

Emotional resilience is associated with having a positive response to adversity.[46] *How do you feel when you're faced with a setback? Are you able to absorb and process the emotional impact in a healthy way?*

Cognitive resilience is associated with the way we think and reflect on past failures and hardships. *How do you perceive the adversity you've experienced? Do you remain bitter about a setback or do you look at past adversity as a learning experience?*

Finally, social resilience refers to our ability to access support from our network of colleagues, friends and family during trying times. A fascinating study out of New Zealand looked at how different entrepreneurs dealt with the failure (bankruptcy, liquidation, etc.) of their businesses. The study highlighted three entrepreneurs in their mid-40s. The first individual was Luke, a tech entrepreneur, who lost his $500,000 investment, as well as control of his 18-employee company after six years in business. Hayden, the second entrepreneur, was forced to liquidate his company and lay off its 20 employees. Ben, the last example, was the founder of a carpet retail business, who laid off his five employees and closed shop after five years.[35]

Each of these founders dealt with the loss of their business differently. Hayden didn't cope well, turning to alcohol "to numb the pain." Ben also struggled. He felt ashamed and isolated himself from friends and family after the business went under.

Luke, on the other hand, found solace by reflecting on his *story of self*. After losing the business he reflected on his "tough childhood and immigrating to a country when [he] had no money and didn't know anyone." He told the interviewer in the study that "hardships stay within you and become your strength. I thought... I had lost money [due to a failed venture], but at least I know people now, so something positive will happen."[35] By reflecting on his *story of self*, Luke could see how far he'd come already. The business failure was a setback for sure, but he felt that with help from those in his network, he could bounce back.

Luke went on to tell the researchers that he envisioned his mind as having two boxes where he could direct his thoughts. "Your mind constantly works on what happened [the failure] and what you could have done better," he said. "That's the old box and you get into a negative spiral. It is not easy, but the longer you focus on the old box, you are not moving into the next chapter of your life, so focus on the new box."[35] What a powerful mindset!

Measuring Resilience

Resilience is something we can learn and measure. We can become "conditioned to cope".[47] The Connor-Davidson Resilience Scale (CD-RISC) was developed in 2003 by Dr. Kathryn M. Connor and Dr. Jonathan R.T Davidson - both affiliated with Duke University. The CD-RISC has been shown to be a reliable instrument in measuring entrepreneurial resilience.

I've adapted the CD-RISC and a few other resilience scales to create a new Entrepreneurial Resilience Assessment that I highly encourage you to take below. Take the assessment now and return to it in a few months, after you've finished studying and implementing some of the strategies in this book.

There are fifteen statements in the assessment. For each statement, select how untrue or true it is of you on a scale of 1 to 5 with 1 being "not at all true" and 5 being "very true":

Not at all true = 1	Sometimes or somewhat true = 2	Moderately true = 3	Usually true = 4	Very true = 5

Question	**My answer (1 through 5)**
1. I have a good sense of how past events in my life have helped lead me to the path of entrepreneurship.	
2. I am able to formulate a series of short-term and mid-term objectives that will help me achieve my long-term business goals.	
3. I believe failure is part of the learning process in business.	
4. When I need help with my business, I know where to find it.	
5. I periodically meet with someone I consider to be my business mentor or coach.	
6. I can achieve my goals, despite obstacles.	
7. I can handle critical feedback, even when it's unpleasant.	
8. My strengths help my business more than my weaknesses hold it back.	
9. I actively seek to learn new knowledge, skills, and abilities that might help my business.	
10. My friends and family are supportive of my entrepreneurial endeavors.	
11. I am able to adapt to change.	
12. I believe that working through a business challenge with someone else is better than figuring it out alone.	

13. If my first attempted solution doesn't solve a challenge, I'm able to try multiple solutions until I find an effective one.	
14. I believe I need to work more than 50 hours per week to be successful.	
15. I find it uncomfortable or intimidating to reach out to someone for help with my business.	

Calculate your results	**Totals**
Add up your numbers for questions 1 - 13	
Add up your numbers for questions 14 & 15	
Subtract your total for questions 14 & 15 from your total for questions 1-13	
Grand Total	

Interpret your results	**Range**
High levels of resilience	48 to 63
Average levels of resilience	19 to 47
Low levels of resilience	3 to 18

"For an optimist, it makes no sense to lose hope. We can always do better (instead of being devastated, resigned, or disgusted), limit the damage (instead of letting it all go to pot), find an alternative solution (instead of wallowing pitifully in failure), rebuild what has been destroyed (instead of saying, 'It's all over!'), take the current situation as a starting point (instead of wasting our time crying over the past and lamenting the present), start from scratch (instead of ending there), understand that sustained effort will have to be made in the best apparent direction (instead of being paralyzed by indecision and fatalism)."

- Matthieu Ricard

Author of *Happiness: A Guide to Developing Life's Most Important Skill*

Optimism is one of the foundations of the resilient mindset and happens to be a well-studied frame of mind for entrepreneurs. Dr. Martin Seligman is the Director of the Positive Psychology Center at the University of Pennsylvania.[48] He has devoted most of his professional career to the study of varying outcomes from optimistic versus pessimistic thinking.

In his seminal book, *Learned Optimism*, he distinguishes between pessimists and optimists, citing the "defining characteristic of pessimists is that they tend to believe bad events will last a long time, will undermine everything they do and are [entirely] their own fault. The optimists, who are confronted with the same hard knocks...think about misfortune in the opposite way. They tend to believe defeat is just a temporary setback [and] that its causes are confined to this one case."[49]

Optimists are more likely to view challenges as opportunities to learn and grow. In a longitudinal study of optimism, it was found that optimists tend to live, on average, about 19 percent longer than the general population.[216] In the context of entrepreneurship, studies have shown that entrepreneurs are more optimistic, on average, than a career professional.[174] It's important to transfer and build optimism into the business' culture because, as the research shows, entrepreneurial optimism is contagious. That means employees will mimic the optimism of the company founder, leading to a happier and more productive workforce.[50] As we learn to think more optimistically, our positivity will be absorbed into our business.

Confidence and Self-efficacy

"Genuine fearlessness arises with the confidence that we will be able to gather the inner resources necessary to deal with any situation that comes our way."

- Matthieu Ricard
Author of *Happiness: A Guide to Developing Life's Most Important Skill*

To build entrepreneurial resiliency you must become more confident in your own business acumen. The confidence you have in your own knowledge, skills, and abilities (KSAs) is also referred to as self-efficacy. Resiliency and self-efficacy are interlocking links in a self-reinforcing chain. Together they help aspiring entrepreneurs start a new business and guide it through the challenges of the startup lifecycle. Stated another way, self-efficacy is the belief that you can succeed in your business endeavor.[51] As an emerging entrepreneur, you'll be faced with unexpected challenges, including imperfect information when making decisions. If you're confident in your KSAs, you'll be better prepared to act in an uncertain environment.

It's not realistic to expect that you'll have the time or bandwidth to be an expert in all aspects of business, but broadening your knowledge on some of the basics, and adopting a regimen of continuous learning will increase your confidence in your own ability to overcome challenges with your own capabilities. For example, having confidence in your ability to effectively analyze your company's financial health or understanding how you might organize an effective marketing strategy can help you increase your own self-efficacy.

Even if you're still on the fence about becoming an entrepreneur, consider taking a few introductory courses about small business. You'll increase your business skills and self-efficacy, which might give you the extra confidence to tip the balance. Many local or regional economic development organizations will offer free or partially-subsidized classes on a wide range of business topics. In addition, there is an increasing number of free or low-cost business courses available online through platforms like www.Coursera.org and www.Udemy.com. Coursera, for example, offers a wide range of business classes taught by credible institutions like the University of Pennsylvania, University of California in Davis, Yale, and countless others.

Confident entrepreneurs are also more likely to remain positive and optimistic when adversity strikes. This is true for nascent entrepreneurs in the startup phase, as well as tenured entrepreneurs facing a setback or business failure. When we fail or face adversity, we can pull from our reservoir of confidence for reassurance that we can overcome and persevere. This is because, as research suggests, confident entrepreneurs tend to expend greater effort – they tend to stick with it through the rough patches, believing that they will eventually emerge, recover, and thrive again.[52]

The opposite end of the spectrum from having too little confidence is being overconfident. Some passionate entrepreneurs are prone to being overconfident and exuberant about their business' chances of success, revenue estimates, positive response from customers, ability to compete, etc. Earlier, we cited that approximately half of all new businesses fail within their first five years. Yet, in a study of close to 3,000 business founders, 81 percent of them rated their chances of success at over 70 percent and approximately 33 percent surveyed estimated their chances of success at close to 100 percent![53] It's hard to imagine that nearly one third of new entrepreneurs believe their chances of succeeding are virtually guaranteed!

Perhaps part of the reason is that some of us are naturally prone to being overconfident.[54] I've surveyed hundreds of entrepreneurs about their levels of confidence. I've seen some survey forms come back with a straight line drawn through the highest-rated option for each question about confidence in their knowledge, skills and abilities (KSAs).

Dr. Mark Simon is a professor of entrepreneurship and innovation at the University of Michigan in Flint.[55] He and his research team found that overconfident entrepreneurs dropped their confidence levels significantly after receiving what they perceived to be accurate, expert information that went against their original beliefs.[54]

In other words, these highly overconfident people plummeted when surprised with a reality that was incongruent with what they previously presumed to be true. This is an important point for the resilient entrepreneur. If we experience a steep fall from such an elevated level of confidence, shocked by unexpected adversity, it will be much harder to bounce back from those unanticipated challenges.

Entrepreneurs need a certain level of confidence to be resilient, but too much confidence – overconfidence – can act as a lubricant for poor strategic decision-making and an overall lack of proper business planning. Overconfidence can lead us to enter a new market where we lack core competencies, overcommit to risky new projects, underestimate our competition and disregard feedback that tells us it's time to stop or pivot in a new direction. [56]

Even the most successful entrepreneurs overextend their confidence at times. Billionaire entrepreneur, Mark Cuban, is no exception. He says that "very often, along with some success comes the feeling of invincibility. I have been in situations where I have told myself that I'm smart, I know what I'm doing, that I will figure things out as I go, so it's okay to take on this new opportunity. Those were usually the times I made mistakes."[79]

So how do we know that we have the right amount of confidence we need to be successful and not so much that we're susceptible to the pitfalls of overconfidence? Where might we find the Goldilocks of self-efficacy? To answer that question, we need to understand where our confidence is coming from.

Confidence can be divided into three buckets. The first is confidence in your own knowledge. We can be overconfident in our knowledge when we're certain about something that isn't accurate.[57] The second is confidence in our skills and abilities. These two buckets combine to form the KSAs of self-efficacy that we discussed earlier. Overconfidence in your skills and abilities might lead to unrealistic goals and missed performance expectations. The third is confidence in the future.[58]

You should strive to become confident in your KSAs and espouse a belief that they will help you shape the future you desire for yourself. Be confident in your ability to learn and master new KSAs. Be confident that if you work hard and apply your KSAs, you will be able to achieve your business goals. All the while be realistic about the fact that you might need to invest time and resources in learning and developing the KSAs that you need to be successful. No startup should believe that their chances of success are guaranteed. Be realistic about overall startup failure rates while being confident that you can outperform the 50 percent of business startups that fail within the first five years.

To summarize, degrees of entrepreneurial confidence or self-efficacy can be plotted on a spectrum. The right amount of confidence lies somewhere in the middle. Successful entrepreneurs need confidence to be successful, but not so much confidence that they underestimate the risks or believe that success is somehow predetermined. Be confident in your KSAs, but not over-confident in your chances of success.

Self-efficacy is about believing you have the KSAs to be successful at your chosen endeavor. However, research has shown that many potential entrepreneurs may be subconsciously discounting their own KSAs, and therefore limiting their own self-efficacy due to implicit or subconscious bias.

Bias

The Kirwan Institute, at the Ohio State University, defines and explains implicit bias as the "attitudes or stereotypes that affect our understanding, actions, and decisions in an unconscious manner. These biases, which encompass both favorable and unfavorable assessments, are activated involuntarily and without an individual's awareness or intentional control. Residing deep in the subconscious, these biases are different from known biases that individuals may choose to conceal for the purposes of social and/or political correctness. Rather, implicit biases are not accessible through introspection."

Project Implicit is a nonprofit organization convening professors from some of the top universities around the country. According to their website[B], "the goal of the organization is to educate the public about hidden biases and to provide a 'virtual laboratory' for collecting data..."[59] The Researchers associated with Project Implicit created the Implicit Association Test (IAT), which is an assessment designed to measure our own implicit biases about various subjects like gender, race, religion, and age.

For example, a common implicit bias might be that males are associated more with being medical doctors and females are associated more with being nurses. Even though we know for a fact that not all doctors are male and not all nurses are female, in the blink of an eye, the synapses in many of our brains will subconsciously trigger an initial association of male doctors and female nurses.

This same bias is often present when we think about the association of females with any career at all, outside of caring for the family at home. Project Implicit reports that 56 percent of those who have taken the gender-career association assessment show either a moderate or strong association between males and professional careers compared to females. In comparison, only 4 percent of respondents either moderately or strongly associate males with family and females with careers. Although the U.S Bureau of Labor Statistics reports that 52 percent of all people employed in management and professional occupations are female, our biased minds seem to

---

[B] https://implicit.harvard.edu/implicit/aboutus.html

be thinking in a period before living memory.[60] Even at the turn of the 20th century, women accounted for approximately 20 percent of the workforce.[61]

What's even more surprising is the fact that we often show implicit bias against our own self-identifying groups. Let's look at an example. Working professional females, albeit to a slightly lesser extent compared to males, are likely to demonstrate implicit bias in their associations with males in the workforce when compared with females in the workforce. When it comes to thinking about doctors, women are likely to think of a male doctor before they think of a female doctor. Results show that similar biases exist for race, religion, age, and weight.

Again, our implicit bias is almost completely unfounded when we consider that the education gap between men and women in the U.S. has almost completely closed. According to the National Center for Education Statistics, females earned approximately 57 percent of all undergraduate degrees, 60 percent of all master's degrees, and 51 percent of all doctorate level degrees.[68] However, when we dive into the specific fields of study, we find that some gaps still exist - women still trail men in degrees earned in engineering, computer sciences, math, and physics.[62]

The Project Implicit research results led me to ask whether similar findings might be found in implicit biases associated with entrepreneurial intentions and self-efficacy as they relate to gender and race. Dr. Vishal Gupta, Associate Professor at the University of Alabama, found that both men and women thought of entrepreneurship as a primarily male-dominated endeavor.[63]

In another study, Dr. Ali D. Farashah, a researcher at the Umea School of Business and Economics in Sweden, looked at a Global Entrepreneurship Monitor's dataset that included information on over 86,000 female entrepreneurs. His research showed that aspiring female entrepreneurs, on average, are 30 percent less likely to believe in their own entrepreneurial knowledge, skills, and abilities compared to their male counterparts.[305]

I encountered an example of this while facilitating a group mentoring session. The group consisted of five entrepreneurs and five mentors. Each entrepreneur took a turn pitching their business model and value proposition. Afterward, the mentors took turns asking questions and offered feedback on the pitches. One female entrepreneur, let's call her Tina, gave a pitch about her window blinds cleaning business. She uses a specialized technique and ultrasonic technology to clean the blinds. When a male mentor asked her how the technology worked, she hesitated and then discounted herself before responding, "I'm a woman," she said. "I don't really understand the technology."
Then, she immediately gave an impressive and convincing overview of the technology and how it worked to clean blinds better than alternative methods.

During the feedback session, I asked her why she discredited her knowledge about the ultrasonic technology.
"I don't know," she said. She was surprised and a little embarrassed. I don't think she had realized what she said or how self-doubting and degrading it sounded. Tina had a blind spot, but she's not the only one. Regardless of our stated egalitarian views on equality, the truth is that the majority of us are susceptible to this kind of implicit bias.[64]

Another female entrepreneur, Melinda, who had been sitting quietly across the table from Tina chimed in, "Yeah," she agreed, "I was a little offended when you said that." Melinda utilizes software and additive manufacturing technologies to design and manufacture her jewelry. She obviously understands technology, and so does Tina. We encouraged Tina to speak confidently about her business' use of technology and her knowledge of how it worked. She nodded and thanked us for the feedback. Several weeks later, we hosted an event and Tina had the opportunity to pitch her business. She pitched with confidence about her business and the technology she uses.

Why does Tina's confidence and self-efficacy matter when it comes to her business' bottom line? For aspiring female entrepreneurs, it matters a lot. Studies have shown that when women are less confident in their own entrepreneurial capacity, especially financial management skills and fundraising abilities, they're less likely to apply for lending, and when they do apply, they request smaller funding amounts compared to men. This is also true for African American entrepreneurs, regardless of gender.[65] Similar results were found when looking at females' implicit bias against themselves when asking for a raise or negotiating salary in the workplace. There are significant differences in African American entrepreneurs' ability to access capital compared to white entrepreneurs and I'll discuss some of the implications of that limitation and how it relates to resiliency in a later chapter on funding.

Lending data shows that women are just as likely to be approved for a loan as men.[66] So, when women don't apply or apply for less than what they need, they are literally short-changing themselves and their chances at successfully starting and growing their business.

I'm not discounting or ignoring the fact that there are more barriers and obstacles for women and minority entrepreneurs compared to white male entrepreneurs. Those issues need to be better identified and addressed, but we should also affect change where we have the greatest zone of control and impact - with ourselves.

"No one can make you feel inferior without your consent."

-Eleanor Roosevelt

Although women account for just over half the U.S labor force, they only account for 36 percent of business ownership.[67] This means that there are almost two male entrepreneurs for every female entrepreneur. Exacerbating this disappointing statistic, a study using data from the Kauffman Foundation found that women are also less likely to create high-growth, job-creating startups compared to male entrepreneurs.[68]

This is concerning because empirical research has shown that female entrepreneurs are perhaps more resilient than their male counterparts. A study conducted by Professor Hechavarria at the University of Cincinnati found that male entrepreneurs are statistically more likely to quit their startup business compared to female entrepreneurs.[143] In another study conducted on a sample of over 300 small business owners across the U.S., African American women entrepreneurs showed the highest levels of resilience compared to any other gender or ethnicity included in the study.[69] Part of the reason for this, the researchers explained, is that women are often better able and more willing to access social resources when they need support.

Female entrepreneurs' resiliency advantage isn't just some abstract ideal – it may be affecting the bottom line. In another study, it was found that women-owned businesses increased their revenue by 35 percent between 2007 and 2016, which was 30 percent higher than the national average during the same time.[70] This is even more impressive when we remember that several of those years included the Great Recession and its recovery.

So, how might we encourage more women to pursue entrepreneurship? One way is to showcase more female entrepreneur success stories. A quick look at best-selling business biographies on Amazon reveals a disparity. As of this writing, in mid-2018, the top entrepreneur biographies include Elon Musk, founder of Tesla and Space-X; Phil Knight, founder of Nike; Donald Trump; Jeff Bezos, founder of Amazon; Steve Jobs, co-founder of Apple; J.P. Morgan; Ed Catmull, co-founder of Pixar, etc. Sheryl Sandberg, the Chief Operating Officer at Facebook, was the only female-focused biography in the top twenty best-sellers in the entrepreneur biography category. When aspiring female entrepreneurs are exposed to more female entrepreneur success stories, they are more likely to feel confident in the entrepreneurial knowledge, skills, and abilities needed to start their business and have the resilience to persevere in the face of business challenges.

Let's look at one such success story with Therese Tucker, the founder and CEO of Blackline. BlackLine is a leading provider of cloud software that automates and controls various finance and accounting functions.[71] BlackLine brings in more than $123 million in annual revenue and is valued at approximately $1.75 billion.[72] Therese studied Mathematics and Computer Science at the University of Illinois at Urbana-Champaign. After graduating her journey eventually led her to SunGard, a financial tech company that has since been acquired. While at SunGard, she worked her way up to Chief Technology Officer. In 2001, she left to found BlackLine, engineering her startup's entire technology infrastructure from the ground up. Tucker's resilience shines through in both her entrepreneurial endeavors and personal life.

Tucker founded BlackLine in the wake of a recent divorce - one made more painful because she and her ex-husband had two children together. A few years into the startup, a professional divorce led to another bad break when her Chief of Sales left Blackline to start a rival company. That startup was later purchased by one of BlackLine's major competitors. Yet, Tucker's resiliency helped her see the silver lining. Instead of focusing on how she was wronged, she credits her competitors for helping bring overall legitimacy to an emerging trend of outsourcing and automating financial and accounting functions.[73]

Therese bootstrapped Blackline through its most financially challenging times until she was forced to borrow money from friends just to cover payroll. "It was difficult and humiliating and scary," she reflected in a 2016 interview with Business Insider.[74] Years later, she's able to look back at that time with humility and humor. "It was so stressful," she says. "I'm sure that's why I have gray hair."[75] Today, her gray hair has been reinvigorated with what has become her signature dyed hot pink hue.

Therese has proven wrong those whose implicit bias would lead them to second guess her financial and accounting acumen, technical savviness, and entrepreneurial and business leadership capabilities based on her gender. When asked whether she's experienced any negative bias because she's a female tech entrepreneur, she responded with an inspiring testimony to the power of entrepreneurial resilience:

> *"I have certainly encountered some weird things over the years, but that's not [sic] stopped me. An entrepreneur, by definition, will encounter difficulties and the reason that you're successful is because you persist through those difficulties. If you find someone – and they are out there – that has extreme bias against women, then you drop that person from your life and you take a different route. Yes, the bias exists, but why would you focus on it? Why wouldn't you focus on the things that you need to do to build a successful business? I mean, who cares what anybody else thinks?"*[76]

Therese isn't defined by the adversity she's experienced - she defies it, and derives from it the strength and motivation to be a more resilient entrepreneur. Yet, bias does still exist, and leadership in existing businesses should play their part in actively encouraging more female tech leaders and entrepreneurs.

As Microsoft CEO, Satya Nadella, pointedly reminds us, "Any advice that advocates passivity in the face of bias is wrong. Leaders need to act and shape the culture to root out biases and create an environment where everyone can effectively advocate for themselves."[9] Nadella goes on to cite mentorship as an active strategy to encourage more female business leaders, especially in tech businesses.

Mentorship is a great idea and not just for tech companies, where mentorship is commonplace. Mentoring offers support, advice, and guidance for the budding entrepreneur pursuing a startup in any industry. Mentoring can also help existing business owners. Mentors with significant experience in entrepreneurship can increase confidence and self-efficacy in their mentees.[77] Later in the book, I devote an entire chapter on finding the right mentor and building a valuable mentoring relationship.

Balance

Some entrepreneurs might believe that they can accomplish whatever they put their minds to by sheer willpower or brute force. This might prove true in the short-term and in small bursts, but in the long-term, it is unsustainable and may have the opposite outcome. Burnout is often cited as one of the top reasons why startups falter.[23] That's why it's important for entrepreneurs to work hard and effectively without overworking an excessive number of hours.

You might be thinking, "But wait, I've heard dozens of success stories from business owners who practically worked non-stop, from the early hours of the morning through the evening to become successful." That's true - I've heard these success stories too, but at what cost? How often do you enthusiastically and proudly hear about the lengthy hours worked from the perspective of their family and friends?

Yet, not all superstar entrepreneurs sprint non-stop day in and day out. Those that have learned to be resilient have incorporated balance into their work routine. For example, take Daymond John, founder of FUBU and co-star of ABC's reality TV show Shark Tank. In an interview with Inc. Magazine, he says he avoids burn-out because he "puts in the time to take time off."[78]

When he's had enough and needs to recharge, he takes a day for himself and turns off his cell phone.

It's not about the number of hours you work. As billionaire entrepreneur and investor, Mark Cuban, says in his book, "It would have been easy to judge effort by how many hours a day passed while I was at work. That's the worst way to measure effort. Effort is measured by setting goals and getting results."[79]

Jeff Bezos is known for working his employees hard at Amazon. He created a company culture that demands hard work and long hours from its employees. In Brad Stone's book, *The Everything Store: Jeff Bezos and the Age of Amazon*, he cites a telling example of Amazon's culture when he describes a meeting in which a female employee courageously challenges Bezos about the company's lack of work-life balance. According to Stone, Bezos responded, "The reason we are here is to get stuff done; that is the top priority. That is the DNA of Amazon. If you cannot excel and put everything into it, this might not be the place for you."[31]

Some Amazon employees joke that an employee who fits in well at Amazon becomes an "Amabot," referring to a lost sense of self in exchange for becoming an obedient and subservient input into a machine.[80] They say that employees who choose to remain human instead of becoming an *Amabot* don't last long. According to a survey conducted by PayScale in 2013, the median tenure for an Amazon employee is only about one year, giving it one of the highest turnover rates in the Fortune 500. For everything great that Amazon has accomplished, and for all the valuable products and services that they deliver, it's important to remember that they've done all these things despite a healthy work-life balance for those employees who help make it happen.

Peter Thiel, another billionaire entrepreneur and co-founder of PayPal, admitted that although he and his team were working 100-hour weeks, it was counterproductive.[81] They were spending too much time trying to destroy a competitor. Looking back, Thiel realizes this wasn't where his team's focus should have been. It's a great lesson to heed because it's a symptom of waste often left unnoticed. If we find ourselves with less time, working increasingly longer hours, we need to ask ourselves if we're focused on doing the most important things.

The University of Minnesota study mentioned earlier suggests that working exceptionally long hours may have a detrimental effect on a business. The number of hours worked is positively correlated with business success up until a workweek of approximately 56 hours, at which point the additional hours worked contribute more to fatigue and damaging important relationships with family and friends. This is particularly troubling because 17 percent of small business owners report working 60 hours or more per week.[82]

An unrelenting habit of working hellish hours each week leads to higher rates of stress and that higher stress will often result in additional health risks.[83] Entrepreneurship isn't a 40 hour a week, 9 to 5 endeavor, but it also doesn't need to be a 60+ hour per week commitment either. Like so many things in life, a balance somewhere in the middle of two extremes is where we often find both happiness and success.

Everyone's home-work situation is a little bit different, and what works for one entrepreneur might not work for you. Yet, in the face of seemingly impossible constraints, we are often poised to discover the most innovative solutions. This was true for Gay Gaddis, the founder and CEO of T3, the largest female-owned advertising agency in the U.S.[84]

One year, 4 out of her 24 employees got pregnant around the same time. To help her employees transition into being working mothers, she invited them to bring their babies to work. Thinking back on having four newborns in the office, Gay admits, "it was a bit daunting at first, but we all quickly got into a groove. If a baby cried, whoever was not on the phone grabbed it and waltzed it around the office. When they were asleep, we worked like fiends. We all laughed and said this is what growing up on a family farm must have been like, and it was."[85]

That sense of community became so powerful that Gay decided to make bringing your baby to work a permanent benefit called T3 & Under. Since 1995, more than 100 babies have gone through the program, and two of those first four babies returned to T3 in 2016 as college interns. Gay advises parent-entrepreneurs to get help when they need it, "Don't let the cost of help be an obstacle. Build the cost of help into your business plan. One or two new business successes or raises can be more than enough to cover the costs." [85]

We can also find work-life balance with the help of techniques like mindfulness meditation, which has been shown to help build entrepreneurial resilience.[86] Mindfulness meditation is a way to focus awareness on the present moment and stop our minds from wandering into the past or the future, racing from one worry to the next. It's an effective technique that's been scientifically shown to help us deal with the stress, anxiety, frustration, disillusionment, burnout, and cynicism that we're likely to experience at some point along our entrepreneurial journey.[214] In short, mindfulness meditation helps reduce our emotional exhaustion and enhance our well-being.[87]

Mindfulness meditation involves sitting peacefully, sealing ourselves off from outside distractions (turn off the smart phone and put it out of reach!), closing our eyes and focusing on our breathing. This process helps to "facilitate a separation between self and an [adverse] event and this in turn facilitates the reflective choice of actions and reactions such as greater hope, efficacy, resiliency, and optimism."[214]

Mindfulness practice has also been shown to help us reduce our biases, including the implicit biases we discussed earlier.[88] This is because when we practice mindfulness, we are intentionally redirecting brain activity from our reactionary "lizard brain" to our more rational and logical thinking capabilities in the prefrontal cortex.[89] This helps us be more open to new information and embrace the diverse perspectives of others.[90] We can realize the benefits of mindfulness with as little as 10 to 15 minutes of meditative practice each day. This should be part of the daily routine for every resilient entrepreneur.

Michael Acton Smith founded Mind Candy, a children's gaming and Entertainment Company, in 2004. Their signature products include Moshi Monsters, Petlandia, and World of Warriors. By 2012, the company had more than 50 million users throughout the world, helping to value the company at $200 million.[91] As the company grew exponentially, so did its challenges.

In 2014, Michael stepped down from the CEO role, admitting that the business' "challenges had gone from being more creative to more operational...there are better people to run that. I think it's about self-awareness, and in life it's very important to know what we're good at."[92] Reflecting back on his departure a few years later, he said those challenges and transition took their toll on him. "I was not sleeping well, I was exhausted all the time and I had headaches," he recalled.[93]

It was around that time that he started trying mediation. Speaking to the British daily newspaper, The Guardian, he said that, "like a lot of people, I thought mindfulness or mediation was weird and woo-woo. I assumed it was religious, and I just didn't really get it."[93]

Still, he gave it a try and started to notice the benefits. If you feel like Michael did, just remember that the opposite path to greater mindfulness is a much less desirable state – mindlessness.

"Meditation has benefited me hugely throughout my life because it produces a calm open-mindedness that allows me to think more clearly and creatively... It helps slow things down so that I can act calmly even in the face of chaos..."

-Ray Dalio
Founder, Bridgewater Associates

Give it a try, and like Michael, you might experience something transformational. In fact, his experience was so positive that it inspired him to create Calm, a smartphone app that helps people relax, meditate, and sleep. As distracting as smartphones can be, if we leverage them in the right way, they can help us be more mindful. In 2017, Calm was awarded app of the year by Apple. Now, with more than 30,000 app downloads each day, Calm's valuation is estimated to be approximately $250 million.[94] You can also check out Headspace and Brain.fm, other meditation apps comparable to Calm.

Social Resilience

Let's look at how helpful support networks and resources make us more resilient. Of all the research on resilience, the most consistent finding is the relationship between the number of high-quality relationships in our lives and our ability to overcome adversity.[95]

Immigrant communities are a great example, as they regularly access diaspora and familial networks to support one another's entrepreneurial endeavors.[12] Research conducted by Dr. Rocio Rosales, Associate Professor of Sociology at the University of California Irvine, highlights one such community in Los Angeles. Dr. Rosales estimates that there are more than 1,000 fruit vendors or *fruteros* operating in Los Angeles County - many of them self-employed immigrants.[96]

These *fruteros* often operate their businesses illegally because local permitting regulations and ordinances restrict their commerce due to concerns about health, public safety, and the right of way. Setting aside the various policy debates about immigration and local permitting regulations, what intrigued me most about these entrepreneurs is how they came together to overcome their shared challenges. Dr. Rosales refers to their coping mechanisms as survival strategies.

Ricardo is one of the *fruteros* she discusses in her study. When Ricardo's fruit cart was seized by the local health department regulators, he borrowed $1,000 from his cousin to purchase a new one. This new cart was again seized about two weeks later, and again his cousin lent him the money to purchase a new one. When this cart too was eventually seized, the same cousin who lent Ricardo money twice, hired him as an employee in his own business. While working to pay off his debt, Ricardo moved in with his cousins to save on rent and other living expenses. The responsive support offered to Ricardo is typical of many immigrant communities. We can learn from Ricardo's resilience by identifying our own support networks that we can call on during times of need.

Similarly, when early-stage entrepreneurs are seeking seed investment, they're usually advised to turn to friends and family first. Close friends and family are more likely to invest in a risky, unproven startup because they're betting more on their confidence in and love for the entrepreneur, rather than an objective view of the proposed business model's feasibility. Even if your inner circle isn't in a financial position to invest money in a startup, these people may still represent an invaluable asset to early-stage entrepreneurs. Resiliency, as it relates to funding a business is discussed in greater detail in Chapter 5.

When it comes to building entrepreneurial resiliency, it makes sense to tap into the support system of close friends and family, but there is also support outside these first-level networks. Our ability to access various networks outside our close friends and family is known as social capital. For example, when we network with other business owners, we're investing in our social capital with them.

These peer networks can serve as a good source of advice and camaraderie.[97] This can be especially true for online-based businesses that are prone to isolation from social interactions with their customers, suppliers, partners, etc. Some entrepreneurs engaged in e-commerce have found that online peer-networking groups can be effective sources of support.

For example, artisans selling their crafts online are joining forces to create seller teams whereby they offer cross-promotion, critical feedback, fresh ideas, as well as emotional and psychological support to team members. In a survey of over 300 artisans selling handcrafts on the online handmade goods retailer Etsy, 97 percent reported having had received some type of support from other sellers at one time or another. In addition, those who were most actively engaged in seller teams had online stores that performed significantly better than those who were only passively engaged.[97] In highly competitive environments, such as the artisan crafts industry, these peer networks serve as a support mechanism that help build more resilient entrepreneurs.

Kristine Kuhn, Associate Professor of Management and Operations at Washington State University, was the lead researcher on this study of artisans. She and her research team interviewed several artisans. Here's an excerpt from one of those interviews:

"I've asked [other artisans] for advice on just about every aspect of running my business – they voted on a new banner/avatar for my shop, they've suggested new product ideas, they've referred me to different sites for shipping supplies, they've helped me get ready to take my virtual shop into the 'real world' of craft shows. My top-selling item was actually a suggestion from another member!"[97]

We can see how this artisan's seller team provided a wide range of benefits. It takes time to find the right network to invest in. Use your social intelligence to know when you've found the right network with the right people who can help you solve your challenges and provide a rejuvenating, optimistic environment.[150] You might not feel the right fit with the first, or even the first few networks you encounter, but don't give up. Keep trying out new groups until you find the one that's right for you.

Interacting with others for support isn't fluffy, feel-good advice. There is scientific evidence that active encouragement and peer support can have a direct impact on a startup's bottom line. In fact, entrepreneurs who display higher levels of social resilience are quicker to reach a financial break-even point.[98]

A longitudinal study of 94 business owners, conducted by the University of Minnesota, suggested that greater commitment from a spouse or significant other was exponentially correlated to the number of months it took an early-stage business to reach its break-even point. The study found that a two-fold increase in the perceived commitment shown by an entrepreneur's spouse or significant other resulted in the business breaking even in 15 fewer months, on average, compared to entrepreneurs who never had that supportive commitment. There are real benefits in engaging your support networks.

Dr. Henry Jones, co-founder of Kopis Mobile, was selected in Inc. Magazine's 2017 list of America's fastest growing companies. Kopis specializes in technologies for soldiers and first responders. When asked about the hardest challenge of being a business owner, Dr. Jones replied, "My spouse had not been through this process before in any way and had no entrepreneurs in her family. This has been a foreign and very scary experience for her."[99]

I followed up with Dr. Jones to learn more about how he and his team manage a work-life balance with such a fast-growing company. He acknowledged that he hadn't done as good a job as he would have liked, especially in the beginning. His spouse came from a family where you go to work, do a specific job, and get paid every two weeks. Dr. Jones didn't receive any compensation from his startup for the entire first year, so when he went to work, he was doing a job and not getting paid. That just didn't make sense to his spouse, and understandably, put a lot of stress on their marriage.

He admits that he isn't a relationship expert, but that he and Kopis' co-founders rely on one another to help out when someone needs a little more family time. "As a team, we trust each other, and we rely on and support one another when we need help – that trust is important," Jones said of his co-founding team.[100]

Without exception, every entrepreneur who wants to maintain their personal and familial relationships while they build their business should read *For Better or for Work: A Survival Guide for Entrepreneurs and Their Families* by Meg Hirshberg. I would go as far as to say it should be required reading for every entrepreneurship class. Meg is the life and business partner of Gary Hirshberg, co-founder of Stonyfield Farm, Inc.

Stonyfield Farm is the largest organic yogurt manufacturer in the world with more than 250 employees and annual sales exceeding $370 million[101] Meg has over 30 years of experience as both a spouse working in the business, and more recently, as a spouse who has pursued her own life and career outside of Stonyfield. Speaking about Stonyfield's early startup days, she echoed sentiments of Dr. Jones'; "With little exposure to the trials of entrepreneurship, I had no conception of the endurance it would require. If you've never owned a company or lived with someone who owns one, you cannot imagine the emotional whiplash it can induce."[101] Being aware of the strains and level-setting expectations with those closest to you can make the difference later on when challenges arise.

Just about every entrepreneur struggles with finding the right balance between work and family or social life. Tensions and challenges with family will arise, especially in the beginning when things adjust. It's hard not to over-commit yourself to a new business opportunity. It will be frustrating when things don't go as planned and there is disagreement between the vision for the business and the vision for life outside of it.

One thing to avoid is starting a new business or making major changes in an existing business while a big life event is happening at the same time. Planning to get married in six months? Moving across the country? Having your first child? These enormous life changes are going to test your personal resilience. You will be required to adjust existing habits and form new ones. You'll need to be flexible and adapt to new circumstances. Give yourself time to fine-tune life before adding on the stress from business. Dr. Art Markman says, "making a lot of changes at the same time is a recipe for failure... Focus on making the most important changes first. Add new changes to your life only after you have established some new habits and the stress of those initial changes has faded."[138]

Sometimes a bit of life experience can help you strike the right balance. A study of self-employed nurses found that the older, more seasoned nurses were more likely to place a greater emphasis on personal meaning versus financial metrics or productivity. They were also more resilient, had a clearer sense of their own strengths and overall, encouraged themselves more than they self-critiqued.[102] Perhaps we can learn something from the wisdom they've gained over the years.

We can also try to set realistic expectations. When discussing your business plans and goals with your significant other, don't simply notify them of your entrepreneurial intentions. You should have a serious sit-down discussion about the risks and rewards of going into business. This is especially true if other big life events are happening at the same time.

Lori Greiner, the "Queen of QVC" and co-star of ABC's reality TV show, Shark Tank, has some good advice in this area. She should know; her business partner, Daniel, is also her husband. "It's easy for inventors and budding entrepreneurs to be so excited about a dream that they underestimate the impact their pursuit of those dreams will have on their partner or family, or they dismiss their concerns," she says. She goes on to advise: "if your partner questions the wisdom of accepting a loan or the terms of an investment, do not accuse the individual of being unsupportive."[257]

One of the best strategies for maintaining balance is the ability to work from areas supported by your core strengths and delegate the rest. We'll dive much deeper into those strategies in later chapters.

Choosing a support network is critical to developing social resilience, and choosing that network wisely is just as important. As you embark on your journey, you need to surround yourself with people who can positively encourage you and constructively guide you along the way. The people around us shape us, so choose to spend more time with the people who will help you realize your entrepreneurial dreams and less time with those who won't.

Summary

Six years after discovering an entrepreneurial idea, 66 percent of aspiring entrepreneurs either give up on entrepreneurship altogether or are still stuck spinning their wheels in the idea/startup stage.[20] You are not going to contribute to those stats because you're on your way to becoming a more resilient entrepreneur!

The resilient entrepreneur views their adverse experiences as opportunities to grow and develop new knowledge, skills and abilities (KSAs). These KSAs help them better prepare for future trials and challenges. If you want to become a more resilient entrepreneur and you are willing to apply yourself toward that goal, you can grow into the entrepreneur that overcomes adversity and emerges from it even stronger and more determined.

The resilient entrepreneur has confidence in their KSAs. Yet, they're humble enough to admit when they don't know something and could use some help. This is when reach out to those around us for support. The resilient entrepreneur is also mindful of their biases and blind spots, and they strike the right balance between working hard and taking time to relax and refuel.

Take Action!

1. Before moving to the next chapter, list significant people in your life who might be able to help you along your entrepreneurial journey. These are the people you can call on to help you persevere toward your business goals and lift you up when you stumble:

   A. ______________________________

   B. ______________________________

   C. ______________________________

   D. ______________________________

   E. ______________________________

2. Take the Entrepreneurial Resilience Assessment, if you haven't already.

3. Start practicing mindfulness for 10 to 15 minutes each day. Download the Calm, Headspace or Brain.fm app today and try some beginner meditations. Set a reminder on your phone to take a short break each day for mindfulness practice. There are also several books and audiobooks that can help get you started and guide you through the process.

Chapter 2: Stories of Entrepreneurial Resilience

"Adverse fortune is more beneficial than good fortune; the latter only makes men greedy for more, but adversity makes them strong."

-Jonathan Haidt
Social Psychologist and Best-selling Author

We often see news headlines about natural disasters. The frequency of which seems to be every increasing as we feel the effects of climate change. Severe storms, flash floods, and tornadoes leave wakes of destruction through centers of economic activity. Wildfires consume thousands of homes and businesses each year. The 2017 hurricanes Harvey, Irma, and Maria cost the United States more than $300 billion in damages and economic losses – a significant and disproportionate percentage of those losses were accrued by small businesses.[103]

Small "mom and pop" businesses have a difficult time surviving under the best of circumstances, but when a natural disaster strikes, it can be devastating. Yet somehow some businesses can overcome the trauma and destruction, while others are lost forever. In this chapter, I share inspiring stories from some of the most resilient entrepreneurs who faced the worst that Mother Nature could dole out and still found a way to carry on. Multiple studies have shown that entrepreneurs can benefit from hearing stories of perseverance from their peers.[39] These stories of resilience during extraordinary times of adversity can teach us important lessons for how to face our own challenges, even if we're not facing an earth-shattering crisis.

John's story of entrepreneurial resilience began on Memorial Day weekend in 1981, when the city of Austin, Texas experienced one of its worst floods on record. Thirteen people lost their lives that weekend.[104] Beyond the humanitarian tragedy, there was an enormous economic loss, felt most acutely by Austin's small business community. John's small specialty grocery store, only in its first year of business, was one of many hit hard by the unexpected deluge.[105]

As the relentless rains poured down, the store's employees reinforced the front door with sacks of grains and rice. Yet, when the flood waters rose above 4 feet, the weight of the water broke through the glass door and completely flooded the store. The young business didn't have flood insurance. Like most young businesses, that wasn't a priority startup expense. As John watched cars float by on the street in front of his store, he thought for sure he would have to file for bankruptcy.

The next day, when John returned to his store to begin cleaning up, he was amazed to find himself surrounded by neighbors and customers who had come to help. Not only did they assist with the cleanup efforts, but they also helped organize a fundraiser to finance some of the store's reopening costs. Additional financing came in the form of a small loan. While the financing processed, the store's employees worked without pay, so that more money could be reinvested to help the store get back up on its feet[106].

"We only survived because of the outpouring of love and support from local businesses, customers, neighbors, supplier partners, and dedicated team members," said John, looking back decades later[107]. It was because he invested in creating strong social ties that he was able to tap into those resources during a crisis. Not only did his specialty grocery store survive the flood, it thrived over the next 36 years, and in June of 2017, John Mackey sold Whole Foods, with its international portfolio of 460 grocery stores, to Amazon for $13.7 billion[108].

The resiliency of John Mackey and Whole Foods is at least partially attributable to the access he had to the responsive community. Few expect their business to literally go underwater due to a natural disaster, but when the unexpected happens, the ecosystem of established support mechanisms can make a huge difference in whether a business is able to resurface.

A few weeks after I wrote this section about Mackey and Whole Foods' flood experience in Austin, Hurricane Harvey hit Texas and devastated its coastline. There are probably thousands of stories of resilience that can be told in the aftermath of Hurricane Harvey, Irma, and Maria, but one in particular touched my heart.

In 2013, Jim, a business owner in Houston, began feeling tingling sensations in his face and down into his arm. He immediately called his doctor and learned that there was something wrong with his heart.[109] The doctor told him he was suffering from a condition known as Patent Foramen Ovale or PFO. It happens when a naturally-occurring hole in the heart fails to close.[110] Fortunately, Jim's doctor diagnosed the condition early, and a procedure to repair the hole was performed successfully. His operation was on August 29th, and by Labor Day, Jim was already back to work with high spirits, saying that "a setback is just a setup for a comeback!"[111]

He should know. Jim McIngvale, affectionately known as "Mattress Mack," has had his share of setbacks. He and his wife, Linda, launched their furniture retail business with only $5,000 back in 1981.[112] In 2009, one of his furniture stores was intentionally set ablaze by a disgruntled former employee who was terminated after he'd been accused of operating an illegal side business while on the job. The fire damages temporarily disrupted business operations and cost between $18 and $20 million to rebuild.[113] At the time, Jim's Furniture Gallery business was bringing in revenues exceeding $100 million annually.[114]

The former employee-turned-arsonist was arrested and spent several years behind bars awaiting trial. In 2013, four years after the fire, during pretrial hearings, it was discovered that the employee had a severe brain tumor, and the judge ruled that he was too mentally incompetent to stand trial. Jim was undeniably a victim of a crime, but his response to the judge's ruling underscores the measure of a resilient entrepreneur: "The court system is the court system, and if they say he's incompetent, we certainly respect whatever the court system rules. We've been through so many ups and downs with this thing since it first happened, but that's life. You take your licking and keep on ticking."[115]

As the local news outlets reported on the fire, Logan Burnaman, an 11-year-old boy who lived nearby, watched and wondered how he might be able to help. He had $200, mostly in loose change that he had been saving to buy an Apple iPod. When he heard about the fire at the store, he decided he wanted to donate his savings to the rebuilding effort instead. The boy's parents tried to dissuade him, reassuring him that Jim's business would recover with the help of insurance payouts. Logan insisted, saying, "Even millionaires need to know somebody cares." So, his parents drove him over to another one of Jim's store locations and they met with Jim to donate the boy's savings. Jim tried to refuse, but when pressed, accepted the donation as an example in the art of giving and receiving. Later, he gifted the boy an iPod and made a $200 donation to a charity focused on mental health services. When his store was rebuilt, he displayed the bag of coins as a reminder of Logan's good deed and his renewed faith in the next generation.[116]

Jim McIngvale is a recipient of the Point of Light Award created by President George H.W. Bush. The award is given to "individuals who find innovative ways to meet community needs; efforts which often lead to long-term solutions and impact social problems in their local communities."[117] Almost four years to the day after his heart surgery, Jim's inspiring words, *"A setback is just a setup for a comeback!"* would prove inspiring not only for him, but for the entire Houston metropolitan area.

As Hurricane Harvey devastated the Houston area, Jim converted his furniture delivery trucks into rescue vehicles. After rescuing approximately 200 people from the flood waters, they were brought back to Furniture Gallery, where Jim converted his showrooms and warehouses into temporary shelters.[118] He posted a video online inviting anyone who needed refuge to seek shelter at his stores, saying, "We can take strength from the fact that for hundreds of years Texans have banded together to help each other, and we will help each other now to get through this crisis. If not for our struggles, we would not have known our strengths. We will get through this together".[119] Our ability to band together and help each other during difficult times is part of our humanity and the reason why our species is so resilient.

McIngvale says, “You can’t give up when things look bad. You can’t slow down when things are good.”[112] Speaking at a small business leader’s luncheon, he praised the resiliency of small business owners and their ability to persevere through changes. “As small business owners, we get knocked down every day,” he said. “Our job is to overcome.”[120] That’s exactly what the entrepreneurs in our next story did.

> “Great external upheavals aren’t necessarily what distress us most… Natural disasters sometimes bring out the best in humankind in terms of courage, solidarity, and the will to live. Altruism and mutual assistance contribute to greatly reducing the post-traumatic stress associated with tragedies. Most of the time it is not outward events but our own mind and negative emotions that make us unable to maintain our inner stability and drag us down.”
>
> - Matthieu Ricard
> Author of Happiness: A Guide to Developing Life’s Most Important Skill

---

In season 9 of the ABC reality TV show, Shark Tank, husband-wife entrepreneurs, Maranda and Joe Dowell, pitched Joe’s Fish Fry, a gourmet Cajun-inspired seasoning. When I reached out to Maranda, she graciously agreed to speak with me. I was surprised to learn that this wasn’t their first attempt to pitch on Shark Tank. About a year earlier, they auditioned but didn’t make the cut. Where most people would have said, “Oh well, tough luck” and moved on, the Dowell’s worked on building their business and polishing their pitch. When they auditioned the next year, they were accepted on to the show.

I asked Maranda why they tried again after being rejected the first time. She responded that they were able to better communicate their business' value when they tried again. "Being cut was the best thing that could have happened," she said, "because when we came back the next year, we were stronger and sharper. We were more authentic to who we are."

Failing and getting back up to try again seems to be part of the Dowell Household ethos. Joe's Fish Fry is the Dowell's third attempt at business. Joe started his first restaurant in Atlanta at the age of 28. The business did well – so well in fact that he wasn't able to properly manage the growth, and the business eventually imploded. He learned some hard lessons with that first restaurant, but he wasn't ready to pack it in and go back to the 9 to 5. The Dowell's possess what they call a 'never give up attitude.' They are exemplars of entrepreneurial resilience.

After the restaurant in Atlanta failed, Joe moved back to his hometown of New Orleans to open a "small hole-in-wall Po Boy restaurant." The business started to do well, and after about a year, he opened a second location. Less than a year later, Hurricane Katrina hit New Orleans and destroyed both restaurants. His business was devastated. Among the rubble and flood waters, there wasn't much left to salvage except a couple of fish fryers. Where others might have saw those last two fryers and seen 99 percent of their business destroyed, Joe saw them as his business' salvation. He grabbed the fish fryers and got ready to start again. This time, he decided he would feed festival-goers back in Atlanta. In his first weekend frying fish, he made $5,000. He was back in business!

I asked Maranda why they didn't decide to stay in New Orleans and apply for aid to reopen their restaurants.

"Joe wasn't about that," Maranda said of her husband. "He's not the type to sit around and wait for help."
When Joe looked at those fryers, he saw an opportunity to get himself back in business. They decided to leave New Orleans because the location they were in was just too devastated to be viable again anytime soon.

Joe now does about 40 events and festivals every year. While most of those events fall on the weekend, he's able to spend family time with Maranda and his kids during the week. Maranda says, "Joe's passion is feeding people and that's what he focuses on. He stays true to himself and lets the rest of the pieces fall into place around the vision he has for the business. When he stays focused on working from his strengths, he's able to attract the resources and knowledge he needs to be successful. In that way, we make a great team because we can complement each other. If we weren't together, I'd be back in the corporate world where I was before. Now, I can use my business skills to help manage the operations while Joe focuses on the product and customer."

I finished our interview by asking what advice Maranda would give to entrepreneurs experiencing an unexpected setback or failure. Her response epitomizes the resilient entrepreneur's mindset:

"So, you've had a lot of failures along the way, but it's what you do with those failures that matters. You can use them as fuel for the negative or to fuel the positive. All our battles are won and lost in our head – it's about how we interpret our own circumstances.

We've had some major setbacks, but the real battle is internal –

how you're thinking about things. Do you stay there and allow it to overtake your thoughts or do you keep hope? If you preserve hope, you can overcome anything. It's when your thoughts escape you that you become a failure. Believe in yourself and have hope for a better future. Recover from failure in your mind and the rest of the recovery will fall into place."

While all business owners should be aware of and prepared for the natural catastrophes that might affect them, entrepreneurial resilience is about more than overcoming Mother Nature's periodic devastation.

The American Red Cross offers a free service to learn about disaster preparedness through their Ready Rating™ Program. You can learn more at www.readyrating.org

Additional resources for disaster preparedness can be found at www.restoreyoureconomy.org

Additional information for economic development organizations can be found in the appendix section titled: *The Role of Entrepreneurial Development Organizations.*

Battling Illness while Building a Business

Tiffany Krumins is the inventor of Ava the Elephant, an innovative product that makes it fun and easy for children to take their medicine. She came up with the idea when she was caregiver to a young boy with Down Syndrome who became petrified when it was time to take his medicine. Her fun-loving medicine dispenser resembled a happy elephant, making medicine time much less terrifying.[121]

Tiffany reached a major milestone along her entrepreneurial journey when she secured a $50,000 investment on national television through ABC's reality show, *Shark Tank*. She was riding high, ready to scale and distribute her product through retail when, three months later, she was grounded by the devastating news that she had thyroid cancer. Getting well became a priority and she began radiation treatments almost immediately.

Her specialized radiation regimen required that she be in isolation for seven days at a time after treatment. While in isolation, she kept working on the business.[122] Most people might have called it quits on the business to focus on getting well, and Tiffany considered it on several occasions. Yet, each time she thought about closing the business, she thought about all the sick children that might benefit from her product.

With them in mind, she kept going. When she shipped Ava the Elephant out to a group of kids in the hospital battling leukemia, she received stories back about how much they loved the product. Tiffany's radiation worked, and her cancer went into remission, but she's since had several related health scares. In an interview a few years later with the Huffington Post, Tiffany said she believes that God put her on her entrepreneurial path for a reason. She said her personal experience increased her compassion for the children she helps and the difference her product is making in their lives keeps her motivated every day.[122] Today, Ava the Elephant is in over 10,000 retail stores across the globe.[123]

Tiffany's story gives us an inspiring lesson in resilience. The bio on her website says, "buried in the darkest of wrappings, [Tiffany] unearthed a treasure trove of business opportunities and valuable connections when she redirected her focus from her own troubles to helping others."[124]When we have the strength to shift our focus and energy toward others in need, our own adversity, by comparison, doesn't seem so insurmountable.

Vesta Garcia co-founded Stitch Texas in the summer of 2013. The company specializes in apparel design, development and production. Not long after founding her company, Vesta, at age 42, was diagnosed with amyotrophic lateral sclerosis (ALS).[125]

According to the ALS Association, "ALS is a progressive neurodegenerative disease that affects nerve cells in the brain and spinal cord." After diagnosis, those with this terminal disease have a life expectancy of two to five years.[126] Vesta probably understood her prognosis better than most - before starting her business, she received a master's degree in neurobiology from the University of Washington.

I first met Vesta in 2017. By that time, she was already confined to an electric wheelchair and labored to speak without losing her breath. I was facilitating a group discussion to help the economic development department get input from the community about local government's role in supporting small businesses' workforce needs.

Vesta and her business partner were in my group. She was friendly and professional, and when it came to sharing her opinion on policy issues, she was candid and direct. She was there to represent Stitch Texas, but she also spoke as an unofficial representative for many local small businesses. As a CEO of a company with about ten employees, she certainly had enough on her plate to keep her busy. On top of that, she was battling a horribly debilitating disease. Yet, she was there at the community meeting to give her input because she believed that people who are civically engaged can make a difference.

A few months later, Vesta applied and was accepted into the City of Austin's Accelerator Program designed to help local businesses grow and scale their operations. The program is an intensive 12-week opportunity to learn and connect with other small business owners facing similar growing pains. It adds about 4-6 hours of work per week to the already full plates of business owners, but they emerge from the program with a well-defined strategy for growing their business. Through that program and in several one-on-one meetings, I got the privilege of getting to know Vesta and her business.

It was in one of our meetings that I learned Stitch Texas wasn't Vesta's first business endeavor. Her entrepreneurial journey started after her daughter was born. "I found myself at home after my daughter's birth and looking for a way to stay intellectually stimulated and contribute to the family finances," she said in a 2017 interview with Austin Woman Magazine.[125] She started designing and producing wraps and carriers for babies.

She did well in that business and other related entrepreneurial endeavors. That was until an unscrupulous supplier/manufacturer overseas cheated her out of tens of thousands of dollars, forcing her out of business. She recounted the story and lessons learned without a hint of bitterness. For Vesta, it was only a temporary setback.

With her years of experience, she co-founded Stitch Texas to help other fashion and apparel industry entrepreneurs navigate and avoid common pitfalls that occur during the process, from concept to a completely manufactured product. In an industry where more than 90 percent of domestic demand is fulfilled by imports from overseas, Stitch Texas is resurrecting a domestic apparel manufacturing capability that focuses on high quality, Made-in-the-USA products and superior customer service.[127] That value has led to tremendous growth in her business. Vesta introduced me to some of the wonderful employees at Stitch and gave me a tour of the production and manufacturing space. It was obvious that from the downfall of the previous business, she was able to build something much greater.

As the weeks went on, Vesta's disease worsened, and her voice became softer and quieter. By the end of the 12-week program, she had almost completely lost her ability to speak. Using assistive technology, she gave her final presentation through synthesized speech, calling it her "ALS accent." The last time Vesta and I met in person, she told me that she just wanted to get the business healthy and stable before she was no longer able to work. She passed away a few months after finishing the accelerator program. In our final correspondence, she shared that her business' revenues were up over 50 percent. I think she can rest knowing she accomplished what she set out to do. How she was able to fight a two-front battle in life and in business while remaining so gracious is an inspiring example of resilience that I will remember and be inspired by for the rest of my life.

Chapter 3: Goal Setting

"I realized that the satisfaction of success doesn't come from achieving your goals, but from struggling well. To understand what I mean, imagine your greatest goal... Now imagine instantaneously achieving it. You'd be happy at first, but not for long... Just look at people who attain their dreams early – the child star, the lottery winner... They typically don't end up happy unless they get excited about something else bigger and better to struggle for. Since life brings both ups and downs, struggling well doesn't just make your ups better; it makes your downs less bad."

- Ray Dalio
Founder of Bridgewater Associates and author of *Principles*

There is contentious debate about the costs and benefits of formal business planning. Some argue that it takes too long, it's too academic and everyone's plan is obsolete as soon as you put it up against reality. However, business planning has been found to significantly increase burgeoning entrepreneurs' chance of success. In fact, when researchers followed over 1,000 entrepreneurs during their first five years in business, from 2007-2011, they found that those who had formal, written business plans were up to fifteen percent more likely to have a viable business compared to those who did not.[128]

There are many benefits of business planning. Planning encourages us to create systematic goals and well-defined objectives that keep our efforts coordinated and organized – the focus of this chapter.[129] Planning has also been shown to improve our strategic decision-making ability by forcing us to question and address assumptions baked into the early versions of our business models.[130]

It's nearly impossible to find outside sources of capital for our business without a formal business plan or pitch deck to present to lenders or investors. For the resilient entrepreneur, the question is not whether to plan, but how to plan so that we are better able to persevere through adversity and quickly bounce back from failures.

I'm not going to cover every aspect of business planning in this book, but I do want to get you on the right track with the first step in business planning – goal setting. Whether or not you've already created your goals, I encourage you to read through and study this chapter. I introduce some helpful variations into the typical goal-setting processes that entrepreneurs might be familiar with.

Regardless of planning format or startup methodology, whether you have a new or existing business, goal setting is a foundational aspect of entrepreneurship.[300]
If you're just starting your entrepreneurial journey, goal-setting is an important first step in moving out of the idea or concept phase and taking action. It's not enough to simply muse over or envision business goals in our minds; goals need to be written down if you're to have any chance of attaining them.

Challenging goals become easier to achieve when we define what it is we're trying to accomplish. It's often much more satisfying to dream about the end-state, basking in the glory of triumph. It's much more difficult, on the other hand, to focus on each individual step up the steep staircase to success. Some of the most successful entrepreneurs have had this same realization.

Tony Hsieh, the CEO of Zappos, reflected on one of his first entrepreneurial endeavors in his best-selling book, *Delivering Happiness*. He recalled that he "loved the idea of owning and running a business, but the reality ended up being a lot less fun than the fantasy."[131] Yet, if we're only imagining ourselves at the end of our journey, we're less likely to take those first steps up from the bottom. Don't get me wrong, it's important and necessary to start with a vision of the higher purpose that we're trying to achieve, but don't stop and hang out there for too long.

When we pursue challenging goals, it is important to think about them in terms of what we can accomplish in the near-term and long-term. There should be a balance between both to maximize the effects they have on our motivation. Our larger goals and vision should clearly connect to what we're actively working to accomplish in the near-term. There's a lot of research that shows that when we break down larger goals into smaller sub-goals, we're significantly more likely to persevere toward our bigger, more audacious vision.

Envisioning

To illustrate how we can do this, let's try a mental exercise. Imagine that you've become the successful entrepreneur you desire to be. What does that look like? Do you imagine the financial and intellectual independence you've achieved by becoming self-employed? Do you relish the flexibility and autonomy you have by being your own boss?

Whatever it is you're working toward, imagine what that success looks like. Write it down in a short free-flowing narrative. I teach this technique in my classes and one of my students shared her beautifully-articulated vision. With her permission, I've shared a short excerpt below as an example to reference:

> *"I had always hoped that this day would come, but I could not have imagined that it would be this liberating. To not have to count down the hours until a schedule is posted, hoping that my requested days off have been approved; to not need to come into work on the weekends, but to want to come in; to not worry that I must micromanage every possible detail, but to trust those who work beside me and for me; to have both a work life and a personal life and ne'er the two shall be forced to meet. These are the things that you can't find without forging your own path, without working purposefully toward that end.*
>
> *I have always worked hard, and I find work, structure and purpose to be fulfilling and rewarding, but I also want to work hard toward something I believe in, I want to work on my own terms, and that is what becoming my own boss enabled me to accomplish. I still work overtime, I still fuss over minor details in my pursuit of perfection, but I do this by choice, not necessity.*
>
> *The sacrifices for my work are fewer and less serious, never anything dire, and decisions at work don't bleed over into my personal life any longer. My creative drive is amplified, and my energy and attention are both focused on the task at hand, at continuing to grow and adapt my business. The work is never done, but these days, I rest easy knowing that I am working towards something worthwhile."*

It feels good to envision what our achievements will look like in the future. It has been scientifically proven that dreaming about a better future makes us calmer and more relaxed.[132] While this might sound like a positive outcome, if we're not careful, it can become a contributing factor for not achieving our goals. How can that be? Doesn't positive visioning and dreaming help inspire hope and optimism for success?[133] Sure it does and at first glance, it would seem intuitive that if we're more relaxed and calmed by our vision and dreams, we'll be in a better state to accomplish what we want. If we're not stressed thinking about the challenges we're going to face, we will be more likely to succeed, right?

Research suggests that the exact opposite might be true. When we're calm and relaxed, dreaming about being successful entrepreneurs, we're physically less motivated to act. Our blood pressure decreases, our muscles relax, and we exhale deeper breaths. On the other hand, when we imagine the obstacles that stand in the way of our dreams, our blood pressure rises, we tense up and our adrenaline gives our bodies the energy it needs to act. In other words, we start to feel stress.

The way we respond to this stress is key. If we react anxiously, we might feel overwhelmed and we won't be able to accomplish much. Conversely, if we leverage the energy that stress gives, we can find the motivation to start tackling obstacles.

These findings were validated in several studies conducted by NYU Professor of Psychology, Dr. Gabriele Oettingen.[134] Her experiments involved asking hundreds of people to either imagine having already achieved success or imagine their success and then the various obstacles they needed to overcome to become successful.

Oettingen and her research team measured participants' changes in blood pressure and consistently found that those who only dreamed about success showed a decrease in blood pressure, while those who imagined both the success they desired and the obstacles they needed to overcome experienced increased in blood pressure. When we imagine what we need to overcome to achieve our goals, we can become physically energized to get it done. This gives support to the adage that we're better off with our head in the clouds and our feet planted firmly on the ground.

Good stress, also known as eustress, can help us reach the highest levels of productivity and enter a mental state of complete focus, known as *flow*.[135] The effects of eustress on a group of 21 entrepreneurs were studied using a series of semi-structured interviews, self-reporting through journaling and a three-day monitoring of the entrepreneurs' heartrate variability. When these entrepreneurs entered a state of flow, their pulse increased, but they reported that they felt productive, not overwhelmed.

One entrepreneur, a 38-year-old consultant, described her physiologically stressful experience as productive and enjoyable. "It is like dancing on water, like getting wings," she said. She went on to say that when she felt pressured by the challenge, it was because of that pressure that she was able to find a resolution.[136] For her, the eustress made her more productive.

It's important to remember the differences between negative stress, or distress, and eustress. When channeled appropriately, stress can become the eustress that puts us into a state of flow where we can be most productive.

Laddering

"I'm all for dreaming about things I might achieve. Dreams are the basis of creativity, and I don't want to stop imaging things I might accomplish, because it leads to creating new ideas to be explored and developed. I just refuse to live my entire life in my dreams, and so should you."

- Robert Herjavec
Entrepreneur and Investor

Ryan Holiday, the author of *The Obstacle is the Way: The Timeless Art of Turning Trials into Triumph*, reminds us "when you have a goal, obstacles are actually teaching you how to get where you want to go – carving you a path."[137] You shouldn't view these obstacles as impenetrable barriers, but rather as signals, telling you where you should focus your time, energy and resources.

With that in mind, let's revisit our ultimate vision of entrepreneurial success. Now that we've imagined achieving our entrepreneurial dream, let's build a ladder to that ultimate vision of success by working backward from the top-down. We can do this by asking a simple question - *what's one thing standing in the way of achieving your entrepreneurial dream?*

For many business owners, seed funding and financing early-stage growth is a commonly-cited barrier. If you've identified funding as one obstacle to realizing your dream, let's explore that hurdle and determine some of the things standing between the business and financing. We're working our way down the ladder, and we repeat the same questions we asked previously: what's one thing preventing us from obtaining seed or growth-stage capital for our business? We identify a reason and then we repeat the question to see what else might be blocking us. *What's another possible reason we haven't been able to get financing?*

Perhaps we haven't had any luck funding our business because we don't yet have a very well-crafted business plan or pitch deck. Again, we'll repeat our series of questions: What's one reason why our business plan or pitch deck is lacking? Maybe we really didn't have a good foundational understanding of how to put a business plan or pitch deck together. Maybe we're unsure of how everything should be formatted. It could be that we need help with the financial section of the business plan.

What's another thing blocking you?

As we work backward, we start to identify, with more and more specificity, the types of challenges we're up against. This process should help uncover actionable tasks we can start doing in the near-term that will eventually lead to achieving broader, long-term goals.

Returning to our example, now that we've identified a knowledge gap in our understanding of crafting a persuasive pitch-deck or business plan, we can look for relevant solutions. We can sign up for a business planning class or work with a business coach to improve our pitch materials. These goals represent positive or achievement-based actions – they're things we want to accomplish. It's important to frame goals in this positive, growth framework, as opposed to goals for things we want to avoid.

For example, I encounter a lot of entrepreneurs who are anxious about someone stealing their business idea. Some of them are outright paranoid, telling me snippets of their business model in the abstract with code names for their products. One guy even refused to communicate electronically with me for fear someone could intercept our communications and steal his idea. Every step these entrepreneurs take is clouded by the avoidance goal of not having their idea stolen. This fear should be set aside. Ideas are a dime a dozen – it's a motivated, resilient entrepreneur who can execute on an idea that's in much shorter supply.

If we expend all our energy on what we don't want to happen, we'll find we have nothing left to focus on. You couldn't fill a book with enough stories about stolen business ideas, but you could fill volumes with failed entrepreneurs who didn't succeed because they were paralyzed by their own paranoia.

Thinking again about our ultimate entrepreneurial dream, let's work our way backwards to something we can accomplish in the near-term to make that dream a reality. It's important to always think of that vision as our anchor that keeps us grounded in terms of what's important. When things don't go the way we hoped, we should always be able to call back to our original vision and find motivation to persevere.

Once we've created a ladder to our ultimate entrepreneurial dream, we can look more closely at each rung along the way and decide what needs to be accomplished to overcome each obstacle. Again, going back to our original example, stating our intention to sign up for a business planning class is an important thing we can accomplish as a near-term goal.

I've often found that many of the clients I coach know and even say what they need to do next, but for some reason, they just "haven't gotten it done yet". They've "been meaning to" and are "going to," but for whatever reason they just haven't done it. Why not? You can insert any excuse imaginable as an answer; I've heard just about all of them, many of them legitimate and understandable. One underlying reason is that we imagine ourselves walking out of the classroom with all the knowledge and resources we need to finally get that business plan or pitch deck finished. The positive emotions we get by imagining we've already accomplished our goal saps our energy and leaves us without the motivation we need to sign up and show up for the class in the first place. We've dreamed too long and allowed the day-to-day things that are part of our normal routine to block us from action. Don't just daydream while following the same routine. You're going to have to change some habits and create some new ones to make your dream come true.

It's not enough to state our goal. We must put a deadline on it and envision ourselves taking the steps to achieve it. When will we take that business planning class? After the New Year? Sometime in the next couple of months? Those timeframes are too vague to be action-oriented. By which specific date will we complete the class?
I looked online and found a class that takes place every second Tuesday of the month. I'm going to sign up for that next class on 'x' date.

This might seem overly meticulous, but it's not. Our habits are often engrained so strongly that they control many of our behaviors unconsciously. Dr. Art Markman is a professor of psychology at the University of Texas. In his book, *Smart Change*, he says "to put your long-term goals on an equal footing with your short-term goals, you need to recast the activities that will pay off for you in the long run in terms of specific goals you can achieve on a daily basis that will ultimately lead to long-term success."[138]

We need our daily activities to lead to the completion of our short-term goals, which help us achieve our longer-term goals. If we're used to coming home and continuing our favorite TV series, we might head straight into that routine and lose sight of the small task we wanted to accomplish toward our business goals.

Answering these questions with this level of specificity makes our goals time-bound and action-oriented. For example, when and where will we register and pay for that business planning class? Instead of turning on the TV or checking social media, imagine yourself in front of your computer for 10 minutes after dinner this evening. Envision yourself registering and paying for that business plan class. Then put a reminder in your calendar about when and where the class will be held. We are much more likely to act on an intention when it is planned to that level of specificity. Dr. Oettingen's research shows that creating these specific, actionable plans is critical to following through on goals.[132] From our dream, we've worked backward down to signing up for a business planning class online this evening after we've had dinner and put the kids to bed. The accompanying graphic outlines this example:

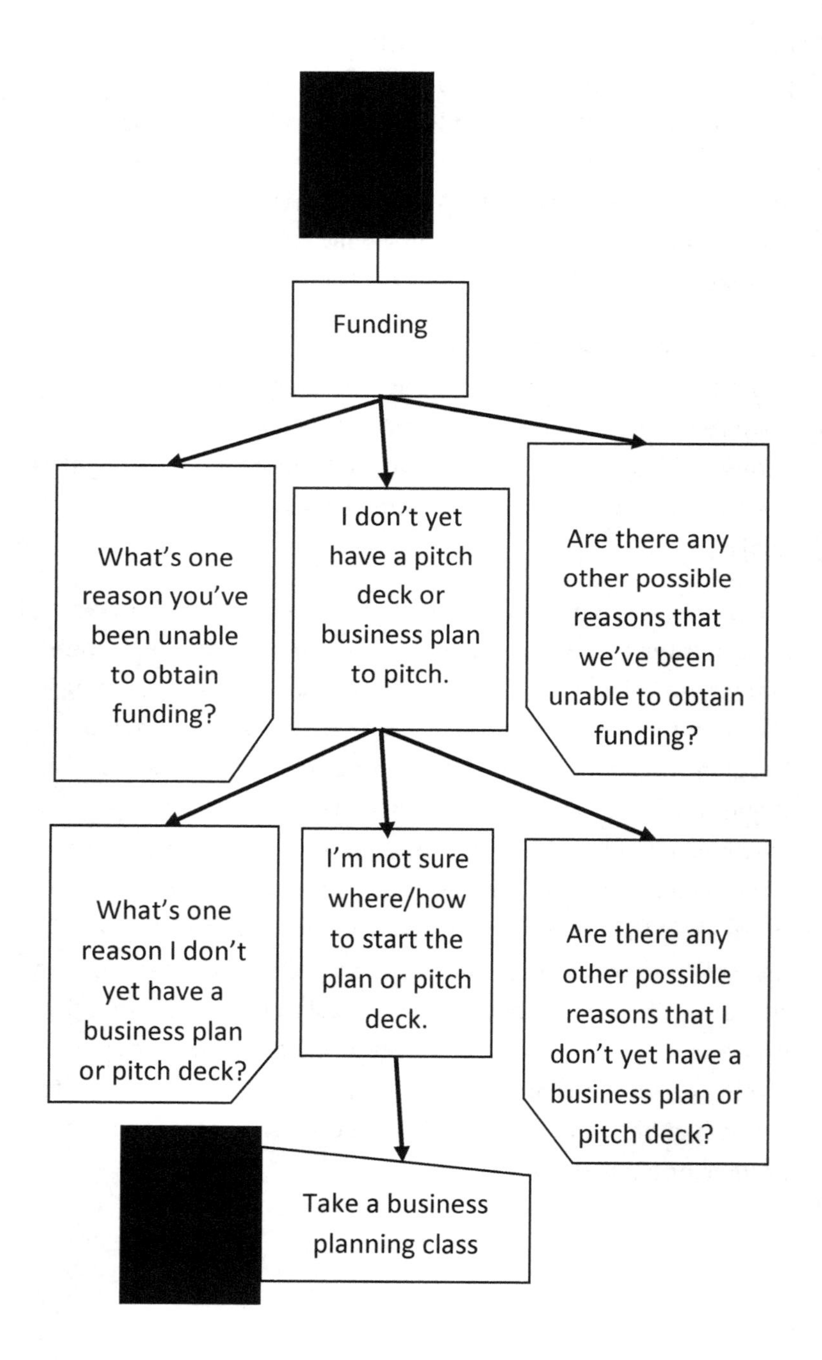
Funding
What's one reason you've been unable to obtain funding?
I don't yet have a pitch deck or business plan to pitch.
Are there any other possible reasons that we've been unable to obtain funding?
What's one reason I don't yet have a business plan or pitch deck?
I'm not sure where/how to start the plan or pitch deck.
Are there any other possible reasons that I don't yet have a business plan or pitch deck?
Take a business planning class

Try creating your own ladder to your ultimate entrepreneurial dream. Start at the top and imagine your ultimate goal first. Then, work backward down the ladder, identifying the various obstacles standing in your way.

This technique, developed and validated by Dr. Oettingen's research, is called mental contrasting. Mental contrasting acts like a bridge between your dreams and reality. When entrepreneurs who believe that they can succeed use mental contrasting as a goal-setting strategy, they are more likely to achieve their goals compared to equally confident entrepreneurs who only imagine an end state where they've already achieved success.[139] Mental contrasting is a technique adopted by the most resilient entrepreneurs.

Similar findings are supported by the studies conducted by Dr. Thomas Stanley, a former professor at Georgia State University and the author of the New York Times Bestseller, *The Millionaire Next Door*. Dr. Stanley found that people are more likely to accumulate wealth and attain financial independence when they're "able to visualize the future benefits of defining their goals."[29] They are skilled at the art of mental contrasting. By using the mental contrasting technique, we can imagine our ultimate goal, as well as the obstacles that stand in our way of achieving it. With this technique we can retain the motivation we need to act on our intentions, while still honoring our broader inspirational vision.

Once we've identified some of the known obstacles standing in the way of our entrepreneurial journey, we can determine how to overcome those challenges. There will be dozens of obstacles we'll need to overcome. If we look at these tasks all at once, the amount of work that lies ahead might feel demoralizing. If we take one task at a time, however, we'll begin to gain momentum toward our goals. When we are faced with a large, difficult, boring, or seemingly meaningless task, we tend to avoid it for as long as we can. Breaking down these tasks into more manageable chunks can reduce our resistance to the required effort. We are more likely to accomplish smaller, more proximal goals. Those small achievements demonstrate progress and motivate us to keep going.[140] Remember, these are the goals we will work toward as we set out to reach our entrepreneurial dreams.

"When you go through the mental process of combining dreams with reality, you begin to see a road map of what you need to do to achieve your dreams. Dream big, and then be realistic, tenacious, and steadfast in taking the steps to make them come true."

- Gay Gaddis
Founder and CEO of T3, an Award-winning Innovation Agency

Performance Goals

"When people set and identify specific goals, it leads to higher performance 90 percent of the time..."

- Daymond John

Founder of Fubu and Investor

We've discussed a framework for how to go about setting goals. Now we need to consider which goals a resilient entrepreneur should be setting. When goal-setting in the context of entrepreneurship, we're often focused on creating performance goals.

Performance goals are competitive and achievement-based. They're often about evaluating how well we're doing compared to others.[264] Sales targets, for example, are often performance-based objectives – you've either reached your targeted $10,000 sales figures or you haven't. Performance goals are typically unforgiving because they're used to compare you to someone else. Yet, performance goals are an important metric in business.

When creating performance goals, consider using the SMART goal method. SMART stands for Specific, Measurable, Attainable, Relevant and Timely/time-bound. When we combine the SMART goal-setting method with cutting-edge goal-setting research in the field of psychology, we'll be more likely to achieve our SMART goals. The following sections provide a basic overview of SMART goals. If you're already familiar with SMART goals, I still encourage you to refresh your knowledge by reviewing what you've already learned.

Specificity

When we set our performance goal, we need to ensure that they're crafted with enough specificity to be clearly understood. Research has shown that entrepreneurs with specific, formalized goals, are more likely to still be in business compared to nascent entrepreneurs who did not specify or formalize goals.[141] Specifying our goals reduces ambiguity and focuses us on the next steps required to move forward.

For example, if you're starting a wellness business, you might be endeavoring to "transform our nation's current healthcare culture into one built upon a foundation of holistic wellness". While this is a noble vision, it's much too broad. To help us make that goal more tangible and actionable, we can ask ourselves, "What's one reason *why* we want to transform the culture of healthcare?" It might be that our current healthcare economy is too focused on reactive care, as opposed to preventative medicine. By identifying the reasons why we're pursuing our grand vision, we can start to recognize, with greater specificity, the challenges we are trying to solve.

Okay, now we can ask ourselves, "What's one way we might encourage more people to engage with preventative medicine?" One way might be to provide people with a variety of wellness services, like mental health therapy, yoga, massage, nutrition coaching, etc. By continuing to ask ourselves why and how we might achieve our higher-level vision, we begin to identify the specific products and services we might offer. We can continue this process and get even more specific with our product and service offering goals, as well as other important business metrics.

I often hear new entrepreneurs say that everyone is their potential customer. While we might like to believe that's true, the reality is, we'll likely be more successful if we've defined our target market and customer segments. Instead of thinking that everyone is our customer, think about who will most likely be our best customers.

Study after study has confirmed Pareto's rule, which says that about 20 percent of some input or effort usually results in about 80 percent of the outcome. This is also true of the products we sell – 20 percent of our customers are likely to account for approximately 80 percent of our sales. Concentrate on the 20 percent that accounts for 80 percent of results. Our broad goal of marketing to everyone might be made more specific if we tailor our marketing efforts to females, aged 25-34, for example. That specificity helps us focus our efforts and limited resources.

Here are a couple additional examples:

Unspecified: "Increase sales"

Somewhat specific: "Increase sales by 21 percent"

Very specific: "Increase sales of product 'X' by 10 percent and product 'Y' by 11 percent, for a total increase in sales of 21 percent."

Unspecified: "Find a location for my business"

Somewhat specific: "Find commercial real estate for my business in the Austin Metropolitan Area"

Very specific: "Find an available commercial space with 3,000 square feet and a commercial kitchen in or within three miles of the 78704 zip-code."

"Whenever I hit a roadblock, I found a way around it. If I couldn't get around it, I went under it. If going under didn't work, I'd go over. I did whatever it took. In return, I accomplished my goal."

- Lori Greiner
Entrepreneur, Investor and "Queen of QVC"

Measurable

Making goals measurable creates a yardstick we can use to quantify progress. It also helps ensure our goals are specific. Whether it's revenue, profit, customer satisfaction, number of customers, etc., we can find a way to quantify most of our goals. By quantifying what we're trying to achieve, we can see how we're performing through metrics.

For example, many businesses aspire to have "superior customer service," yet few define how they plan to achieve that goal and even fewer outline how they're going to measure their progress. Online review platforms like Yelp help us quantify and compare how satisfied or dissatisfied our customers are. So, instead of having a "superior customer service" goal, we might strive to maintain a 4-star or higher average rating on Yelp. That's a measurable goal.

Many other small businesses use a net promoter score (NPS) to measure customer loyalty. The NPS is measured on a scale of 0 to 10 by asking customers one simple question: "How likely is it that you would recommend [business name] to a friend or colleague?" The formula behind the NPS counts scores of 0 to 6 as *detractors* to your business, 7 to 8 as *passively satisfied* and 9 to 10 as *promoters* of your business. The NPS is calculated by subtracting the percentage of detractors from the percentage of promoters. A business with a NPS score of 75 to 80 percent has achieved exceptional, best-in-class customer loyalty.[142] So, if you claim that you will have exceptional customer satisfaction and loyalty, the NPS formula is one way to make that goal measurable.

There are all types of things we can measure in a small business, but it's important to make sure you're measuring the right things. Talk with a business coach or mentor to get some feedback about your metrics. Here are just a few additional ideas and examples of measurable goals:

- Revenue targets and rate of growth
- Average size of sale
- Profitability
- Number of customers
- Number of repeat customers
- Customer satisfaction and customer loyalty
- Referral source

Below are a couple of examples:

Immeasurable: "Have superior customer service and loyalty."

Somewhat measurable: "Achieve superior customer service and loyalty measured through positive reviews on Yelp."

Very measurable: "Achieve superior customer service and loyalty, measured by 4 starts or higher on Yelp and a NPS of 70 or higher."

Immeasurable: "Find new customers."

Somewhat measurable: "Find new wholesale and retail customers."

Very measurable: "Find a list of 10 new wholesale leads and 25 new retail leads and convert 20 percent of those leads into new customers."

Attainable

Research has shown that challenging goals lead to greater sustained effort compared to informal goals that might be easier to attain.[143] Yet, if we set goals that are too grandiose – goals that we're unlikely to accomplish – we risk inflating expectations with what we are realistically capable of completing.

I recently worked with an entrepreneur who had found the perfect location for her business. She thought that all she needed was some funding to secure a lease and get started. Then, she found out that she needed a business plan to get the funding. So, she started writing her business plan, but she quickly realized how much work goes into preparing this strategic document and estimating financial projections. When I met with her, I sensed she was very frustrated. She had self-imposed a goal and deadline of signing a lease and opening her business in sixty days. As we reviewed the requirements of a fundable business plan, she got very quiet. I could see her eyes starting to water. She had set an unrealistic, unattainable goal of completing a business plan, securing financing and signing a lease in eight weeks. Anyone who has completed those tasks will tell you that getting them all done in eight weeks is almost impossible and trying to force them in such a tight timeline is a recipe for burnout, mistakes and oversights.

This young, aspiring entrepreneur didn't realize the amount of work it would take, and she needed resiliency to handle the shock of reality contradicting her expectations. Setting goals that we cannot realistically achieve can lead to a deflated belief in our capability to be a successful entrepreneur. Therefore, our goals should be attainable – challenging, yet realistically achievable. Setting attainable goals helps us become more resilient entrepreneurs.

Remember, entrepreneurs are often overly optimistic and therefore prone to setting outlandish goals that they truly believe they can accomplish. If we have an unattainable goal, there is often incongruence between what we believed we were going to accomplish and the true outcome.[144] This dissonance can lead to a negative self-perception - a misbelief that we're a failure or that we were never really cut out to be an entrepreneur in the first place. If we haven't built up entrepreneurial resilience, the shock of not reaching our goals can be deflating and might lead to an early exit of the venture.

Resilient entrepreneurs, on the other hand, set goals that they can achieve, especially when they're just starting out. Early wins and accomplishments build confidence. Over time, as entrepreneurs learn and establish their business infrastructure, they're able to set increasingly challenging goals.

Likely unattainable: "Obtain financing, sign a lease, build out my commercial space and be open within 90 days."

Likely Attainable: "Complete my business plan and obtain financing for a commercial space in the next six weeks."

Very attainable: "Complete my business plan in the next six weeks and identify potential financing options."

Relevant

We can ensure that the goals we've set are relevant if we can logically match them with the most pressing challenges or most promising opportunities facing our business. If our nearer-term goals aren't methodically leading to the removal of barriers standing in the way of achieving mid and longer-term goals, then we might not be focused on the right things.

For example, I recall working with Kendra, a personal fitness trainer who was looking for space to host her fitness classes. It was very difficult to find affordable space that also fit her needs. As Kendra and I worked the challenge from different angles, sub-letting an existing commercial space emerged as a viable option. We identified several martial arts studios that had after-school programs, but underutilized space on the weekends and in the mornings. I thought she might be able to sub-let at a cheap rate. Although sub-letting didn't align with her dream of having her own exclusive space, it was an option that would allow her to start to build a customer base in the near-term. She could grow that customer base until she was able to afford and grow into a space of her own.

Yet, instead of reaching out to these studios to inquire about a possible sub-letting arrangement, Kendra started evaluating different sound system technologies that she might use to facilitate her classes. The most pressing obstacle to opening her business was finding a location; finding the perfect sound system was far less relevant. She started ignoring what was most relevant because the path was getting difficult and the sub-let option was a sub-par entrepreneurial dream. Leasing her ideal space seemed like less of a reality, so she began to focus on something that still made her feel like she was building a business that looked like her original vision. Remember, it's much more pleasant to envision our dream business than to focus on the things we need to overcome to make that dream come true. I coached Kendra on staying focused on the most relevant goals and objectives and encouraged her to make a few phone calls, which she did.

When you're in the day-to-day operations of business, it's easy to get distracted from the goals you've set. It's also easy for competing goals to emerge. Take time to assess that you're working toward relevant goals. Make sure there is a clear line to what you're doing today and where you want to be next month, next quarter and next year. Choosing not to do something or to stop doing something is just as important as choosing what to do.

Time-bound

"Measuring what matters begins with the question: What is most important for the next three (or six, or twelve) months? Successful organizations focus on the handful of initiatives that can make a real difference, deferring less urgent ones."

- John Doerr
Venture Capitalist and author of *Measure What Matters*

Studies have shown that time constraints or deadlines on our goals leads to increased effort.[145] This makes sense, especially for those that are prone to procrastination. How many times have you waited until the night before a deadline to finish an assignment, file your taxes, answer a request for proposal, etc.? Making sure you don't miss strict deadlines is a strong motivator.

It's also helpful if we align our deadlines with temporal markers. Temporal markers are milestones like birthdays, anniversaries the end of a quarter or calendar year, etc. Research has shown that we're significantly more likely to achieve a goal if we set its accompanying deadline along these temporal milestones.[146] So, for example, if it's January 1st, we might set a goal to finish our business plan in four weeks. However, instead of saying four weeks, we're better off committing to finishing it by the end of January. A deadline of June 21st is a better stated due date compared to saying the first day of summer. There are numerous milestones to attach your deadline to, and although it's a seemingly subtle difference, science shows us that it's meaningful.

As you place self-imposed deadlines on your goals, keep in mind that incorporating a bit of flexibility is okay too. If you need to push a deadline back to make a goal more attainable, then do so. My colleague worked with an entrepreneur who literally tattooed their arm with the date they wanted to launch their next product. That's quite a sign of commitment, but leaves little room for the inevitable delays and unexpected things that are bound to happen.

Give yourself a little slack when needed. Don't make a habit of kicking goals down the road, but bending when necessary is what resiliency is all about. A wise Confucianism says, "it doesn't matter how slowly you go, as long as you don't stop."[147] Entrepreneurs are often restless and anxious, but remember that the entrepreneurial journey is a marathon, not a sprint.

Mastery Goals

"People with a teachable spirit approach each day as an opportunity for another learning experience. Their hearts are open. Their minds are alert for something new. Their attitudes are expectant. They know that success has less to do with possessing natural talent and more to do with choosing to learn."

- John C. Maxwell
Leadership guru and bestselling author of more than 70 books

Performance goals are undoubtedly very important, but they're not the only type of goals that matter for a resilient entrepreneur. It's important to combine performance goals with at least a few entrepreneurial mastery goals.

Mastery goals are things that we want to learn how to do better – new knowledge, skills and abilities (KSAs) that we want to master to help our business thrive. For example, we might not be the most confident at bookkeeping or financial management, so we might set a goal to improve our knowledge in that area. Specifically, our goal might be to work with a mentor who has a finance background, or to take a finance or accounting class.

When we achieve our mastery goals, we increase our overall confidence as entrepreneurs. By taking that finance, marketing or management class, we feel better prepared to confront business decisions with confidence. It's that confidence that helps us become more resilient entrepreneurs. Setting mastery goals encourages us to remain curious and interested in learning and mastering new knowledge relevant to our business or industry.[148] This is equally important for both startups and growth-stage businesses.

According to Edward Hess, Professor of Business Administration at the University of Virginia's Darden School of Business, consistently high-performing companies are those that are continuously learning. Entrepreneurs who set mastery goals are more resilient because they're more likely to seek out bigger opportunities, persevere when faced with obstacles in the way of realizing those opportunities, and look at the challenges they face with a positive attitude.[149]

As much as possible, we should frame our business goals as learning goals – things that we can master and improve upon. We can often buttress our performance goals with mastery goals. For example, as a performance goal, we might want to increase revenue by five percent over the next six months. So, what can we do to master new knowledge, skills and abilities that will help us achieve our performance goal? Perhaps we can deepen our knowledge about strategic marketing, negotiation strategies, creating better sales funnels, etc. Numerous scientific studies on goal-setting have shown that mastery goals can lead to significantly better chances of achieving performance goals.[150]

Yet, creating mastery goals and committing to them are two different things. Mastery goal commitment requires that we have a growth mindset. The *growth mindset* is a term championed by Dr. Carol Dweck in her best-selling book, *Mindset: The New Psychology of Success*. The growth mindset is embodied by people who believe that they can edify themselves by working diligently to learn new KSAs. The growth mindset enables entrepreneurs to learn from failure and reflect on those lessons learned so that they're better prepared to avoid similar mistakes in the future.[166] For example, challenges with decreased sales might be a performance problem, but we can frame it as an opportunity to learn and master new knowledge about strategic marketing, negotiation, product innovation, etc.

Adopting a growth mindset gives you permission to ask, listen and learn from the feedback given by customers, mentors and advisers. It allows you to keep an eye on industry and market trends and continuously improve. Let's look at an example from the Caribbean.

"Why can't businesses change and adapt? A large part of it is because they lost the ability to learn. They stopped being students. The second this happens to you, your knowledge becomes fragile."

- Ryan Holiday
Author of Ego is the Enemy

Aruba Aloe Balm, Inc, founded in 1890, is the oldest aloe-producing company in the world.[151] About 60 years after their founding, they produced 30 percent of the world's aloin, which at the time was a popular aloe-based ingredient for many pharmaceuticals. However, as the pharmaceutical industry innovated and evolved, the demand for aloin tanked. Aruba was over-invested in a single product category, and they weren't actively learning to productize and market aloe in new ways. As a result, Aruba's primary source of revenue plummeted, forcing the company to shutter its manufacturing plant.

12 years later, the company reopened the plant and invested heavily in product research and development. These investments allowed Aruba to develop a broader and more diversified product mix, making the company more resilient to a decline in any one product category. More than fifty years later, the company is still a leader in product research and development.[152] They've made continuous learning and innovation part of their organization's culture. The company has embraced a growth mindset as a strategic priority.

The most successful and resilient entrepreneurs are those who aren't afraid to admit when they don't know something. For them, learning is something that gives their company a competitive advantage. Take Walt Disney for example: One of Disney's clerks described him as having "the drive and ambition of ten million men." [153] Aside from sheer determination, Disney had an inquisitive mind that lasted throughout his entire career. When something piqued his interest, he concentrated, almost exclusively, on that one thing. He obsessed over it. When his first animation company, Laugh-O-Gram, went bankrupt, he reemerged "tougher, more determined and inured to failure."[153] The Disney studio we're familiar with today is a conglomerate with diversified business segments outside of animation. Disney pushed the limits of what was possible because he had a growth mindset and a deep desire for continuous learning.

Entrepreneurial resiliency and the growth mindset go hand in hand, as Dr. Dweck espouses in her book: "The passion for stretching yourself and sticking to it, even (or especially) when it's not going well, is the hallmark of the growth mindset. This is the mindset that allows people to thrive during some of the most challenging times in their lives."[154] Entrepreneurs with a growth mindset will seek out challenging activities because they believe that even if they fail, they will learn from that failure and do better the next time around.

The fixed mindset, on the other hand, is the belief that we have innate talents and gifts that we are born with and don't really change over time – we either have them or we don't. A fixed mindset is dangerous because it can trick us into thinking we already have all the KSAs we need to be successful, and if we're not successful, that must mean that we weren't born with the prerequisites to be an entrepreneur. This mindset can lead us to give up and quit early – the antitheses to resiliency. If we're unsure where our mindset resides, take a quick growth mindset assessment for free on Dr. Dweck's website: www.mindsetonline.com/testyourmindset

By intentionally including mastery goals alongside our performance goals, we're acknowledging the importance of the growth mindset and committing to continuous learning and development as entrepreneurs. This helps us become more authentic and self-aware entrepreneurs, a topic we'll discuss more about in later chapters. Still not convinced that we need mastery goals? Studies have shown that those who adopt and achieve mastery goals are more likely to achieve their performance goals.[155]

Entrepreneurs with the growth mindset understand that it takes time to learn the applicable KSAs to be successful, and so they persevere through adversity, knowing that they are learning and improving every step of the way. We can't control all the obstacles that challenge us along our entrepreneurial journey, but we can control our mindset. Our perspective is an important ingredient in the recipe for goal achievement. Obstacles might seem insurmountable at first glance, but with a growth mindset and the incorporation of mastery goals into our entrepreneurial journey, we can learn to overcome any hurdle that stands in our way.

A cautionary note for those who love to learn for the sake of learning. Those with an insatiable curiosity should be careful that they're learning new knowledge that they can implement in the business – actionable knowledge.

The difference is subtle, but important. You need the ability to distinguish between passive learning and deliberate practice. Only through focused, deliberate practice are we able to improve performance to the highest levels possible.[156]

For example, I love to read. In conducting research for this book, I read more than 20 books and even more peer-reviewed studies on entrepreneurship and psychology and that was just in the first six months of writing.

However, reading can be a very passive learning activity if you're just flipping through the pages. When I did my research, I did so with the purpose of gaining knowledge to create innovative goal-setting techniques, templates and activities to be included in this book and other entrepreneurship curricula. As I read, I highlighted helpful passages and took notes in the margins. Later, I revisited these notes and highlights. This forced me to think critically about what I might be able to implement in my work to be a more effective business coach. If you like to read, make sure you take notes and make highlights as you do. You're more likely to retain and apply what you've read if you do. Also, consider joining a book club so you can interact with peers about what you've learned and how you might apply those lessons to your business.

Deliberate practice should also include candid and recurring feedback that forces you to reflect on your performance.[157] There are plenty of opportunities for deliberate practice in our pursuit for entrepreneurial mastery. In forthcoming chapters on funding and coaching, we'll look at deliberate practice for improving your pitch and getting feedback from coaches and mentors.

Goal Alignment and Commitment

"One needs practice to achieve mastery, a body of experience before one achieves real success. And if what we are missing when we fail is individual skill, then what is needed is simply more training and practice."

- Atul Gawande
Surgeon, Bestselling Author and Public Health Researcher

We've discussed performance goals and mastery goals, now let's touch on the alignment of those goals with our personal lives. It's very important that our personal goals match up with our business goals. For example, research has shown that entrepreneurs are more resilient when their personal financial goals are aligned with the realistic financial potential of the business opportunity.[158]

If our personal goals are aligned with our business' goals, we are more likely to persevere through times of adversity.[144] We will expand more on this topic in the next chapter. Alignment is also important for commitment. If our business and personal goals are aligned, then we're more likely to be genuinely committed to the goals we've set. Psychologists refer to this as *goal internalization*.

Internalized goals are more aligned with our personal goals, values and beliefs. In other words, our goals should be meaningful. Meaning refers to the value that we find in specific goals. If the goals in front of us are not seen as meaningful, our engagement with these goals is reduced and we become less motivated to pursue them. We can find meaning by connecting them to our long-term goals and our ultimate business vision. Finding how these goals take us closer to the finish line is an effective way of finding meaning.

Another way to find meaning in our goals is to find how they relate to the themes in our own stories. Researchers found a correlation between goal internalization and our ability to self-reflect (*story of self*).[159] If we're more inclined to self-reflection, we will be in a better position to create goals that align with our *story of self* (internalized goals), and we will therefore be more likely to achieve those internalized goals.

If we're having trouble internalizing our goals and we find ourselves constantly thinking about them, we might be ruminating. Rumination isn't the same as reflection. Reflection is about productive introspection, learning and growth. Rumination, on the other hand, describes the obsessive worry, distress and anxiety-filled thoughts that run through our mind when there is a lack of integrity between who we perceive ourselves to be and our actions, planned actions or current performance. If we're ruminating on our goals, it might be because there is dissonance or conflict between our goals and sense of self. Our distress comes from a belief that we will not be able to handle the challenges we anticipate we will encounter.[160] Distress, unlike eustress, is debilitating as opposed to motivating.

The following tables include different statements that might help in distinguishing between rumination and reflection. See which statements yours most closely relate to. If you're identifying more with the first table, you might need to reexamine your entrepreneurial goals to ensure they align with your *story of self*.

Rumination statements
It's difficult for me to stop worrying about activities and experiences related to my future goals.
I often obsess over memories related to my past.
I spend too much time second-guessing my efforts and decisions.
I wish I could stop thinking about events related to my past entrepreneurial endeavors.

It's hard to break the cycle of rumination, but one way we can help ourselves is to take breaks when necessary. Give your mind a break if it's stuck in a negative cycle. Go do something that you enjoy and have fun. Trying to stop rumination by sheer willpower oftentimes proves fruitless, so stop banging your head against the wall and give yourself time to reset and recharge. The mindfulness mediation techniques that we introduced earlier in the book have also been shown to reduce rumination and anxiety.[214]

Another good strategy is to consider is speaking with a business mentor or coach and collaborate on ways you can overcome the challenges that might be holding you back. Oftentimes coaching is an opportunity to talk through some of the things that are on your mind, which can be extremely therapeutic. There will be more about coaching and mentoring in later chapters.

If you find that you relate more to the example statements of reflection, you are more likely to internalize your entrepreneurial goals because they are more closely associated with your entrepreneurial identity and *story of self*.[159] These statements have been adapted from research conducted at the University of Aarhus in Denmark and published assessments by Dr. Paul Trapnell, Professor of Psychology at the University of Winnipeg.[161]

Reflection statements
I enjoy meditating and reflecting on my entrepreneurial activities and experiences.
I like to analyze the causes of outcomes from my past entrepreneurial endeavors.
I like to find the meaning in my past entrepreneurial experiences.
I maintain a broad perspective when thinking about lessons learned from past entrepreneurial endeavors.

After setting your goals, go back and evaluate how committed you are to each goal, on a scale of 1 to 10. Any goal with a score of 6 or below should raise some serious red flags about what you're trying to accomplish in the first place. A score of 4 to 7 means you're just lukewarm and you should revisit the goal and ask yourself why your level of commitment isn't higher. Is there conflict between the goal and your self-identity? Are you unsure if it's a goal you should be focused on? This is an important exercise because you're more likely to accomplish goals that you are genuinely and passionately committed to.[162]

Keep in mind that just because you've set goals it doesn't mean that you've set the right goals. The goal-setting framework outlined in this chapter helps you optimally structure your goals, but the content of the goals requires deeper strategic introspection. [163]

From the earliest stages of planning your business, setting business goals together with a spouse or significant other helps create initial buy-in from people who are important to you. Later, those people might serve as a source of encouragement and accountability for you when difficulties arise. It might seem challenging to get feedback on your goals from someone with whom you have a complex interpersonal relationship with but remember these are the people who care about you the most. Asking for their objective feedback (as well as their help implementing it) is a great way to get buy-in and create a partner or collaborator in the process. On the other hand, if someone criticizes your goals but refuses to help you improve and reach them, then you might need to consider having an altogether different conversation with this person.

For existing businesses, setting goals together with your upper management team is a good idea. If you're a new or solo entrepreneur, have your goals reviewed by your mentor or coach. They cannot set your goals for you; your goals will only become meaningful and achievable if you have committed to them through your own volition. With that said, there are benefits to peer group goal-setting or goal-setting alongside your mentor. They can give you feedback and an outside perspective to check if you have the right goals or if you might be missing anything. If you haven't already, schedule some time to review your goals with your partner, coach or mentor.

Another good strategy, if possible, is to set goals alongside other entrepreneurs. *Goal contagion theory* surmises that when observing a peer or mentor's goal-oriented behavior, we are more likely to absorb their motivation and pursue their goals as if they were our own.[164] Goal contagion is so powerful that it can happen unconsciously.

This is especially true if we perceive those peers or that mentor as being like us. Imagine you're observing a racquetball match. It's an extremely competitive game - the players are sprinting and diving after the ball. One of the players you're watching represents the same school that you attended. The other players represent schools that you aren't affiliated with. Keeping this in the back of your mind, let's add on to this scenario.

We're going to switch sports for a moment. Imagine that I ask you to make a coaching decision about a hypothetical scenario in an American football game. You're the head coach of a team that's ahead of your opponent by 17 points and there are only 25 seconds left in the game. Your offense is on your opponent's 15-yard line. You can choose to take a knee and end the game graciously with a win, or you can attempt to run up the score with one last second touchdown. What would you do?

This scenario was presented in a study that Dr. Chris Loersch, Assistant Professor of Social Psychology and Neuroscience, conducted on 132 students at the University of Colorado.[165] He split the students into two groups. One group watched the same competitive racquetball match that I prompted you to imagine. The other group watched a much more informal racquetball match, where the players walked around leisurely and cooperated more with one another.

It was shown that the students who observed the competitive racquetball match with a player they perceived to be part of their own social group were more likely to model competitive decision-making in the mock football coaching scenario. The students who observed the competitive player representing their own university were significantly more likely to choose to run up the score in the simulated football game.

This study illustrates how observing competitiveness can help us be more competitive in our own pursuits. Entrepreneurship is inherently competitive. Setting and working toward goals with other entrepreneurs helps to motivate us much more than if we set goals alone. If we see a peer entrepreneur making progress, we're more likely to exert effort and energy to catch up. Therefore, it's important to set and pursue goals alongside your peers.

I facilitate a peer goal-setting activity in the entrepreneurship class I teach. First, I ask entrepreneurs to work independently on setting some goals for their business. After about 15 to 20 minutes, I split them in to groups of two or three and have them walk through the goals they've created with their peers. As they go through this process, the others in the group are free to ask questions or make suggestions. This usually leads to the entrepreneur adding new goals or more clearly defining goals they've already set. Besides the benefit of having another entrepreneur serve as a thinking partner, goal-setting together creates a sense of accountability. Just the act of telling someone else what goal you plan to achieve can make you more motivated to achieve that goal. Join an entrepreneur networking group and see if you can find an accountability partner in reaching your business goals.

Finally, we need to revisit our goals on a regular basis. As an entrepreneur, you're inherently operating in an uncertain environment, and for that reason, you will need to continually adjust your goals as your business develops.[166] You should find a cadence that works best for you, but many small businesses reexamine their higher-level goals every six to twelve weeks.

In the interim, they keep a pulse on monthly and weekly goals that help them stay on track toward the broader quarterly and annual goals. Go to your calendar and set some recurring holds in your schedule with reminders to revisit your goals. This will help you hold yourself accountable throughout the year.

Summary

Let's revisit the steps to take to set resilient goals for your entrepreneurial journey:

1. Imagine you've achieved success as an entrepreneur. Describe what that success looks like for you. Take a few minutes and write down your vision of success in a free-flowing narrative.

2. Build a ladder to that ultimate vision of success by working backward from the top down.

3. For each rung on the ladder, identify what you will do to overcome the hurdles that stand in your way.

4. Ensure that you describe each goal you set using the SMART methodology: specific, measurable, attainable, relevant and time-bound.

5. Once you've set your SMART goals, make them action-oriented by writing down an action plan that describes when and how you will accomplish any necessary prerequisites to achieving those goals.

6. Finally, come back to your goals periodically and adjust as needed. Celebrate the goals you've achieved and set your sights on the next group of goals you want to achieve.

Chapter 4: The Authentic Entrepreneur

"The more precisely an entrepreneur understands their strengths and weaknesses – and then builds strategies to maximize their strengths – the higher probability that they will build something of significance that creates millions or billions of dollars of value, thousands of good jobs and something that changes the world a little to a lot."

- Jim Clifton
Chairman and CEO of Gallup

As a business coach, I've encountered two distinct mindsets when it comes to an entrepreneur's strengths and weaknesses. The first is the entrepreneur who is insecure and inhibited by their weaknesses. They're too focused on what's missing and have become paralyzed, worrying that they don't have what it takes to be successful. They might spend a lot of time and energy stressing about their weaknesses while their strengths go stale.

The other is the entrepreneur who embraces and invests in their strengths while looking for ways to manage around, outsource or delegate in areas where they're not as strong. This entrepreneur has acknowledged and accepted their weaknesses, but instead of ruminating on them, they're empowered by their strengths. This mindset allows them to learn quickly and helps keep them energized to perform at their highest capacity.[167]

As Ray Dalio, billionaire founder of Bridgewater Associates and, according to Forbes, one of the 100 greatest living business minds, says, "Successful people change in ways that allow them to continue to take advantage of their strengths while compensating for their weaknesses, and unsuccessful people don't."[168]

Resilient entrepreneurs are authentic – meaning that they recognize and embrace their true selves. When we are authentic, our decisions are guided by our core values and our work leverages our strengths, personality and learning style. Authentic entrepreneurs who can acknowledge and scale their strengths while minimizing the impact of their weaknesses on their business have been shown to be more resilient.[169] Furthermore, research has shown that authentic entrepreneurs are more motivated to be creative, explore alternative possibilities and successfully grow a business. The bottom line is that businesses led by authentic entrepreneurs perform better overall.[170]

To be clear, minimizing our weaknesses doesn't mean we deny their existence or ignore them. Instead, authenticity demands that we understand which weaknesses are unlikely to improve significantly and which ones have greater potential to improve with time and attention. As entrepreneurs, we wear many hats. Understandably, you might have to stumble along in an area, just to get through the day.

Yet, when we're at our best, we should be leveraging our strengths in our work at least 80 percent of the time. That percentage is justified by Pareto's 80/20 rule, which consistently shows that approximately 20 percent of any input produces about 80 percent of our results. There are numerous examples of Pareto's rule showing up in business cases. For example, 80 percent of a business' profits are earned from the top 20 percent of its customers, or the top 20 percent of the sales team generates approximately 80 percent of the sales.[171] Similarly, 80 percent of the work we do (our output) should leverage the top 20 percent of our capabilities.

While leveraging our strengths is important, it's also important to improve in areas where we're weak through learning new knowledge and skills. However, improving in areas that are less innately aligned with who we are is more difficult. For example, trying to adopt a new personality trait can be quite difficult.[168]

Robert Herjavec is a successful entrepreneur and investor on ABC's reality TV show, Shark Tank. He sums it up best when he says, "No matter how hard you work on your weak points, you are unlikely to ever make them better or even as good as the things that come naturally to you. Your natural talents won't improve because you're spending all that time and energy on that weak spot. Instead of becoming 'well-rounded,' you will become merely mediocre. And guess what? The world does not reward mediocrity. It rewards greatness and exceptional results."[172]

This chapter offers some practical frameworks that will help you identify and analyze your values, preferences, strengths and weaknesses. We'll also look at ways to scale strengths while minimizing weaknesses. To do that, you must have genuine self-awareness about who you are and how others see you.

Self-Awareness

> "What is rare is not raw talent, skill, or even confidence, but humility, diligence, and self-awareness."
>
> - Ryan Holiday
> Author of *Ego is the Enemy*

Our ability to take an honest, introspective look at our own values, strengths, personality and problem-solving style can have a significant direct effect on our business' performance, measured in terms of sales growth, market share and net profit.[173] When we invest time in better understanding who we are, we develop a better understanding of others, including customers, partners and collaborators.

You might take for granted that you know your strengths and weaknesses better than anyone, but studies have shown that we are often not very good judges of our own performance, knowledge, skills or abilities. Worse yet, the least self-aware people are often the most confident in their performance and KSAs.[174] Psychologist refer to this cognitive bias as the Dunning-Kruger effect.[175] This denial, according to research published in the Harvard Business Review, "can be the greatest hurdle that leaders face in becoming self-aware."[178]

Luckily, we can improve our self-awareness. Organizational Psychologist, Dr. Tasha Eurich, is the author of the bestselling book *Insight*. In the book, she outlines seven things that self-aware individuals are more consciously aware of compared to those who are less self-aware:

1. *Values (the principles that guide them)*
2. *Passions (what they love to do)*

3. *Aspirations (what they want to experience and achieve)*
4. *Fit (the environment they require to be happy and engaged)*
5. *Patterns (consistent ways of thinking, feeling and behaving)*
6. *Reactions (thoughts, feelings and behaviors that reveal their capabilities*
7. *Impact (the effect they have on others).*[174]

I encourage you to take Dr. Eurich's free Insight Quiz online (http://www.insight-book.com/quiz.aspx). It will ask you and a close friend to take a very brief quiz to see how self-aware you are from your internal perspective and from an outside perspective. This is important because research shows that, "those who are more self-aware and have developed their own identity demonstrate higher levels of resiliency."[176]

How might we become more self-aware entrepreneurs? Start with your mastery goals. You must invest in becoming more self-aware and a commitment to that investment of time and energy is an important first step. If you glossed over the section in goal-setting that covered mastery goals, go back and think about adding improved self-awareness as a goal.

You can also work on self-awareness through mindful meditation, a practice we discussed in detail earlier in the book. Remember, a consistent daily practice of just ten minutes of meditation creates enough space to pause and reflect. It is a mechanism by which we can be introspective and better assess our strengths and weaknesses without judgement.

Finally, the assessment tools outlined in the rest of this chapter will help you become a more self-aware entrepreneur and therefore more authentic and resilient.

"Truly knowing yourself is one of the hardest things you can do, but it's also one of the most valuable. The sooner you begin, the sooner you'll begin to see the payoff. Today's a great day to start the journey."

- Annie Bogel
Author of *Reading People: How Seeing the World through the Lens of Personality Changes Everything*

Values

"Learning to deploy that unique blend that is you, to make extraordinary things happen in business and your life, is the central challenge of authentic leadership."

- Karissa Thacker
Management Psychologist and Author of the *Art of Authenticity*

Have you ever been stuck in a job doing work that seems to go against your value system? Have you ever been bothered by an aspect of your company's culture? When you feel forced to do something that doesn't fit with your inner principles, it causes dissonance and discomfort. Many people become entrepreneurs because they want to create businesses and autonomous work environments that allow them to live a life more aligned with their values.[177] What are the values that drive your entrepreneurial purpose?

You might have a pretty good idea about which values matter most to you, but have you ever taken time to purposefully reflect on them? Can you name the top five values that guide your life? Do you know if you're living your values consistently each day? It's difficult to explicitly know our values until they've been put to the test.[178]

The following exercise asks you to focus introspectively and identify the top five values that you hold most dear. Because we start with a list of 82 values, this is a harder activity than most people realize.

A team of researchers from the University of New Mexico developed the list of values, and while their list is quite comprehensive, they couldn't possibly capture every value that exists. So, if there are values that are important to you and you don't see them on the list, you can simply write them in. Here is the starting list:

Accuracy
Achievement
Adventure
Attractiveness
Authority
Autonomy
Beauty
Caring
Challenge
Change
Comfort
Commitment
Compassion
Contribution
Cooperation
Courtesy
Creativity
Dependability
Duty
Ecology
Excitement
Faithfulness
Fame
Family
Fitness
Flexibility
Forgiveness
Friendship
Fun
Generosity
Genuineness
God's will
Growth
Health
Helpfulness
Honesty
Hope
Humility
Humor
Independence
Industry
Inner peace
Intimacy
Justice
Knowledge
Leisure
Loved
Loving
Mastery
Mindfulness
Moderation
Monogamy
Non-conformity
Nurturance
Openness
Order
Passion
Pleasure
Popularity
Power
Purpose
Rationality
Realism
Responsibility
Risk
Romance
Safety
Self-acceptance
Self-control
Self-esteem
Self-knowledge
Service
Sexuality
Simplicity
Solitude
Spirituality
Stability
Tolerance
Tradition
Virtue
Wealth
World peace

The most practical way to do this activity is to print out the list of values and cut them up so that each value is on its own small piece of paper. Then, we can start by separating the list of values into two piles: The first will consist of the values that are **important** to you, while the second pile will contain the values that you don't think are as important. This should only take you about five minutes.

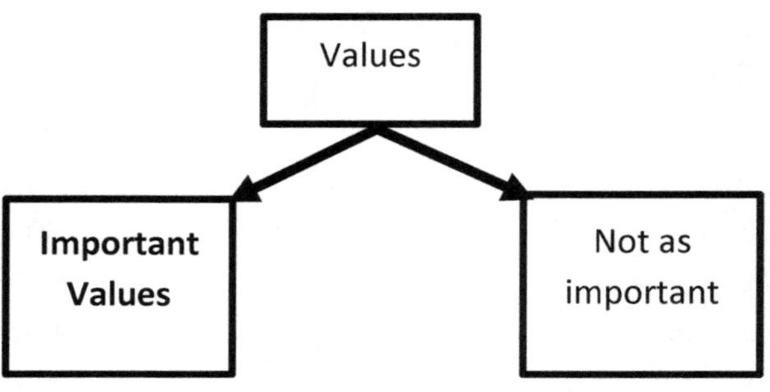

Once you have the two piles, put the **not as important** pile off to the side. Now, go through the stack of values you identified as **important** and create a new stack by pulling out the values that are **very important** to you. Again, this should take about five minutes.

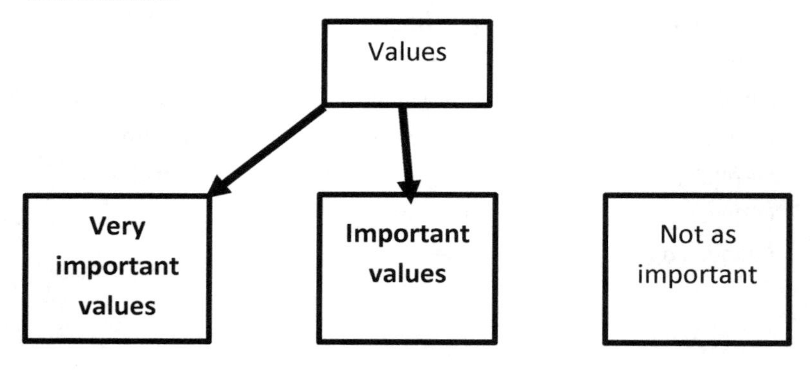

You will repeat this step of filtering out the values that are most significant until you're left with only a small pile of 15 or fewer values from which you will select your top five. For example, if you still have a large pile of value cards after separating out into a **very important** pile, create a new, **very, very important** pile and repeat the exercise.

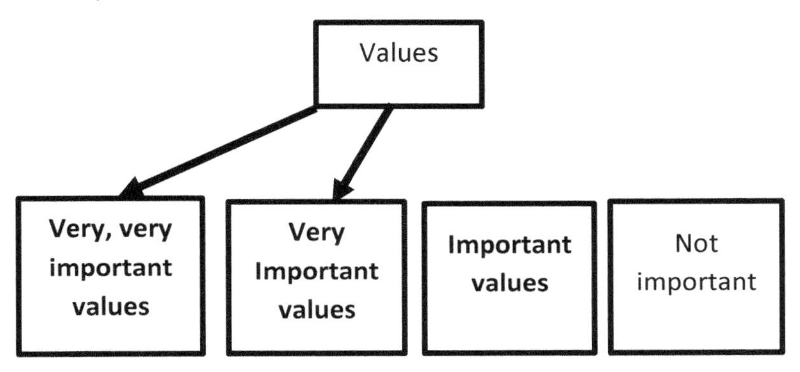

Each round presents increasingly difficult decisions about which values to filter out, but keep going until you've narrowed down your top five. You might be tempted to stop before you've narrowed down to five, but don't. Keep going until you're only left with five. This forces you to ask yourself tough questions about your value system. Once you're finished, you'll be left with the values that are most important to you.

"Values lie at the core of behavior. Yet most people have only a shallow appreciation of the values they hold, where they come from, and how they influence them."

- Lancer, Natalie; Clutterbuck, David; Megginson, David
Authors of Techniques for Coaching and Mentoring

When I first did this activity, I was a bit skeptical, but the process of selecting my top values really forced me to think about what drives and motivates me every day. For example, one of my top five values is family. Sometimes clients ask me to meet late in the evening or on the weekends – time normally reserved for my family. I ask myself if I can accommodate their request while still maintaining a healthy work-life balance. I will often say yes, but if I feel that I'm jeopardizing that balance, I'm not afraid to say no and explain my reasoning. Most of the time the client understands and shows respect for my family-first values. Those few that don't aren't the type of clients I want to work with anyway. Doing business without compromising my values enables me to be the most authentic version of myself that I can be.

Will you be intentional about consistently living your values? It's not always easy to integrate your values into how you do business. It takes courage, especially when challenges arise. Adversity has a way of tempting us with imprudent shortcuts and backward paths, but we can refuse to compromise our values. If you do, you'll lose your sense of self, and from there, everything can come crumbling down.

I encourage you to print your top five values and put them on display them to keep them in the forefront of your mind as you continue your entrepreneurial journey. This exercise isn't a shortcut for deeper reflection on your values. Instead, it's designed to get you started thinking about what values are important to you. It will take continued effort and focus to weave your values into your life and business endeavor.

Now that you've identified your top five values, let's look at our entrepreneurial personality.

Personality

Understanding people based on their personalities helps us increase our own emotional intelligence, which is important for self-awareness, collaboration, leadership, sales and marketing. This has been true for many successful entrepreneurs, especially those with businesses in the service industries. Gay Gaddis, the founder and CEO of the ad agency, T3, has used information about personality to find her own calling, engage her workforce, and design and execute effective advertising initiatives for her clients.[85]

Let's look at a few case studies of how understanding people's personality better can help in sales. Have you ever tried to buy something online, only to discover that you're required to speak with a sales representative over the phone to complete the purchase? As an introverted person, this makes me cringe. I'm the type of person who thinks deeply about what I want and conducts thorough independent research before I decide on a purchase. The thought of interacting with a high-energy salesperson who wants to "better understand my needs" so they can recommend unwanted add-ons is typically enough to send me shopping on a different website.

For others, especially those more extroverted in nature, a phone number on the home page or live chat to connect with a human is a first option. Extroverts tend to be more talkative, energetic and assertive, so when shopping, they might say to themselves, "finally, an online store that lets me talk to a real person!"[179]

As a customer, the best experience a business can give is one that accommodates your unique personality. Zappos, the online shoe store heralded for its exceptional customer service, is an exemplar for how to do this well. When you go to their homepage, their 24/7 customer support number is clearly visible at the top of the page. It's always available while you shop, from start to finish, but it's not mandatory. Whether you are introverted or extroverted, the shopping experience on Zappos is tailored to you. There aren't many companies like Zappos that are this mindful when designing their customers' shopping experience.

I'll offer one more example outside the digital world. A while back, my wife and I were shopping for a new mattress. We did a little bit of research online and then went to the mall to test them out. We stopped by a well-known mattress store we'll call the *Slumber Digits* Store. It was empty except for three salespeople. One of them greeted us when we walked in and asked us what brought us into the store. I returned a polite greeting and offered the standard response, "We're just looking, thank you."
"Sure thing," he said. "May I ask you a few questions about your current mattress and sleeping preferences?"
I deflected. "We're just going to look for a minute, if that's okay?" I said.

He was obviously well-coached in overcoming objections, and thus continued to press. Finally, I said "I just want look around for a minute. I'll let you know if we have any questions. If that's not okay, let me know and we'll leave."
I thought that would be enough for him to back off, but I was shocked when he actually invited us to leave. My wife and I walked out and ended up buying a bed-in-a-box online. We love it!

The problem with our *Slumber Digits* experience was that there wasn't an in-store on-ramp designed for the introverted shopper. A salesperson with a better understanding and appreciation of different personalities might have reacted differently. After my first or second plea, the salesperson probably should have backed off, handed me a brochure (or list of FAQs) and invited me to ask questions at my leisure.

Looking back, our experience might have been better if the salesperson and I understood our differing dispositions, but that's not practical. Being attuned to your customers' unique personality traits takes time. With experience and practice on improving your emotional intelligence, you'll be able to pick up on cues for what makes people tick.

Luckily, when working with internal teams and close collaborators, we can take time to understand personalities better. We can do this with basic personality assessment tools, many of which are available online.

A lot has been written about personality traits and the various assessments that help us identify them. I'm not going to go into detail rehashing the psychology behind personality, but I want to highlight the relevance of personality within the domains of entrepreneurial authenticity and resilience.

You might have heard about the Myers-Briggs Type Indicator (MBTI), a popular personality assessment. 2.5 million people take it each year, and it's the personality tool of choice for the majority of companies in the Fortune 500. Although it is well-known and widely used, in the last several years, prominent psychologists across the country have been "breaking-up" with Myers-Briggs, citing its unreliability, among other shortcomings.[180] I mention Myers-Briggs because it's so widely used, despite is unreliability and it's important that we're utilizing the best tools available to us.

A more reliable personality assessment, according to many of those same psychologists, uses the scale associated with the Big Five Personality Domains, also known as the Five Factor Model: Extraversion, Agreeableness, Conscientiousness, Neuroticism (emotional stability), and Openness to experience (Intellect/Imagination). Let's look at each of these domains in a bit more detail:

Extraversion

Extraversion/Introversion is probably the most studied of all the personality domains. Extraversion is a trait typically characterized by outgoingness and sociability. Highly extroverted people are more comfortable interacting with external stimuli. They thrive at large networking events, social gatherings, concerts, etc. They're also prone to thinking out loud.

Introversion, on the other hand, is a trait characterized by an inward focus. Those with higher levels of introversion typically prefer small group or one-to-one interactions, as opposed to large parties and events. They also typically do their best thinking when given time and space to reflect independently.

Agreeableness

Agreeableness relates to how warm and personable our connections are with others. Agreeable people are typically more trusting and compassionate.[181] On the other side of the spectrum, disagreeable people are often curt with others, which can be negatively perceived as detachment or even rudeness.

Conscientiousness

Conscientious people are very intentional. They're typically well-organized, dependable and responsible. They also tend to plan, making them good at establishing and working diligently toward goals.[182]

Less conscientious people are often more spontaneous. As an example, think about how you prefer vacationing. Do you plan every stop, restaurant and landmark you want to see ahead of time? Or, do you prefer to arrive without a strict agenda and go with the flow?

Neuroticism (emotional stability)

People with higher levels of neuroticism tend to worry more, even when things seem to be going well. They tend to be susceptible to negative thoughts and emotions.[183] Conversely, people with lower levels of neuroticism show greater levels of emotional stability.

Openness to Experience (intellect/imagination)

High levels of openness to experience indicate that you are a daring, original, and innovative thinker with broad interests.[184] As an example, you might be someone who looks at new experiences as learning opportunities and you actively seek them out whenever possible.

On the opposite end of the spectrum, you might prefer more familiar routines and ways of doing business.

You might have recognized your own personality in some of these descriptions. If you want to learn more precisely which of your personality traits are strongest, I recommend taking a free personality assessment online at
http://webspace.ship.edu/cgboer/bigfiveminitest.html
It only takes a few minutes to complete.

As you analyze your results, it's important to keep in mind that personality traits aren't binary. For example, you're not either extraverted or introverted. Instead, your unique personality falls along a spectrum that might represent various degrees of each trait. When you get the results from the assessment linked above, you should receive a score ranging from 8 to 72, which tells you whether you land on the low, average or high end of the spectrum:

Range	Numerical Score
Low	8 to 29
Average	30 to 50
High	51 to 72

It's also important to remember that even though many personality traits are believed to be biologically derived and relatively stable, there are many more flexible characteristics important for entrepreneurship previously mentioned in Chapter 1 (risk tolerance, entrepreneurial self-efficacy, believing you have control of your own destiny, etc.) that you can adapt and develop.

For years, researchers at prominent academic institutions across the globe have been on the quest to uncover "the entrepreneurial personality" – those personality traits that predict success in business. They've found interesting correlations linking individuals with higher levels of extraversion, conscientiousness and openness, and lower levels of agreeableness and neuroticism, to stronger entrepreneurial intentions and better business outcomes.[185] However our personality doesn't predetermine whether we have what it takes to be successful entrepreneurs, at least not directly.

Our personality traits are more important for understanding the potential blind spots that might affect how we grow and develop as entrepreneurs. For example, individuals with higher levels of extraversion tend to be less risk averse. Extraverts are less deterred by the thought of "putting themselves out there" in front of people. Compared with entrepreneurs high on the introversion scale, extraverts are more comfortable attending networking events, approaching a potential customer or partner to make a new connection, speaking in front of an audience, etc.

This doesn't mean that introverts cannot do these things. It just means that these activities might not come as naturally to them. The perceived risks of failing at these activities might weigh greater on an introvert. To get more comfortable with the idea of networking, we might create a goal of attending 1-3 business networking events each month. Another goal might be that while attending these events, you create 2-4 new connections, exchange business cards and schedule one follow-up meeting afterward. Achieving these goals will increase how comfortable an introvert is interacting among larger groups of people.

Another, perhaps more surprising example, is that people with lower levels of agreeableness are more likely to become entrepreneurs. They're also more likely to introduce disruptive business models that go against conventional ways of doing things. Malcolm Gladwell writes about this paradox in his bestselling book, *David and Goliath*. He says "Innovators need to be disagreeable. They are people willing to take social risks – to do things that others might disapprove of. That is not easy. Society frowns on disagreeableness. As human beings, we are hardwired to seek the approval of those around us. Yet, a radical and transformative thought goes nowhere without the willingness to challenge convention."[186]

Some of the most disruptive entrepreneurs of our time (e.g. Steve Jobs, Mark Zuckerberg, Jeff Bezos) have been known to be a bit crotchety.[187] In his book, *Onward*, Howard Schultz, the long-time Chairman and CEO of Starbucks, admits that his "tendency to let enthusiasm morph into impatience was a trait widely known throughout the company – generally appreciated, but occasionally the cause of frustration."[188]

So, what does this mean if you have a more agreeable personality? It certainly doesn't mean that you need to start being grumblier toward others. It does, however, mean that you need to be aware of agreeableness as a potential blind spot. Your agreeable personality might cause you to hesitate and miss an opportunity because you're too worried what a person (or people) might think.

There is also a significant relationship between higher levels of conscientiousness and entrepreneurial success. It makes sense that someone who is a natural planner and highly organized is more likely to be successful in business. These individuals tend to be more focused and seek out efficiency in their work wherever possible. Again, if that doesn't sound like you, it doesn't mean you cannot be a successful entrepreneur. Instead, it might mean that you need to work with a coach or mentor to help keep you on track with your goals, and/or hire a consultant to help you establish an organized business process.

The key take-away is that we shouldn't feel limited by our personality or the traits that make us who we are. Instead, we should embrace the positive aspects of our personality while recognizing any drawbacks that might slow us down. Now that we have a better understanding of the foundation built by our values and personality traits, let's continue our self-assessment and learn about the unique talents and strengths that will help us build and grow our business.

Talents and Strengths

"My advice to every budding entrepreneur is to actually take seriously the notion that the most important assets in your entire company are your people, starting with you."[190]

-Paul Allen
Co-founder of Ancestry.com

Paul Allen is the co-founder of Ancestry.com, the popular genealogy platform that boasts over 2.7 million subscribers.[189] Two decades before hitting that milestone, the startup was selling CD-ROMs filled with information for people interested in family history. That product was well-received, and the company began making money. As the Internet took shape, the business evolved into an online resource with revenues exploding from $2.6 million in 1998 to $23 million by 2001.[190] In 2012, Ancestry.com was acquired for $1.6 billion.[191]

Reflecting on his company's growth, Allen admitted in an interview with Gallup that although his company was doing great, he was "unaware and unappreciative of the diverse talents" of those he worked with. He didn't invest in "self-awareness, team awareness, leadership development [or] management."[190] That changed in 2012 when Allen was introduced to Gallup's CliftonStrengths® assessment.

Donald O. Clifton invented the CliftonStrengths® assessment to help people identify their top five strengths from an inventory of 34 distinct talents. The difference between a talent and a strength is that talents are latent, and they will only turn into strengths if we actively cultivate and develop them. The CliftonStrengths® assessment is accompanied by a reference book and report that dives into the details of each talent. Those 34 talents are grouped into four broad domains: **strategic thinking**, which helps you conceptualize and analyze information while remaining focused on goals and outcomes; **executing**, meaning you make things happen; **influencing** and convincing others; and **relationship-building**, which helps create meaningful social connections and cross-pollinate ideas.[192]

When Allen took the assessment, he was struck by how accurately it described his top strengths, all five of which fall within the strategic thinking domain. He was also taken aback when he discovered that his top talents didn't include anything in the relationship building domain.[193]
This was a blind spot for Allen during much of his entrepreneurial career. He admits that he wasn't very team-oriented and has a lot of regrets about the culture that he could have built at Ancestry.com. He says, "It could have been a very mindful culture, inclusive and aware of all the amazing talents that human beings possess."[193] It's ironic that a company built for customers wanting to know themselves better through genealogy, didn't really know itself very well.

Allen is a serial entrepreneur, founding seven other businesses besides Ancestry.com. His latest venture, Strengths, Inc., was inspired by his desire to "help more people identify, develop and use their natural talents."[194] (The Strengths Inc. platform matches individuals with coaches who can help them leverage their strengths). We will talk more about coaching in a later chapter.

How well do you know your own strengths? How well can you recognize the strengths of those you work with – your employees, partners, contractors, suppliers, collaborators, etc.? Are you leveraging your strengths and the strengths of those around you to build a more resilient business? Like Allen, even the most successful entrepreneurs have blind spots, but your ability to acknowledge them and continue to work from a position of strength will help you become a more authentic, more resilient entrepreneur. (We will explore this point more in the next section when we discuss how to delegate based on you and your teammates unique talents).

According to Gallup, more than 18 million people have already taken the CliftonStrengths® assessment, so there's a good chance you've heard of it before. My intention isn't to rehash a well-known tool as something novel. Instead, I encourage you to take the assessment if you haven't already, or revisit it if you have, and utilize the information in a way that will make you a more authentic and resilient entrepreneur.

Through my experience coaching entrepreneurs, I've found that many lose sight of their talents and let the immediacy of urgent problems create lasting habits that diminish their focus on working from a position of strength. This is especially true for small businesses entering a growth spurt.

For example, two of my clients are a husband and wife team offering residential remodeling and interior design services. They are artists in their respective crafts. They've done little to advertise, but their business has grown exponentially over the last couple of years because the quality of their work results in strong word-of-mouth marketing. Their business model requires significant time spent triaging customers' needs, individualizing consultations and educating the customer on multiple options. This front-end of the pipeline is extremely important and requires relationship-building and patience, among other unique skills.

Admittedly, they recognized that their strengths were designing and building and the time they spent at the beginning of the new customer development process was time away from their core competencies. In its infancy, the business required the two-person team to wear all the hats, but as the business grew, trying to do everything on their own became unmanageable.

In our coaching session, they said they were looking to hire their first employee. This made sense based on their strong growth. When I asked what they envisioned that person doing, they described an apprentice's job – someone to shadow them and develop the remodeling trade. My advice was to think about that job description for a second position and instead consider bringing in someone whose role is to manage the front-end of the customer funnel. This strategy results in delegating those time-consuming tasks that don't leverage their strengths.

If they could hire an employee with relationship-building strengths to focus on business development, they would create a job intentionally aligned with that employee's individual strengths while increasing their own productivity at the same time. The CliftonStrengths® assessment is one tool that enables us to make important decisions about such things as hiring and strategic outsourcing.

It's important to think about this now because the costs of hiring the wrong person are staggering. Aside from the financial loss, there's often a significant hit to productivity, morale and management's reputation.[195]

Ian Pettigrew is the Director of Kingfisher Coaching. He coaches entrepreneurs on how to leverage their strengths to become more resilient using the CliftonStrengths® tools. Pettigrew's top two strengths are R*elator* and *Winning Others Over (WOO),* both of which are activated by strong social connections and relationships with others. He and Paul Allen, the co-founder of Ancestry.com, would likely complement each other quite nicely if they worked together, combining their strategic-thinking and relationship-building talents.

In reflecting on his strengths, Pettigrew says that, "With *Relator* and *WOO* as my top two strengths, I know that periods of time when I try to work alone are always the most difficult for me, as I'm not getting to apply my dominant talents. If I continue to work alone without addressing the needs of my *relator* and *woo,* this could lead to feeling hopeless and fatigued – in a word, burnout."[196] His ability to self-reflect on his strengths helps him recognize when he might need to rebalance his work tasks.

"While it's true that your greatest successes will be in your strength zone," says leadership guru and bestselling author John C. Maxwell, "it's also true that your best failures will occur there." When we falter from a position of strength, we're more likely to bounce back quickly, learning and improving from that setback and emerging even stronger. When we fail in an area of weakness, we might not even know why we failed - it's much harder to reflect on and learn from these types of failures.[21]

The reality is that entrepreneurs, especially sole proprietors, wear many hats. At the end of the day, they must get things done, and many of those tasks might not leverage their strengths. However, if you find yourself frequently and consistently slipping into work that doesn't leverage your strengths, it might be time to look to others for help.

"Be completely honest with yourself about what you do well and what you don't. Pour your energy into your strengths. Find others who can shore up your weaknesses and learn that great teams are built this way."

-Gay Gaddis
Founder and CEO of T3, an Award-winning Innovation Agency

> "When you're the leader of a company, be it large or small, you can't do everything yourself. In fact, you can't do much of anything by yourself. The more talented people you have to help you, the better off you and the company will be. One of the challenges you face as a company grows is that you tend to get a little too close to your own strengths and weaknesses, and it's hard to be objective. I've heard this referred to as 'believing your own press,' but I prefer to think of it as 'breathing your own exhaust.' It doesn't sound healthy—because it isn't."
>
> - Michael Dell
>
> Founder, Dell Computers

Tasks that don't align with your entrepreneurial strengths should be delegated to someone else. The ability to delegate is fundamental to business growth. In fact, a Gallup survey of 143 of Inc. Magazine's 500 fastest-growing private companies in the U.S. revealed that CEOs who were adept at delegating generated 33 percent more revenue, on average, than those who weren't.[197]

Entrepreneurs who have difficulty delegating make themselves vulnerable to the stress of an ever-expanding plate of responsibilities and tasks that need to be done. These entrepreneurs take on more and more work, believing that only *they* are capable of correctly executing the task. Eventually, this behavior leads to burnout. The resilient entrepreneur guards themselves against burnout and makes themselves more effective by delegating tasks that are least aligned with their strengths.

All-star entrepreneurs are celebrated by society because of the tremendous amount of hard work and long hours they put into their businesses. The reality is that the heroes of entrepreneurship have learned to delegate and lead their business by leveraging their strengths.

"Sure, I deal with operational issues," says billionaire entrepreneur, Mark Cuban, "but pretty much every other strategic element of my businesses I have learned to delegate – that's not easy for an entrepreneur to do. In the past, I would have taken on anything and everything that I thought I could add value to. I had to be in the middle of everything. No longer. I've learned to hire people in whom I can build trust and let them take the ball and run with it."[79]

Even if you're the only person in the business, you need to be thinking about creating an effective team if you want to grow your business. Peter Drucker, the "Founder of Modern Management," advises, "Long before it has reached the point where it needs the balance of a top management team, the new venture has to create one. Long before the time has come at which management by one person no longer works and becomes mismanagement, that one person also must start learning how to work with colleagues, has to learn to trust people, yet also how to hold them accountable. The founder has to learn to become the leader of a team, rather than a 'star' with 'helpers.'"[30]

If you're not able to hire an employee yet, consider a temp or contractor instead. There is a plethora of freelancing platforms available that literally bring you a world of talented people waiting to enhance your capacity and complement you in areas that don't leverage your strengths. Sites like 99Designs,

Upwork, Freelancer and Fiverr are great ways to outsource tasks that take you away from your core competencies. Make a list of the tasks that consume your time without leveraging your unique talents and plan to delegate or outsource them. Whether you're outsourcing or hiring, think about how you will lead people from their unique positions of strength.

Learning Styles and Creative Problem-Solving Preferences

"At a fast-growing start-up, effective leaders keep firing themselves from jobs they did at the beginning. Like many founders, I handled accounting and payroll, which drained a lot of time. One of my first objectives and key results was to offload the financial tasks and focus on product and strategy, our big-picture objectives."

- Brett Kopf
Founder of Remind, as told to John Doerr in *Measure What Matters*

I worked as a consultant with the City of Austin's Office of Innovation for two and half years. During that time, we trained hundreds of people on creative problem-solving techniques and how to work better as a team. Our curriculum was grounded in methodologies developed by Humantific, a New York-based innovation consultancy, and Basadur, a leader in applied creativity and organizational effectiveness. Part of Basadur's process is to understand our preferences when it comes to taking on a new project with an uncertain outcome.

Are you most comfortable getting things started by pulling in important collaborators and pieces of information that can help you better understand the challenge or opportunity? If you answered with a strong 'yes,' your preferences align you more with those of a ***Generator***.

Are you most effective at making sense of all those pieces of information, finding patterns in the data and defining the challenge or opportunity? If that sounds like you, then you likely have strong ***Conceptualizer*** preferences.

The ***Generator*** and ***Conceptualizer*** preferences represent *divergent thinking*. Divergent thinkers often prefer "generating many diverse ideas for one problem by perceiving the world beyond the conventional viewpoints."

On the flip side, some of us are *convergent thinkers*. Convergent thinkers help us take existing ideas or processes and make them better, more efficient and practical for the real world. There are two preferences strongly aligned with convergent thinking. The first is optimization.

If you're good at taking data and forming actionable, well defined plans with steps clearly laid out, you are likely an ***Optimizer***.

If you're of the *"get 'er done"* mindset, performing your best when you're knocking out tasks and checking things off the to-do list, you're probably an ***Implementer***. Implementers help us make things happen.

While we all might have to work in each of these areas at various times, we typically resonate more strongly with one or two of these preferences.

Contrary to what you might expect, Michael Dell isn't best known for inventing breakthrough computer technology.

Instead, he built his business by addressing inefficiencies in the computer industry's value chain.[204] Dell built and differentiated his business based on optimization of business processes within the computer industry. For example, he adopted just-in-time delivery into his supply chain to reduce inventory and warehousing costs. He also maximized cash flow by receiving up-front payment from his customers while obtaining favorable, longer-term accounts payable arrangements with his suppliers.

Gay Gaddis, Founder and CEO of T3, admits that she's not a details person. In her book, *Cowgirl Power*, she says, "I try to write down the details. I make all kinds of lists, but then I misplace them... the good news is that I always remember the big issues. But I suck at even finding those lists, much less executing them."[85] Gay is most likely a Generator or maybe a Conceptualizer. She might not be great at details or checklists, but she is certainly comfortable in the abstract and ambiguous space of creative design and advertising.

Interestingly, Dell became one of T3's largest customers. They consistently received exemplary feedback from them for their advertising work. Part of the successful relationship between these two companies was the complementary learning styles and creative problem-solving preferences of the two founders and their company cultures. Dell wouldn't claim that he is best suited to creative advertising, but he could take credit for recognizing those strengths in Gaddis and delegating that business function to her firm.

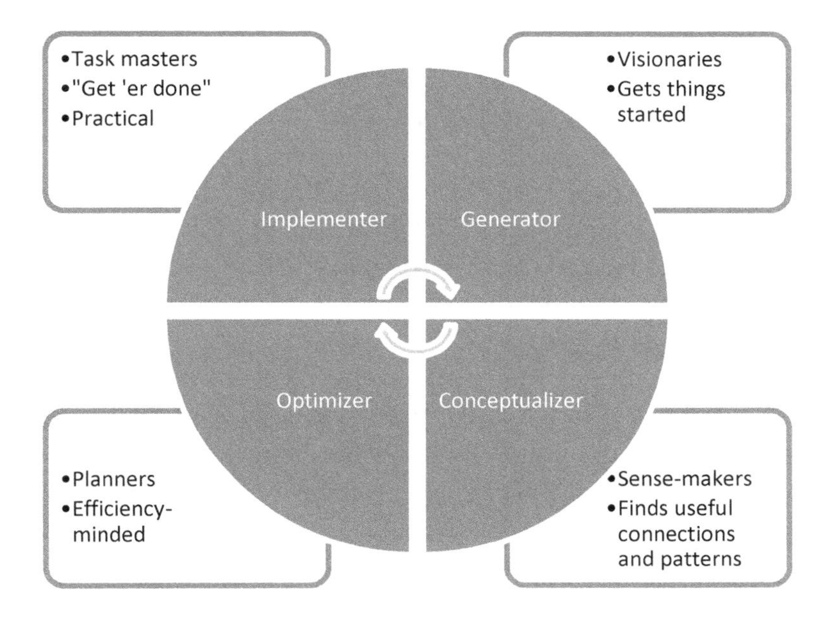

Figure 3: Adapted from Basadur's Innovation Profile Inventory Matrix

Basadur has a well-developed online assessment (https://www.basadurprofile.com/default.aspx) that can measure which style of thinking you are most productive working in. There is a small fee to take the assessment, but I highly recommend it. It's a helpful tool for both authentic self-reflection and collaboration. Let's look at a couple of different styles in action with an example from one of America's most culturally iconic businesses.

Walt Disney is a household name, but Walt's brother, Roy Disney, was arguably just as deserving of the credit for the animation studio's success. Yet, the brothers couldn't have been more different in their business approach and managerial mindset. In Walt Disney's biography, Author Neal Gabler says that Roy Disney always "emphasized fiscal accountability [as opposed to] Walt's own management style, which was capricious, idiosyncratic, extravagant and hopelessly inefficient."[153]

For example, after a film screening one day, Roy's first question to Walt was "how long was the run time?" Walt was incensed. "We work for years creating these pictures and all Roy can say is, 'How long does it run?'"

This is a classic example of the friction we often see between generators and optimizers. Walt was the creative generator and Roy was the operational optimizer. Although they often clashed, together they made Walt Disney Studios an ambidextrous organization - both creative and striving toward greater efficiency.

Think of other companies you've done business with recently. Was their business model founded on creativity or efficiency? As they've grown, have they changed or expanded their approach? What about your own preferences? Are they aligned with your business' core competencies?

Related to our creative problem-solving preferences are individual learning styles. Dr. David Kolb, Professor Emeritus at Case Western Reserve University in Cleveland, has researched learning styles for more than four decades. At the core of his findings is the premise that there are basically two different ways that we learn about something. One way is by experiencing it directly or hands-on learning. The other is by thinking and reflecting deeply on it.[199]

Through experience, we gain situation-specific knowledge. Would you agree that having 25 years' experience running several successful restaurants would make someone an expert in that industry? Probably so. That individual probably knows the ins and outs of nearly every facet of operating a restaurant because they've experienced it all, first-hand.

Now, let's say you want to start your own restaurant after a few years working on the wait staff. Your experience, although valid, pales in comparison to the 25-year restaurateur. Luckily, you don't have to wait tables another 22 years to learn as much as the veteran. You can sit down with him or her and pick their brain. As challenges arise, you can rely on their advice. This mentoring relationship, which we will cover more in-depth later in the book, will help you shorten your entrepreneurial learning curve.[198]

If you learn equally well through both experience and reflection, you have what Professor Kolb calls a flexible or balanced learning style.[199] That's a good thing. It would be difficult to get through life if we didn't learn through both experience and reflection. However, like Basadur's Creative Problem-Solving Styles, many people will typically prefer one learning style over the others. If you have a strong preference, you might try to partner or collaborate with someone who can complement your preferences and styles with their own.

A good example of complementary learning styles and creative problem-solving preferences is found in the genesis of Honda Motor Company. Co-founder Soichiro Honda was an engineer and knew before he even started the company that his talents and preferences would be best focused on the research and development side of the business. Furthermore, he knew that there was more to business success than research and development. So, even before starting the business, he sought out a complementary co-founder. He found that partner in Takeo Fujisawa, who handled the finance, logistics, human resources and marketing functions.[30]

Kolb's research has shown that "engineers often experience difficulty moving from the role of individual contributors, which allows them to focus on the strength of their learning styles, to the role of manager or leader, which requires them to flex to other styles."[199] From its inception, Honda Motor Company was formed by founders working from their perspective areas of strength because of Mr. Honda's self-awareness and authenticity.

Like Disney and Honda, many of the most disruptive, visionary companies in history have had similar balancing co-founder relationships: Steve Jobs and Steve Wozniak with Apple; Anne Wojcicki and Linda Avey as co-founders of 23andMe; Evan Williams and Biz Stone, co-founders of Twitter, etc. Each of these co-founding teams complemented each other's strengths, creative problem-solving preferences and learning styles.

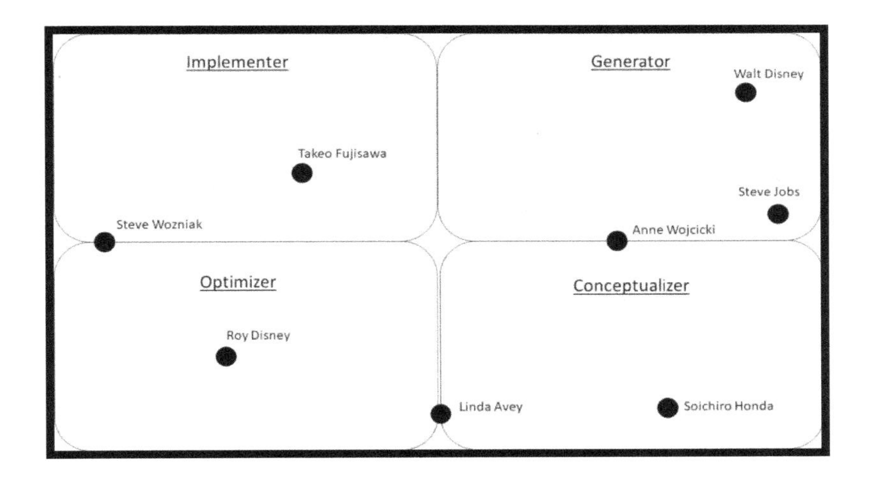

*Figure 4: Renowned Co-founders Presumed Creative Problem-Solving Preferences.**
**The graphic above shows several renowned co-founder teams and where they might land on the Creative Problem-Solving Preferences Matrix. Note that this wasn't created with actual assessment data, but presumed based on their respective company roles.*

If you're a balanced learner, you're probably comfortable with bouncing back and forth between both reflective observation and active experimentation. On the other hand, if you have an extreme preference for one or the other, you need to be aware of your potential blind spots.

Research conducted at the Georgia Institute of Technology revealed some interesting findings about learning styles and how they relate to entrepreneurial success. They found that entrepreneurs with task-oriented problem-solving preferences and practical, hands-on learning styles were more successful in terms of market share, growth and profitability.[198] This is especially true for entrepreneurs pursuing innovative, disruptive business models. One of the best strategic approaches to innovating is to use the lean startup methodology, popularized by Eric Ries, in his bestselling books: *The Lean Startup* and *The Startup Way*.

Lean methodology guides entrepreneurs to a more experimental approach in business by establishing and testing hypotheses quickly and inexpensively without a huge upfront investment. Using lean principles, entrepreneurs fail and learn rapidly, cheaply and with enough resilience that they can iterate and pivot until they find something that works in the market.

I'll give you a brief example. I worked with an entrepreneur interested in starting her own gluten-free bakery and confectionery store. She was interested in startup financing for a brick-and-mortar retail location. She had baked for friends and family for years, but this was her first stint in business. I encouraged her to consider a leaner strategy where she started her business at a local farmer's market instead of going straight to brick-and-mortar retail.

This strategy required substantially less capital and gave her a lot more flexibility. She took the advice, and over the course of a year, expanded from one farmer's market into three while she refined and improved her menu and worked to reduce her cost of goods sold. All these discoveries would have been much more expensive with a storefront.

No matter how long and hard you think about your business idea, it's never going to become an actual business without trying it and seeing if it works. If you find yourself stuck on the hamster wheel of ideation, you might try to design an initial experiment to test your idea. If that sounds daunting, it might be because your learning style, problem solving preferences and strengths don't align well for experimentation. If that's the case,

I suggest you look for a cofounder, coach or mentor that can complement you in this area.

Regardless of our industry or business stage, we can use frameworks like Basadur, CliftonStrengths® and Kolb's learning styles to better position ourselves for success. I have a strong preference for conceptualizing and reflective observation. They help make me a great researcher. I'm able to dig deep for facts and data, find underlying patterns and trends, and then put them all together to create a framework to better understand a challenge or opportunity. Without my conceptualizing preference and reflective observation learning style, there's no way I would have been able to write this book.

With that said, I know I'm not going to meet the tasks of marketing and promoting my book with as much gusto as I have in the research and writing. It will be a challenge to find flow in those activities. Executing an effective promotional strategy might be better suited to a diligent implementer. I know that as soon as I finish this book, I'm going to want to take another deep dive into a related field of research or keep building on the ideas I've presented. What I really should do though, is find someone who can help me with marketing and promotion. That will allow me to continue to focus on what drives and motivates me. It will enable me to keep working from a position of strength.

The flip side of these examples is having an extreme or inflexible preference for implementation and action. I typically encounter entrepreneurs with these symptoms after they've already started the business. They tell me that they've never been busier, but they feel like they're treading water. They have difficulty stepping back from the day-to-day operations of the business to think about strategic direction. If you've found yourself in this situation, then working with someone with strategic thinking strengths and a conceptualizer's problem-solving approach can be extremely helpful.

Another common blind spot is when entrepreneurs prefer to act quickly without adequately assessing and mitigating potential risks. The "fire-aim-ready" entrepreneur may also be more susceptible to getting entrenched into a routine way of doing business without reflecting on other possible alternatives. The lean methodology helps mitigate some of the risks through prototyping and testing minimum viable products. We'll explore the lean methodology a bit more in chapter 6.

In Kolb's book, *How You Learn is How You Live*, he says, "When we reflect without acting we have trouble accomplishing change and may become overwhelmed with possibilities, but when we act without reflecting on the consequences of our actions, our decisions become aimless and random."[199]

The point is we all need people who have different strengths, preferences and styles to help us think through business challenges, explore and experiment with new opportunities and execute on all our wonderful ideas. The trick is to recognize when the time has come that we need to get help. Recruiting collaborators with diverse skillsets will allow you to focus on your strengths.

It's oftentimes more challenging to work with others who have different styles, strengths and preferences than our own because our different viewpoints can clash. It's much more comfortable to work with others who think and work like we do, but in doing so, we run the risk of complacency and *group think*.

Let's look at a tool I've developed that can help us reduce conflict within a diverse team.

Collaboration Canvas: Putting it altogether

"Don't make business sound more sophisticated than it is. All you need to know is how to work with people. That's all business ever is – any success or failure rests entirely on my ability to work with the people at hand."

- Barbara Corcoran
"Queen of New York Real Estate" and business investor

Now that we've assessed our values, personality, strengths, learning styles and creative problem-solving preferences, let's put it all together in a practical format that we can use throughout our entrepreneurial journey.

One of the most interesting case studies of a company doing this successfully is Bridgewater Associates. Bridgewater is one of the largest, most successful hedge fund management companies in the world. Ray Dalio founded the company out of his apartment in 1975 at age 26.[168] Today, more than 40 years later, Bridgewater manages about $160 billion in assets and employs around 1,700 people.[200]

Every employee at Bridgewater has a *People Profile*. This is an individualized tool that presents things like strengths, weaknesses, values, etc. It helps everyone better understand each other, so they can make better decisions about which "jobs a person can and cannot do well, which ones they should avoid, and how the person should be trained."[168]

Similarly, as entrepreneurs, we can build our own profiles. I've developed a simple *Collaboration Canvas* to serve as a quick snapshot of the values, traits, strengths and preferences that make you uniquely powerful as an entrepreneur. As you complete the assessments highlighted in this chapter, include your results in a canvas. It will serve as a powerful, practical framework for introspective self-reflection, as well as for building interpersonal relationships with co-founders, new-hires, and partners outside your organization. Build out your canvas and encourage those you work with to complete theirs. Then, share and discuss how you complement one another and where areas of friction might emerge.

I've included the Collaboration Canvas on the next page as an example. There is also a blank template included in the appendix.

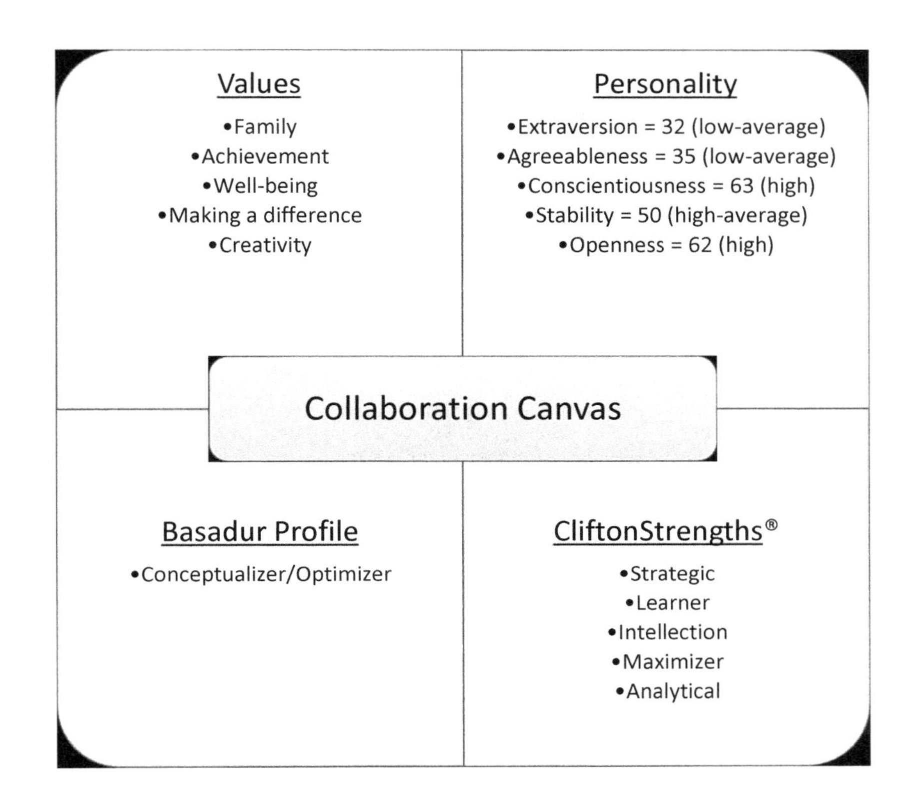

In the next chapter, we're going to switch gears a bit and focus on funding an early stage business. Funding is an area that creates a lot of barriers and stress for new entrepreneurs. Let's examine some new ways of thinking about early stage capital and methods of successfully financing your venture.

Chapter 5: Funding

"The more money you have at the startup stage, the more trouble you're bound to buy for yourself and for your business."

- Daymond John
Founder of FUBU and Investor

True or false: It's impossible to start a business without a loan or outside investment. This is one of the most common myths I hear from new entrepreneurs. Nothing could be further from the truth. Some aspiring entrepreneurs get so caught up thinking about all the funding required to open their dream business that they forget that they need to start small. We can still think big while starting small and growing iteratively. Financial scarcity in the preliminary stages of your business isn't a negative. Often, showing progress despite a lack of financial resources proves your grit, determination, and resiliency. When you need capital to grow your business later, potential investors and lenders will notice and respect how far you've come without outside capital.

Derek Sivers, the founder of CD Baby, started the online music store with only $500 of his own funds. He didn't know how to code or program an online store, so he went and bought a book on programming for $25 and taught himself. Ten years later, CD Baby was sold for $22 million. Sivers' advice is to "watch out when anyone (including you) says he wants to do something big, but can't until he raises money. It usually means the person is more in love with the idea of being *big-big-big* than with doing something useful. For an idea to get *big-big-big*, it must be useful, and being useful doesn't need funding. If you want to be useful, you can always start now, with only 1 percent of what you have in your grand vision."[201]

This is some of the greatest advice an entrepreneur can heed, yet it's often ignored. I've worked with several lawyers who wanted to start their own business. I'm not sure if it's a trend among lawyers or a coincidence, but many of those that I've worked with were trying to start a business outside of the legal profession. I remember working with one lawyer, Harry, who wanted to open a bar and restaurant. He envisioned a family dine-in experience on one half of the building and a sports bar on the other. He spent a large sum of money buying a plot of commercial land. He had no experience in the bar or restaurant business. He had never controlled perishable inventory, created and tested recipes, or managed waitstaff, but he did have a lengthy (108 pages) business plan and was seeking $1.9 million in seed financing to get the restaurant launched.

I suggested he consider scaling down his idea – maybe start with a smaller physical space or even a food truck. In doing so, he could prove that he had great food and service with less than 5 percent of his current plan's startup costs. He heard my advice, but couldn't heed it because it conflicted with the grandiose vision of what he had planned. Think about the time and energy that went into drafting that 108-page business plan. He felt like he had already invested too much to change course. This is just one of the many pitfalls of seeking an unnecessary amount of capital too early – we lose our ability to adapt and be flexible.

Five years after working with Harry, I was surprised when I saw his name in our local newspaper. He was interviewed about all the commercial development happening around the plot of commercial property he owned. I still drive by that piece of property and it's still a grassy field. In the article, Harry mentioned his plans to open a restaurant as soon as he found a business partner. Poor Harry has been on the hamster wheel for half a decade looking for someone with money to show up and make his dreams come true.

Compare Harry with Barbara Corcoran who is probably best known for her role as an investor (shark) on ABC's reality TV show, *Shark Tank*. The incredible story of her entrepreneurial journey began when she left her waitressing job and co-founded a New York City real estate company with only $1,000 in startup capital. She began leasing one apartment at a time, starting with the only properties an unseasoned New York City real estate agent could get her hands on – the ones that were historically difficult to sell. She worked with what she had, and with a bit of remodeling and savvy salesmanship, she started getting leases signed and making commissions.

As the business grew, the partnership soured and eventually they parted ways. Because her co-founder put up the original seed money, he was the majority shareholder with a 51/49 percent split and had final decision-making authority. She left the partnership with less than $15,000. As she walked out the door, her business partner said, "You know, Barb, you'll never succeed without me."[202]

Taking that slight as a personal challenge, she decided to start again. Her limited funds forced her to focus - "instead of buying furniture and equipment, [she] decided to lease phones, typewriters and desks."[202] This allowed her to stretch those limited funds, purchasing only the essentials. Through her scrappiness and perseverance, Barbara was able to rebuild her business, taking it to much greater heights. It became the most profitable real estate company per employee in the United States, and in 2001, she sold her business for $66 million![203] The key to her early success was focus. Limited funding is a great motivator for relentless focus.

Another great example is Michael Dell, who, like Corcoran, started his company with only $1,000 in startup capital. Four years later, in 1988, when he took his computer company public, the business was valued at around $85 million![204] In his book, *Direct from Dell,* he shares his company's secret to success. "Lean beginnings created the strategic management principles that defined our culture: Less is more. Information is better than inventory. Ingenuity is better than investment... when you start a company with as little as $1,000, as I did, you spend each dollar very carefully. You learn to be economical, efficient and prudent. You also learn to only do those things that really add value for your customers..."

As author Eric Ries articulates in his book, *The Startup Way*, "If you passionately believe in a mission but lack the resources to make it unfurl in every possible way, you're absolutely forced to focus. There's simply no extra time and no extra money..."[205] When you're fully bankrolled, it's difficult to maintain the discipline needed to make investments based on evidence and customer feedback. It's much easier to skip the learning process of experimentation with minimum viable products or prototypes and spend that money on vanity projects that don't add any real value to the startup.

Start small and grow your business in iterations. Financiers are much more willing to fund growth as opposed to early stage, *yet-to-be-validated* ideas. Even if an investor or lender is interested, you should expect less favorable terms from them. Regardless of how lucrative the opportunity, without validation, the risk will be priced into an investor's equity stake or a lender's interest rate.

With all that said, most new businesses are going to need some type of funding to get off the ground. In this chapter, I'll share the financing options that resilient entrepreneurs should focus on. These are the options that I've seen work best for new entrepreneurs. With a lot of hard work, patience and perseverance, they can work for you too.

"It's as if the missing link for success in business is cash to get started. It's not. Far more often than not, raising cash is the biggest mistake you can make."[79]

- Mark Cuban

Bootstrapping

"Money is a tool, and nothing more. Don't confuse it with the end-goal."

- Jesse Tevelow
Bestselling author and entrepreneur

In Chapter 1 I told the story of Anthony, the personal fitness trainer looking to evolve his business into a smoothie and nutrition supplement store. Anthony was interested in applying for a loan to help cover the costs of the business expansion. When applying for a loan, it's common for a lender to require a loan applicant to have some skin in the game – bringing in anywhere from 10 to 20 percent equity for the deal. Anthony needed about $100,000 to get his storefront open and purchase the necessary furniture, fixtures, equipment and inventory. He only had about $7,000 to contribute, but he needed closer to $20,000. The loan would cover the other $80,000 in expenses.

Anthony planned on covering the gap through a grant from the Texas Department of Assistive and Rehabilitative Services (DARS). The grant was designed to help self-employed entrepreneurs with disabilities access small amounts of capital for equipment and other business expenses. Anthony's dyslexia made him eligible for the grant program. If Anthony could secure a $10,000 grant along with his $7,000 in savings and cut a few expenses, we believed we could make the financing work.

DARS requested a meeting to review Anthony's grant application and learn more about the business plan. Anthony asked if I would join him in the meeting. As his coach, I could offer moral support, and as a representative of Business and Community Lenders (BCL) of Texas, I could speak to the details of the lending process, showing how all the pieces of the financing puzzle would come together to fund the startup.

BCL hosted the meeting. The two women from DARS sat across from us at the conference table. They listened respectfully as Anthony presented his business plan. I stayed quiet and watched Anthony give an outstanding presentation. He was well-prepared. As the presentation ended and the DARS representatives began asking questions, I could tell they were skeptical.

I thought Anthony responded well to their objections and doubts. I even chimed in to reinforce the work ethic and time he'd spent going the extra mile in researching and strategizing a sound business model. The meeting ended with them saying they would give it some consideration and run it by their supervisor. Through their politeness I sensed that they had already made up their mind. When Anthony informed me the next week that his grant application had been rejected, I called one of the representatives we met with to find out why.

I tried to convince her that they should reconsider their decision. I pleaded my case. "We're prepared to move forward on a loan that accounts for about 80 percent of the risk… We cannot do the deal without the additional funding from this grant…. Anthony has run his business successfully for years and this is a logical expansion for him – one that will allow him to work for himself for years to come with less physical demand."

I listened to the canned responses and objections:
"I understand, but we just cannot… I wish we could, but we just don't believe the project can be successful…" she said.

"Why not?" I asked bluntly.
And then she said it – finally a candid response, "We just don't want to give false hope to the people we work with," she said.
I was stunned! The people they work with are the exact people they should be instilling with hope. In fact, when I work with entrepreneurs overcoming disabilities, it's usually them who inspire hope in me.
"I see," I said, punctured by the finality of her statement.

She seemed unaware that some of the greatest, most resilient entrepreneurs of the last century succeeded in business, despite their dyslexia: Richard Branson, Daymond John, Barbara Corcoran, Charles Schwab, Henry Ford - just to name a few.[206]

Anthony didn't get the funding he needed for the retail store. I talked to him about other financing options, but he decided he would double down on growing his existing services instead. Anthony is still in the personal fitness training business and doing quite well. I'm confident that when he's ready, he will try again for the funding to open his store.

Many entrepreneurs experience financing constraints, but none more so than America's most overlooked and underestimated populations. African Americans are five times less likely to receive supplier credit and twice as likely to be denied a loan compared to non-minority business owners.[207] As a result of these barriers to capital, African American entrepreneurs are significantly more likely to finance their business using their own personal savings.[208] Despite these constraints, they are also more likely to persevere through the startup stage, giving up on their business significantly less often compared to White and Hispanic entrepreneurs.[65] How is that possible? One plausible reason is they have a lot more to lose since everything they have is on the line. This forces them to focus on what's important and leverage every resource at their disposal to gain an advantage.

In 1978, after working for a couple of years as a temp in the magazine publishing industry, Janice Bryant Howroyd decided she was ready for a more permanent position – this time working for herself. She left her job and started her own staffing agency with a single desk, a phone and less than $2,000, including a $900 loan from her mother.

When asked about her business' modest beginnings, she says, "I didn't have a lot of what people typically have to start a business, but I did have a lot of intelligence. Sometimes when you don't have anything, you can be bolder than someone who has something and is afraid to lose it."[209] Today, her company, the Act 1 Group, generates approximately $1.1 billion in annual sales, with 17,000 clients and 2,600 employees across 19 different countries. According to Forbes, Bryant Howroyd's personal net worth is more than $400 million, and in 2015, she became the first female African American entrepreneur to have founded and grown a business beyond $1 billion in annual revenue. She achieved all this with less than two thousand dollars to start!

Despite the financial constraints that Janice and so many other entrepreneurs face, many can find a path forward because they stay focused on providing value for their customers. These lessons of persistence, perseverance and focus aren't shared and celebrated enough.

What *is* over-promoted are the few pots of grant money out there for women and minority-owned businesses. The reality is that these funds are very limited. While there may be some funds out there, those that you do find will be wrought with qualifying limitations and a cumbersome bureaucratic application and reporting process. For many idea-stage entrepreneurs, funding isn't the problem, and sending inexperienced entrepreneurs on a quixotic search for grant funds is distracting them from going out and proving their concept in the market. Once an entrepreneur has accomplished that, it will be much easier for them to find financing to grow and scale a validated business model.

Bryant Howroyd's story is a fitting example of the *bootstrapping* entrepreneur. The term stems from the adage to "pull yourself up by your own bootstraps." Bootstrapping in business is all about finding creative methods of obtaining the resources you need to start and grow your business, especially when obtaining those resources through traditional means is too expensive or otherwise infeasible.

Bootstrapping has its pros and cons. For example, you need patience to bootstrap your business because the bootstrapped path is defined by slower growth and more time between major milestones. "Expect everything to take three times as long as you predicted," warns businessman and bootstrapping expert, Gregory Gianforte.[210]

Yet, for the resilient entrepreneur, bootstrapping a business carves a path forward when there may be few options otherwise. Bootstrapping also enables you to retain complete control over your company because you don't have to answer to outside investors and there aren't any lender's liens on your assets. It's estimated that at least 80 percent of all small business owners have implemented some type of bootstrapping strategy at one time or another.[211] Let's look at some of the bootstrapping strategies used most frequently.

The first set of strategies is internally focused and involves the most self-sacrifice. It includes keeping your day job for the time being while you save up enough money to get started. With this option, you are funding the business with your existing income. Many entrepreneurs take this moonlighting route, working full time during the day while working on the business in the evenings and on the weekends. This makes for long days and can result in a strain on your social and family life. The idea is to get the business rolling, little by little, while you retain the financial safety net of your day job. Almost all the students who take my evening business classes are working full-time jobs during the day. By 8:30PM, we're all burnt out, but every evening we meet, the students learn something new that can help them in their entrepreneurial journey and they're one step closer to realizing their dream.

There is a lot of planning and prep work you can do for your business before you ever make a dime, and you can probably start making some sales on the side while you keep your steady job. I've seen many entrepreneurs take this route. Stepping back from a full-time job to a part-time job, they continue to transition slowly into being a full-time entrepreneur.

Another common strategy is deferring owner salaries. Many founders will cover their personal expenses using their savings while the business is starting out. It took over a year for Walt and Roy Disney to start paying themselves a salary when the animation studio was starting out.[153] Business owners who are already operating also employ this strategy when cash is tight or when they need to purchase a larger batch of inventory or new piece of equipment. Aaron Levie, co-founder and CEO of Box, ensured that he was the lowest-paid employee in his company for its first four years.[81] Again, these strategies might not seem ideal, but they are used more often than you might think by highly-motivated entrepreneurs.

While employing these self-sacrificing strategies, be cautious not to fall into a common trap – something psychologists refer to as an *escalation of commitment*.[212] In entrepreneurship, escalation of commitment might entail continuing to throw money at a flawed idea or failing business strategy because so much effort or resources have already been spent on the cause. It's hard to make objective decisions when you've sacrificed so much for something.

I'll share an example from my work where I met with many entrepreneurs interested in a business loan. I'd help them get their business plan together, complete the loan application and put together a stack of required paperwork. I wanted every entrepreneur I worked with to have the best shot possible when they submitted their loan package, so I'd review everything before they applied. If I thought they could make changes to their plan or application that gave them a better chance at qualifying, I coached them on making the right presentation. This usually took several meetings and hours of work for both the loan applicant and myself.

By the time the application was ready to submit, the applicant and I had usually formed a good working relationship. It was exactly for this reason that I typically wasn't part of the loan committee responsible for making the ultimate decision about loan approval. As much as I might have tried to remain neutral, the truth is that I was biased – I wanted to say *yes*. The loan committee had very little interaction with the applicant, so they were able to make a more objective and unbiased decision.

Bootstrappers are also susceptible to this pitfall because they've invested a greater percentage of their personal savings and sweat equity into the venture. It's hard to make objective and unbiased business decisions when we feel that we have already committed so much of our time and money into something. We ignore key facts and tune out logic. We might also feel like it's too late to change course.

Sunk Cost Fallacy

This mental snare, known as the *sunk cost fallacy*, leads us to believe that we must continue to invest time and energy into something even if it's a better idea to stop and pivot in a new direction. To illustrate the sunk cost fallacy, imagine that you're the final decision-maker in a company that has already invested $900,000 in producing a new battery technology. It will cost your company an additional $100,000 to complete the development of the battery. However, your competitor just announced the release of their brand-new battery, which lasts longer than the one you're developing, and it's cheaper. What do you do? Do you spend the additional $100,000 to finish the project or do you save that $100,000 for something else?

Dr. Hal Arkes is a professor of psychology at The Ohio State University. He and fellow researcher, Catherine Blumer, posed this scenario in a research study. They found that 85 percent of people chose to spend the additional $100,000 to finish developing an inferior and more expensive product![213] A rational decision maker should choose to withhold the additional $100,000 and use it to fund a different project, or at least take the current project in a different direction.

This isn't just academic theory; some of the most iconic businesses you can name have fallen for the sunk cost trap. Take Polaroid, for example. Years after going bankrupt, Polaroid remains a memorable brand, known for pioneering instant photography. Yet few remember Polavision, Polaroid's huge misstep into the video recorder business in the late 1970s. It's estimated that they spent nearly $500 million developing their video recording technology, but when launched, it was overwhelmingly rejected by consumers. It was a hard pill to swallow, but instead of facing reality and cutting their losses, they wasted millions more in failed marketing campaigns. Polavision was eventually discontinued after a $68 million write-off.[277]

So many entrepreneurs, especially those who bootstrapped their businesses using their personal savings, are prone to believe they can control an outcome, despite all evidence to the contrary. This is known as the *illusion of control*. Even though the battery being developed by our hypothetical company costs more and is inferior to a competitor's product, a lot of entrepreneurs will continue to believe that customers will choose to spend money with them. They're aware of the facts working against them, but they disregard the facts because they're not making logical decisions.

An *illusion of control* is an entrepreneur's tendency to overestimate their ability to control the outcome of an event that, in reality, they have very little influence over.

Going back to our battery company example, the development of a costly battery that doesn't measure up against the competition is a swing and a miss, but it doesn't mean that we've failed on a personal level because we invested in the research and development (R&D).

Dell Computers' investment in R&D nets a $6 return for every $1 invested, but even a company as efficient as Dell has missteps.[204] Back when they were developing their early line of laptops, they had invested in several different options simultaneously. As they continued to assess the rapidly-evolving market, they realized that only one of the laptops in development would be competitive. They had a difficult choice – "a no-win situation," as Mr. Dell recalls in his book.[204] "Canceling products in development would be painful and costly," he says, and "by the time we redesigned them and got them out the door, we'd be at the tail end of the product life cycle." So, they had to scrap everything except the one promising laptop. Dell could have easily ignored the market and gone through with developing the inferior products. Instead he made the difficult decision to hit escape and cut his losses. In the long run, this saved his company a lot of money.

Mindfulness

"To dispel the illusion of the ego is to free oneself from a fundamental vulnerability."

- Matthieu Ricard
Author of *Happiness: A Guide to Developing Life's Most Important Skill*

Mindfulness meditation is a scientifically validated technique we can use to check our ego and avoid pitfalls like sunk cost and the illusion of control. As I mentioned earlier in the book, mindfulness meditation is a way to focus awareness on the present moment and stop our minds from wandering into the past or the future. I want to revisit mindfulness here in the chapter on funding because when money is involved, people tend to make mindless decisions.

Taking a moment for mindfulness allows us to make better, less reactive decisions.[214] In a study conducted at the University of Pennsylvania's Wharton School of Business, it was found that as little as 15 minutes of mindfulness meditation each day can significantly reduce our tendency to escalate commitment to a poor decision.[215]

Part of the reason is that when we meditate, we redirect our focus away from ruminating about the past and thinking about things that might have been. Meditation also helps reduce over-speculation about the future. We worry less about how we're going to make up for yesterday's setback, or how we're going to rationalize our actions to others. Meditation rebalances our thoughts and reduces the anxiety of an unsettled mind.

Before making a big decision, try taking a 15-minute break. Sit peacefully with your eyes closed and focus on nothing but your breathing. I've found that having some ambient background music or white noise helps me when I meditate. There are also several great apps like Headspace, Calm and Brain.fm which help guide your meditation practice. I encourage you to give it a try, even if you're skeptical. Remember, an entrepreneur with a growth-mindset is open to learning new things. If you feel you're too busy to make time for mediation, remember it's only 15 minutes per day and it's a scientifically validated method of improving your decision-making. What entrepreneur wouldn't give 15 minutes of their time to have that kind of advantage?

If you still feel a bit hesitant or outright resistant to the idea of mediation, let's switch back to the discussion around ego for a moment. In the book *Happiness: A Guide to Developing Life's Most Important Skill*, author Matthieu Ricard describes the paradox of the ego. I think it's a useful insight: "The idea that a powerful ego is necessary to succeed in life undoubtedly stems from the confusion between attachment to our own image and the resolve to achieve our deepest aspirations. The fact is, the less influenced we are by the sense of our self's importance, the easier it is to acquire lasting inner strength."[216]

Another symptom of an ego-driven entrepreneur is their state of denial about any feedback that goes against what they believe. They will often deny that any alternative possibilities exist.

Another interesting study conducted at Ohio State University found that when executives only consider one course of action, their decisions resulted in a failure more than 50 percent of the time. When decision-makers were given just one additional alternative to consider, the failure rate dropped down to less than 33 percent.[213] When our ego is wrapped up in our venture, we often fail to recognize the other options in front of us.

To counter this challenge, resilient entrepreneurs should be willing to intentionally envision the worst-case scenarios resulting from their business decisions. This exercise, known as a *premortem*, was developed by Dr. Gary Klein, a research psychologist from New York City. A premortem begins with the assumption that a planned course of action has resulted in a negative outcome.[217] As you think about starting or growing your business, ask yourself some of the following questions: What are some of the worst-case scenarios that could result from this business decision? Who might be harmed by the decision? What are some other possible negative consequences? What's the absolute worst that could happen? How might you handle these possible scenarios?

Write down the answers to these questions. Then, ask yourself what might make these negative outcomes more likely. List all the reasons why you might end up with the undesirable result. Are there any patterns or themes emerging from your list? Any glaring pitfalls to avoid? What can you do to minimize the risk of these negative results? What might you change or do differently going forward? If someone else replaced you as CEO of your company, what would he or she do differently?[213]

Sometimes the answer might be that you've done all you can do to limit risk. You won't be able to completely eliminate everything; all business endeavors have an inherent amount of risk. Yet, by identifying and acknowledging the worst possible outcome, you give yourself the opportunity to decide if you can live with its consequences. That way, if the worst possible outcome does happen, you're not as shocked. You can nod your head, accept what you knew was possible, gather yourself, and keep moving forward. This is a great exercise in strategy, planning and becoming resilient.

It's also helpful to identify someone who can help keep you accountable – someone who isn't afraid to tell you when you're about to fall off the prudent decision-making wagon. This person should be someone you trust to give you honest advice. A lot of times a mentor or coach can fill that role. We'll look more at mentorship and coaching later in the book.

Another bootstrapping strategy leverages our social connections. Examples include borrowing tools or sharing office space. Many entrepreneurs will barter their services with other service providers. Need help with marketing? Do you have a good or service that a small marketing business might find valuable? Are there cross-promotional opportunities with another small business that offers complementary goods or services to the same target customer? Why not ask?

Some might feel that there is a bit of stigma around bartering – any cashless transaction can come off as a bit uncouth, but you might be surprised at just how common bartering is. In fact, it's estimated that 11 percent of all transactions in industrialized nations are conducted through barter.[218] Furthermore, a survey conducted by American Express found that about 45 percent of small business owners are open to bartering new goods or services with their customers and suppliers.[219] So although you might be apprehensive, go ahead and ask. You might be surprised at what people will have an open mind about if you present it in the right way.

Strategies that leverage social connections often come without financial cost, but they're not free. When we borrow from others or barter services, we're entering an unwritten social contract. By borrowing or accepting a service, you're expected to return a favor in the future. So, be prepared to accept and deliver the same high-quality product or service that would be expected with a financial transaction.

The final bootstrapping strategy is frugality. An example of frugality would be to negotiate more favorable payment terms with suppliers, allowing you to hold on to as much cash as possible for as long as possible. Larger suppliers might not be willing to negotiate terms with a small business, but efficient *bootstrappers* have learned to test and see what the most acceptable boundaries are with their suppliers.[211] Serial entrepreneur, Sean Murphy, says, "Small firms feel they are not entitled to discounts, but that's not the right attitude. Always ask for discounts."[210] If you are told no, ask what you would need to do to meet the requirements for a discount in the future. If that doesn't work, shop around for a supplier that might be willing to offer discounts to win your business. Be persistent, yet respectful, since you don't want to damage relationships with key partners.

The frugal strategy might also include doing things like leasing or buying used equipment. You might be opposed to used equipment because of maintenance costs, but if you don't have the upfront money, it's an option to consider. I've seen many food businesses get their start by renting commercial kitchen space to manufacture their food products, as opposed to building their own space. I've also seen frugal entrepreneurs buy used furniture and computers for dirt cheap at 'like-new' quality.

Another frugal strategy includes using freelancers as discussed in the section on delegation in the previous chapter. There is a plethora of freelancing platforms available that literally bring you a world of talented people waiting to plus-up your capacity at an affordable price. Sites like 99Designs, Upwork, Freelancer and Fiverr are great ways to outsource tasks for a nominal fee.

Although bootstrapping creates options where few existed before, one of the major potential drawbacks is the constraint it creates on business growth. Companies that bootstrap typically grow at a much slower rate than those who received outside financing. This isn't necessarily a bad thing, as not every company needs to have fast growth. It's perfectly fine to create a lifestyle business for yourself and your family. If you have visions of scaling your business quickly, you should look to outside financing to help fund growth. Next, we'll look at how crowdfunding has become one of those options.

Figure 5: Common Bootstrapping Strategies

Crowdfunding

"Crowdfunding can help take the democratization of innovation, entrepreneurship and finance even further. By giving a voice to people who would otherwise never even have a chance to seek funding, let along provide it, crowdfunding creates opportunities for new businesses and innovations, as well as a new wave of investors."

- Dr. Alicia Robb
Founder and CEO of Next Wave;
Dr. Ethan Mollick
Associate Professor of Management, Wharton School of Business

---

Crowdfunding democratizes startup and growth financing for small businesses. Its openness and transparency make it inviting for any entrepreneur, especially business owners who are less likely to be networked with traditional financiers, like women and minorities.[220] Women-owned businesses, for example, represent only 2.7 percent of all venture capital-backed investments. Minority-owned businesses represent even fewer.[221] The lending world doesn't fare much better for these entrepreneurs. Female-led businesses represent only $1 out of every $23 lent to small businesses (about 4.5 percent).[222]

Part of the reason stems from the legacy effects of primarily white males dominating the organizations representing these financial industries. Calls for more female and minority representation in these organizations can help, but it's not the only obstacle to improved equality. Inherent to these financial mechanisms are due diligence obstacles that oftentimes disproportionately exclude women and minority-owned businesses (collateral, equity injection, credit scores, strong entrepreneurial and financial networks, etc.). Efforts to ease and adapt the due diligence processes to make it more flexible can help, but it's not enough. It's difficult to change these entrenched, bureaucratic financial vehicles, and it will take intentional effort before we see meaningful improvement.

Crowdfunding, on the other hand, has fewer institutional prerequisite qualifications. Do you have poor credit or no credit? Most types of crowdfunding don't check your credit and even for those that do, poor credit or no credit isn't necessarily a deal breaker.

Anyone willing to learn the best practices for crowdfunding and put in the effort can raise funds successfully. Crowdfunding also helps coordinate fundraising from friends and family. Some entrepreneurs are lucky enough to be able to finance their business with help from the proverbial 'rich uncle'. Most entrepreneurs are not that fortunate. Yet, there is still a surprising amount of investable capital dispersed among our familial and social networks. Crowdfunding enables anyone to pool that capital through an organized and transparent process.[223]

The results of decreasing traditional barriers to capital are significant; female-led crowdfunding campaigns are 13 percent more likely to reach their fundraising goal compared to men.[221] In looking at data from 106 companies who raised funds on Circle-Up, a popular crowdfund-investing platform for accredited investors, 34 percent of all money raised went to female-owned businesses.[224]

Another equity-based platform, Republic.co, showed even better results with 44 percent of all investments going to companies with a female founder. The impact on African

American and Hispanic-owned businesses is also promising. Republic reported that 25 percent of all investments went to founders of color.[225] That's significantly better when compared to lending or venture capital.

Also, because all crowdfunding happens online, it also democratizes the geography of entrepreneurial finance, opening the gateway to funding small businesses in rural areas and cities that aren't known for their robust ecosystems (e.g. Silicon Valley, Boston, Austin, New York, etc.). Crowdfunding also holds promise for non-traditional industries (e.g. not just high tech) in favor of other creative industries like the arts.[221]

My first introduction to crowdfunding happened unexpectedly. When Lizz walked into my office in the fall of 2012 with her business plan in hand, I could tell she was a bit apprehensive about our meeting. She hadn't shared her idea with anyone outside her circle of close friends and family, but she was ready to take that difficult step of moving an idea from concept to prototype.

When she handed me her business plan, I read the title on the cover page: "Gypsy Heart Wandering Photo Booths". I thumbed through the plan until I came across a blueprint drawing of what appeared to be a photo booth attached to the back of a bicycle. I looked over the detailed drawings as she explained her business model. "Gypsy Heart Wandering Photo Booths is a fun mobile photo booth that can be easily transported around Austin's downtown hotspots and year-round festivals," she said. Lizz was already a full-time self-employed photographer, and this was an opportunity to expand and differentiate her business.

Lizz looked up at me, half expecting me to scoff at the quirky idea. I hadn't seen anything like it before, but growing up in Austin, I understood how this *weird* local business could work and make money. "So," I asked, "How much is it going to cost to build a first iteration of this *Wandering Photo Booth*?"
"About $6,000," she said.

For various reasons, Lizz wasn't an ideal candidate for a loan, and as I began to list off the barriers she would likely have to overcome to qualify for one, she politely interrupted me, "I'm actually interested in crowdfunding. Can you help me with that?" In 2012, crowdfunding was just starting to build buzz. I was familiar with the concept but didn't know anything about the mechanics. I told Lizz I'd be happy to help in any way I could, but that we'd be learning together about how to launch and manage a successful crowdfunding campaign.

We started by piecing together a rough campaign plan. After a couple of weeks, she launched on Indiegogo, the second-largest perks and rewards-based crowdfunding platform. In just over 30 days, Lizz was able to raise the $6,400 she needed to build her first *Wandering Photo Booth*. Crowdfunding allowed Lizz to take a novel idea and test its validity with early adopters and loyal supporters. The campaign also helped create enough buzz for her to sustain much-needed momentum throughout her first several months of operating.

Lizz's successful crowdfunding campaign inspired me to learn as much as I could about this emerging financial frontier. It offered an opportunity for entrepreneurs to access seed and expansion funding when they might otherwise be denied and rejected by traditional financial institutions.

Gypsy Heart Photo Booths ended up being a difficult business model to scale. Businesses that successfully crowdfund still have a long startup journey in front of them; not all will make it. Yet, without crowdfunding, Lizz might not have otherwise had the funds and encouragement to try something new in the first place. For that reason, crowdfunding can become part of the resilient entrepreneur's toolkit.

I've worked with dozens of entrepreneurs since then, consulting them on the best practices to fundraise successfully through crowdfunding. I'm also an active investor and try to contribute to a crowdfunding campaign every month. In this section, I want to show you how you can use crowdfunding to fund your startup or expansion needs.

There are two types of crowdfunding that we will cover in this chapter: perks and rewards-based crowdfunding (also known as the Kickstarter model or traditional crowdfunding) and crowdfund investing.

Perks and Rewards-based Crowdfunding

These are exciting times for small businesses looking to raise capital for their new venture or growing startup. There are massive amounts of money being contributed through perks and rewards-based crowdfunding – more than nine billion dollars worldwide in 2018. That figure is estimated to grow exponentially to more than $25 billion by 2022.[226]

Perks and rewards-based crowdfunding is the offering of a product, service, or other item of value in exchange for a financial contribution. Entrepreneurs, idealists and innovators alike use crowdfunding to find early adopters and supporters of new products, services and charitable causes. This is made possible at such scale because of social media and online crowdfunding platforms.

Kickstarter and Indiegogo are by far the leading online platforms in perks and rewards-based funding, both in terms of the number of projects they host and the amount of funding those projects raise.[227] Kickstarter is best known for spring-boarding innovative projects around consumer technology, music, film, gaming, art, food and fashion. Indiegogo's flexible platform hosts projects related to almost any industry or social cause that you can imagine.

Indiegogo and Kickstarter were both founded during the Great Recession – in 2008 and 2009 respectively. These platforms, known today for helping hundreds of thousands of entrepreneurs raise capital, had their own difficult fundraising journey. Indiegogo's co-founders bootstrapped the business for three years. During that time, they sought venture capital and received nearly 90 rejections before finally securing seed funding in 2011.[228] It's a good thing they were persistent because Indiegogo and Kickstarter represent one of the most promising financing opportunities for early-stage entrepreneurs struggling to raise capital just like they were.

Although crowdfunding represents an attractive alternative to traditional financing, planning and managing a successful campaign takes a lot of work. You can't just post your project online and watch as the funds magically roll in. That's a common misconception that has contributed to almost two-thirds of all crowdfunding projects failing to meet their fundraising goal.[226] This doesn't have to be your crowdfunding experience though, because resilient entrepreneurs refuse to become a statistic of failure!

On average, you should expect to spend about 15 hours per week for 4 to 6 weeks preparing for a successful campaign. Once you've launched, expect 16 to 24 hours each week managing a 5 to 8-week campaign. Then, after the campaign ends, expect 15 to 20 hours each week for several weeks fulfilling rewards and engaging your backer community.[236] In total, you might expect to invest anywhere between 170 and 330 hours over a 2 ½ to 4-month period. It's like taking on a part-time job on top of whatever else you have going on.

It's a lot of work, but if you invest the time required to learn the best practices and avoid common pitfalls, you'll have a much better shot at reaching your fundraising goal. This is especially true if you set a realistic goal. You might have heard about one of the few hundred crowdfunding projects that raised millions of dollars, but they only received publicity because they're outliers. You shouldn't expect to raise anywhere close to those numbers on these platforms. In fact, 68 percent of all successful Kickstarter campaigns raise less than $10,000.

Another way to think about how to set your fundraising goal is to think about the price of the primary products or services you're going to offer, and how many backers you need to justify going through with the project. If, for example, your average perk/reward will cost the crowd $35 and you'd like to engage at least 100 backers, then you might consider a goal of at least $3,500 ($35 * 100).

When I wanted to author a children's book, I wasn't sure if my concept would be well-received by a large-enough audience to make the endeavor worthwhile. I wanted to see if there was a larger market outside of just my friends and family. So, I launched a crowdfunding campaign on Kickstarter and received support from 78 backers in 7 different countries. That's not a ton, but it was a big enough group of early adopters to validate my concept and give me the confidence to move forward. How big does your crowd of early adopters need to be to give you enough encouragement to keep going? How much do you need to get the economies of scale to deliver at your promoted price?

As you plan for how much you'll seek to raise from the crowd, also keep in mind that you'll want to account for the admin and credit card fees that crowdfunding platforms charge if you reach your goal. Typically, these account for 5 to 8 percent of your total. It's normal to factor those costs into the amount you ask for. Also, don't forget that the funds you raise should be reported as taxable income.

The Coolest Lesson in Crowdfunding

I want to share an interesting case study from Kickstarter - not because of the eye-popping amount of money raised, but because of the resilience of the entrepreneur behind the project. There are important lessons we can learn from some of his mistakes, as well as the way he responded.

Ryan Grepper is the inventor of the Coolest Cooler, a portable ice chest with built-in luxuries like a beverage blender, waterproof speakers, and a USB charger. Ryan's successful crowdfunding campaign launched in the summer of 2014 and raised more than $13 million from 62,642 backers on Kickstarter.[229] Although those impressive figures make it the second-highest funded Kickstarter campaign of all time, Ryan's journey to a record-setting raise started out as a belly-flop.[230]

About eight months prior to launching this famed Kickstarter campaign, Ryan launched a lesser-known campaign for a similar, slightly less-developed version of the cooler. In that campaign, he was able to raise over $100,000 in 30 days, but failed to reach his minimum fundraising goal of $125,000. As a project creator on Kickstarter, you have the liberty to set almost any fundraising goal you want, but if you don't reach the goal you've set, you don't get to keep any of the pledged funds. This all-or-nothing model means campaigns must reach their fundraising goal by the deadline or all pledged contributions are returned to the backers. After his 30-day campaign, Ryan was forced to watch as $100,000 and 279 potential customers slipped through his grasp.

Some entrepreneurs might have given up after such a devastating shortfall, and Ryan admits that his "confidence was pretty low" after the first campaign failed.[231] Still, he chose to focus on the positive takeaways and words of encouragement from early supporters. In an interview with Entrepreneur Magazine, Ryan said that "the biggest lesson from that first campaign was recognizing that failure isn't permanent...it is an opportunity to either give up and move on to the next project, if that's what the data and what the feedback shows, or it is a chance to recognize and learn from those mistakes, dive deeper into best practices and launch again."[232]

Lucky for you, Ryan and thousands of others have made enough well-documented crowdfunding mistakes that we now have a robust compilation of common pitfalls to avoid and best practices to adopt. The table below shows some of the key differences between Coolest Cooler's two campaigns and the best practices I've found through research and experience:

	Coolest Cooler Failed Campaign	Coolest Cooler Successful campaign	Crowdfunding Best practice
Fundraising goal	$125,000	$50,000	Around $20,000 or less
Funds pledged	$102,188	$13,285,226	-
Launch date	November	July	Late March – early September
Campaign length	30 days	52 days	50 – 60 days
Video length	3 min 36 seconds	3 min 21 seconds	Less than 3 minutes
Backer update frequency	Every 6 days	Every 4-5 days	Every 5-7 days
# of words in description	3,000+	2,100	750 – 1,700
# of rewards offered	11	11	3 – 8
Promised delivery timeframe for rewards	About 8 months	About 6 months	About 2-3 times longer than your most optimistic estimate

I'd love to tell you that Ryan's crowdfunding journey had a multi-million-dollar happy ending, but unfortunately his biggest challenges came after his big payday. While Ryan couldn't have predicted such a wildly successful fundraising campaign, he also didn't accurately estimate the costs and lead time for manufacturing the cooler. He optimistically promised to deliver the coolers to backers in about six months, but cost overruns and an employee strike at the cooler's manufacturing facility left him strapped for cash and broke on promises.

By the way, unanticipated manufacturing delays are one of the most common reasons that crowdfunding campaigns fail to deliver their rewards on time.[236] A manufacturing strike might be an anomaly, but if you're manufacturing in China, accounting for delays caused by their holidays is something you can plan for from the beginning. Make sure you're doing your homework. If you're not sure where to start, talk to an experienced mentor. (More on mentoring later in the book). If you have a technology product, Indiegogo partners with a company called Arrow (https://www.arrow.com/en/indiegogo/program-overview) who specializes in helping crowdfunding projects develop their prototype and move it into full-scale production.[233]

Three years after Ryan's fundraising campaign ended, thousands of backers were still waiting to receive their coolers. Complaints from the disgruntled mob made their way to the Oregon Department of Justice who began investing the case in late 2016.[234] By the summer of 2017, Ryan settled with the Oregon DOJ, agreeing to ship coolers to all campaign backers by 2020.[235]

Ryan, like many new entrepreneurs raising funds from the crowd, made a common mistake – he overpromised and under-delivered. When you launch your campaign, make sure you get multiple quotes for manufacturing costs and lead time. Then, take the most pessimistic estimate of both and double them. In my experience, the crowd is very understanding about higher prices and prolonged delivery times if you set those expectations during a campaign. They know you're doing something new and that it takes time to build a business from the ground up.

On the other hand, if you start missing your delivery deadlines and running out of money because you underestimated your costs, you'll be stuck answering lots of angry calls and emails. Set realistic expectations up front and be as conservative as possible in your manufacturing cost and delivery date estimates. Whatever your most conservative delivery estimate is, add additional time on top of that. Your ability to succeed in crowdfunding and entrepreneurship will depend on you and your team's perceived reliability, credibility and overall believability that you can execute on the promises you've made. It all boils down to establishing trust.

Ryan's story is still playing out, but from what I can tell, he's not the type of entrepreneur to quit. He's made some major mistakes along his entrepreneurial journey, and from them, learned some very hard lessons. After his case settled with Oregon's DOJ, he sent an update to his Kickstarter backers, sharing an open confession: "I've had a long, hard road with lots of challenges and a steep learning curve, but the easiest thing would have been to quit long ago and just move on. I've gone into debt to keep this thing going and am doing my best to make good on my commitments. I still can't promise a time frame, but I can tell you we are doing the hard work every day and persisting because it's the right thing to do."[235] Spoken like a truly resilient entrepreneur, Ryan!

As you might imagine, Ryan's crowdfunding campaign garnered a lot of media attention. Most of it, unfortunately, went from good to bad to ugly as his company's manufacturing and fulfillment woes dragged on, but even smaller, less controversial campaigns can benefit from the positive buzz that crowdfunding helps create.

This was true for a client and friend of mine, Nathan Jones, co-founder of the *Freeloader* child carrier – a lightweight backpack designed to carry children over the age of 2 ½. Nathan and his co-founder, Erik, are both dads, and when their young children tired after a couple of hours hiking or sightseeing, they were forced to play the role of porter, carrying them on their hips or shoulders the rest of the afternoon. The *Freeloader* child carrier is designed to make carrying your growing kiddo a lot easier. Nathan and Erik successfully raised over $31,000 on Indiegogo when 265 people from around the world agreed that they needed the product for their kids too.

The founders' story, innovative product design and success of the crowdfunding campaign all helped to get the attention of various media outlets. They also spent a little bit of money on promoting the campaign. That publicity helped land Nathan and Erik on ABC's hit reality TV show, Shark Tank, where they received even more exposure from new customers and potential investors. There are certainly no guarantees that you'll experience Hollywood-level publicity, but nearly half of all successful crowdfunding projects reported that they received press attention because of their campaign.[236] The point is that crowdfunding offers a lot of potential benefits beyond the number of dollars raised.

If you have some funds to invest in the success of your campaign, you might consider paid advertisements, press releases and promotional events. Many successful crowdfunding projects utilized one or more of these marketing tactics.[236]

If you're interested in raising money through perks and rewards-based crowdfunding, I highly recommend your first step be conducting research on Kickstarter or Indiegogo. Go explore these platforms and look for successfully funded projects that are like yours. What did they do well? What might they have done better? Don't just make a carbon copy of their campaign; Adopt the successful strategies that might work for your project.

Before you launch your own campaign, talk to someone who has done it before. Check out some of the useful guides, blogs and tips online. You might notice that many of them suggest recruiting crowdfunding collaborators early on. Planning and managing a successful crowdfunding campaign is a lot of work, so see if a friend or family member might be willing to help out with some of the most important tasks like creating a video, proofreading the campaign description, being an early backer or promoting it through their networks.

It's also important to include friends and family in your crowdfunding campaign as early as possible because they're often the people who will account for most of your project's funding.[236]

Crowdfund Investing

While Ryan's $13 million crowdfunding raise is extraordinary, it's an outlier in terms of the typical amount you should expect to raise in a perks and rewards-based crowdfunding campaign. Remember, about 90 percent of all successful rewards-based crowdfunding campaigns raise less than $10,000. If you need a bit more than that for your next fundraise, you might consider investment crowdfunding.

Through this fundraising mechanism, you can legally raise up to $1,070,000 from non-accredited investors in exchange for equity, revenue share or a term loan.[237] (As I write this, efforts are in place to amend legislation that will raise that ceiling to $20 million).[238] An equity transaction involves giving up a percentage of your company's ownership; revenue sharing means you pay back investors a percentage of every earned sales dollar. A term loan is an agreement to repay investors their principal with a fixed percentage of interest over a set period.

Non-accredited individuals (people who make less than $200,000 in annual income or have a total net worth under $1 million) can invest anywhere between $2,000 and $10,000 (depending on their income) in a small business like yours! These individual investors contribute relatively small amounts, pooling together enough funds to help you reach your fundraising goal. This is exciting because up until 2012, it hadn't been legal to publicly solicit investment from friends, family or other potential investors due to the passage of the Securities and Exchange Act in 1934. Under the old law, investment was regulated for all, except for the 7 percent or so of the households nationwide that qualified as accredited investors.[239] Under the new regulations, an entirely new and very large category of investors can now get involved, making crowdfund investing the most democratic form of financing available.

I've been an active investor in many small businesses through crowdfund investing. One of the first companies I invested in was Smiley Transportation (https://www.smileytransportation.com/home.html), located just north of Fort Worth, in Keller, Texas. Smiley provides transportation for students participating in after-school activities, summer school and camps. They launched their fundraising campaign on NextSeed (https://nextseed.link/lm_apply) and raised close to $100,000 from 37 people including myself. In exchange, Smiley agreed to repay our principal investment, plus 10 percent interest over a four-year period. Smiley basically had a $100,000 loan from 37 lenders.

Rushelle Wetzel established Smiley Transportation in 2007. When she launched her campaign in the summer of 2016, she had nine passenger vans, but increasing demand was putting a strain on the business. The funds they received from her loan helped them hire new drivers and support staff. Two years after they launched their campaign, their fleet has increased to 16 shuttles and they're still hiring! I love checking in with them from time to time to see how they're growing to provide value to their community.

Small businesses like Rushell's are the backbone of the U.S economy, and crowdfund investing is emerging as a powerful financial mechanism to elevate small businesses and job creation across the nation. In fact, businesses that crowdfund successfully create an average of 3 new jobs – in many cases doubling the size of their workforce.[240]

While the potential for so many people to be interested in supporting small business is groundbreaking, it can also be a challenge to manage so many different stakeholders. Crowd investors' individual levels of sophistication and motivations can vary greatly. Thus, we should be prepared for all types of questions. Even if the answers seem obvious, we need to be courteous and responsive to the crowd. All questions and answers are publicly visible on the crowdfunding platform, and if we're short or rude, other potential investors will notice. Besides being potential investors, the crowd is likely to become a loyal customer and brand evangelist. So, make sure that as they invest in you, you invest in building a long-term relationship with them.

Of the more than 1,700 U.S-based companies that have attempted to raise investment from the crowd, (since the JOBS Act went into effect in May of 2016) about seventy percent have been in business for less than three years. Thus far, the funding success rate is over 50 percent.[241] This makes crowdfund investing ideal for early-stage businesses. Before I get you too excited about the possibilities, let's explore some of the important considerations for entrepreneurs looking for crowd investors.

First, because of the nature of crowdfund investing, there is more regulation and oversight compared to rewards-based crowdfunding. As a business offering up equity or taking on debt from the crowd, you will need to disclose your company's financial statements, both historical (applicable for companies already generating revenue) and future projections. If you're looking to raise over $500,000, you will need to have an independent audit of your financials by a Certified Public Accountant.[242]

You'll also be required to provide background information on all current owners who have a 20 percent or larger stake in the company.[239] In addition, you'll need to share your basic business strategy and marketing plan with potential investors. Basically, you should be prepared to open your books, and be as transparent as possible about your business. There are regulatory forms and requirements, and whichever crowdfund investment portal you utilize can guide you through that process.

Crowdfund investment platforms like WeFunder, NextSeed, StartEngine, Microventures, SeedInvest and Republic.co act as intermediaries between the crowd and your business. They ensure that you are complying with all regulations while walking you step-by-step through the necessary paperwork and prelaunch tasks. Legally, you must raise funds through a regulated crowdfunding platform like those noted above – you cannot just start soliciting investments on your own website or social media. You probably wouldn't want to anyway because one of the biggest benefits of these platforms is the curated base of potential investors in their networks. When you list your business on one of these platforms, they typically send out a newsletter announcing your investment opportunity to a large pool of interested investors. In essence, these platforms are introducing you to potential investors in your business.

WeFunder, one of the largest of the largest investment crowdfunding portals, boasts over 155,000 registered investors![243] Because of this massive investor base, they've helped more businesses raise larger amounts of capital compared to any other crowdfund investment platform. For access to their investor networks and the other services these portals provide, you can expect commissions and other fees to range anywhere between 7 and 10 percent, on average.

Like rewards-based crowdfunding, setting a realistic fundraising goal in crowdfund investing is a major factor for success. 70 percent of businesses that seek to raise less than $100,000 reach their goal. It's significantly more difficult to fundraise over larger amounts - only about 33 percent of businesses that look to raise over $500,000 reach their goal.[246] The average successful crowdfund investment campaign is between $165,000 and $245,000.[244] Keep that in mind as you evaluate how much investment you truly need to reach the next milestone for your business.

I worked with Franny (not her real name), co-founder of a healthy foods business, to prepare for a campaign on WeFunder. Her business had done well the past two years and an investment from the crowd would help her finance growth. She needed at least $250,000 to hire a sales executive and launch a new product line. She also wanted to hire a CFO and finance a marketing campaign, which we estimated would require another $250,000. She wondered if she should set her goal at $250,000 or try and finance the grander vision ranging from $500,000 to $750,000.

Luckily, WeFunder and most other platforms allow you to set multiple fundraising goals – floors, stretch goals and ceilings to define the minimum, ideal and maximum amounts of funding. Franny set a minimum fundraising goal at $250,000 and a stretch goal of $750,000. In exchange, she offered 5 to 15 percent equity in her company.

Valuing a startup can be challenging. It's often more art than science because so many factors are subjective. Founders tend to overvalue assets and are overly optimistic about future cash flows. Angels and VCs are typically in a strong negotiating position and will challenge founders on their valuation, oftentimes demanding larger equity positions than what founders are prepared to offer.[245]

Equity crowdfunding helps new companies get a better sense of their valuation using the wisdom of the crowd. If the crowd isn't responding to your investment opportunity, it might be because they perceive your company to be overvalued. Try adjusting the valuation and see what happens. This worked for a UK-based company whose fundraising stalled out about 5 weeks into a 6-week campaign. They decided to reduce their valuation. Once they did, it was enough to attract a few larger investors that put them over their goal within a week.[245]

Unlike perk and reward-based crowdfunding, crowdfund investors are not just interested in your story, product or service; They're also incentivized by the promise of a financial return on their investment.[246] Thus, businesses that have proven themselves beyond an idea or prototype, meaning they have demonstrated market validation through revenue, are more likely to receive investment from the crowd.

In fact, businesses that have some market traction are about 65 percent likely to reach their minimum fundraising target through crowdfund investing.[246] While you might not think that's impressive, it's significantly better than the nearly 66 percent failure rate seen in reward-based crowdfunding. If you are still in the idea or product development phase, you might consider bootstrapping or perks and reward-based crowdfunding before taking on investors or lenders from the crowd.

When you are ready for crowdfund investment, make sure you present a clear exit strategy. How will investors get their money back? Are you planning on raising additional rounds of funding from angel investors or venture capitalists? Do you plan to eventually take your company public? Are you hoping to get bought out by a larger company in your industry? Do you plan on paying out dividends? As an investor, I'm appalled by how few businesses address these questions. I want to know that you've put thought into how you will pay me back with a return on my investment, not just on how you plan to use my money.

For these reasons, I typically invest in more revenue sharing and term-loan deals compared to equity opportunities. With this type of financing, I know how I get a return. Revenue sharing has become increasingly popular for food, alcohol and hospitality-related industries. They will typically offer a 1.2x to 2x return. This means, if I invest $100 in a 2x revenue share deal, I can expect to receive my initial $100 back, plus an additional $100, doubling my money. The average return offered through revenue sharing is around 1.5x and investors are getting repaid, on average, over a period of 46 months.[247]

This is an expensive cost of capital, but investors in your revenue sharing business are more likely to become loyal customers and vocal advocates for your products and services. Because they're receiving a small percentage of gross revenue, they're heavily invested in helping you make more sales.

Revenue sharing has benefits over term loans for companies that have cash flow seasonality.[247] For example, an ice cream store is going to be much busier in the summer months. If they chose debt financing using a term loan, they'd be subject to a fixed debt repayment every month. A two thousand dollar per month debt service might be no big deal between May and September, but come February, that expense will put a huge strain on cash flow. For this reason, this ice cream business might be better off with a revenue share, repaying investors only when they make sales.

Before you decide which crowdfund investment strategy is best for you, speak with a Certified Public Accountant, financial adviser or financially-minded coach or mentor. There are some upfront costs associated with crowdfund investing. Bill Clark, the CEO of MicroVentures, offers a rough estimate of those costs. I've shared those estimates in the table below:

Service	**Estimate costs**
Legal	≈ $2,500
Accounting	≈ $2,000 - $5,000 (depending on the size of the business)
Video Production	≈ $1,500 - $3,000
Marketing/Promotion	≈ $5,000- $10,000 ($5k is a good start, but $10K is ideal)
Total	≈ $11,000 - $20,500

Some might balk at these expenses. However, according to Sherwood Neiss, of Crowdfund Capital Advisers, "there is a direct correlation between how much time and money is spent and how much money is raised."[248]

I've chosen to highlight bootstrapping and the various methods of crowdfunding because I think they're the most accessible forms of capital for new businesses, especially compared to institutional lending, angel networks and venture capital. Financing your business by bootstrapping and crowdfunding isn't easy, but with enough planning, hard work and grit, you can successfully fund your startup. When you bootstrap and/or crowdfund your business, you will grow to become a much more resilient entrepreneur.

Pitch

"Ideas are only as good as the actions that follow the communication of those ideas"

-Carmine Gallo
President of Gallo Communications Group and Bestselling Author

---

An effective pitch for an entrepreneurial concept or business model is an important aspect of new business creation, fundraising and growth. Yet, for many new entrepreneurs, especially those with little experience in sales, marketing or public speaking, pitching your business can seem daunting. For some, it can be outright terrifying.

The *elevator pitch* is a reference to a common pitch format for entrepreneurs. It is a short pitch, normally less than two minutes in length. The time limit of an elevator pitch restricts a complete assessment of the business concept while requiring a well-articulated summary that piques the interest of the audience and entices them into a longer discussion.[249]

In his book *Rise and Grind*, Daymond John advises entrepreneurs to write out a scripted pitch to practice. He recognizes that a rigid script often won't work in real-time presentations and negotiations, but the deliberate practice of writing and reciting a pitch script will increase your confidence when you're ready to pitch it for real.[250]

A study conducted by the University of Idaho's College of Business showed that the more a business student practiced their elevator pitch in an informal setting, the more confident they became. The more confident they became in their pitch, the better their overall delivery and persuasiveness.[251]

Instead of a traditional elevator pitch format, these professors created a more relaxed reception-style networking event, akin to what a conference attendee might experience at an evening mixer. Community members, composed of experienced investors and entrepreneurs, were invited to serve as judges. As the entrepreneurship students made it around the room, they were given the opportunity to practice their pitch multiple times with different judges. Compared to a traditional pitch presentation where students pitch on a stage to an intimidating audience, the more relaxed networking-style format is a less daunting, one-on-one conversation. Write out your script and think about a trusted advisor you can practice your pitch with.

When launching any type of crowdfunding campaign, it's crucial that you have a persuasive pitch in both written and video formats. Businesses crowdfunding without a video pitch were 67 percent less likely to reach their fundraising goal compared to campaigns that do.[252] A video is so important that the majority of the crowd has already made a decision to invest or not just by watching your video.

Crowdfund Capital Advisers (CCA) conducted an analysis of more than 200 crowdfunding campaigns and found ten key components common across effective crowdfunding video pitches:[252] These best practices can be used in a video, as well as the written part of the campaign. Use these tips to help you craft a persuasive message.

1. **High audience engagement** – keep it short and interesting.

Research has shown that since the year 2000, people's attention spans have shrunk, on average, about 33 percent - from 12 seconds to eight seconds![253] No one expects you to give your pitch faster than a bull ride at the rodeo, but you need to be concise. A two-minute video is ideal. If you need a bit longer that's okay, but if your video is longer than three minutes, you risk losing the crowd's attention.

2. A compelling demonstration of the product or service

Even if all you have is a sketch or prototype, include it in the video. It's important to make your product/service as tangible as possible. It's also important to highlight anything novel or exclusive about your product or service. If you present something unique, it's more likely to be remembered.

Each year the City of Austin hosts the [Re]verse Pitch Competition. It's a unique event that helps address a local environmental challenge and zero-waste goal. There are two

---

"If you can't explain your big idea in 140 characters or less, keep working on your message. The discipline brings clarity to your presentation and helps your audience recall the one big idea you're trying to teach them."

- Carmine Gallo
President of Gallo Communications Group and Bestselling Author

---

pitches involved in the competition. The first pitch comes from local organizations whose operations create some form of waste byproduct.

For example, the local food bank receives tons of donated food items, including a lot of damaged and expired canned goods that cannot be served. Due to limited resources, the food bank doesn't have the time to open, rinse and recycle the cans and then compost the food waste. The unfortunate result is that the cans end up in the landfill. The food bank asked social entrepreneurs in the community to take those damaged and expired canned goods and turn them into an input for a sustainable business model.

About 8 to 12 weeks after the first round of pitches, the second round begins. That's when the social entrepreneurs pitch their ideas about how to turn that waste into a new business model and income stream. The best pitches receive innovation prizes to seed fund their ideas.

One of the best pitches I've ever heard in this competition was by Robert Olivier, the founder of GrubTubs. His idea was to collect the food waste from the Austin Food Bank and other local food service businesses, feed it to grub worms who eat the waste faster than a typical compost process, and then sell those grub worms to local chicken farmers at cheaper prices than the standard, less-nutritious chicken feed. It's a terrific example of a *circular economy* at work.

The thing that makes GrubTubs unique is their hermetically-sealed six-gallon buckets that keep the food waste from smelling. When the buckets get full, GrubTubs comes to collect them. When Robert pitched this concept to the judges during the competition, he brought a "grub tub" filled with food waste and grub worms to demonstrate how the tub worked. When he opened the lid to show the judges the worms chowing down, he gave them all a remarkable experience. The audience burst out in laughter watching the squeamish looks on the judges' faces.

Most people at the competition will have forgotten the other pitches, but no one, especially those judges, will ever forget Robert's product demonstration. Robert won the [Re]verse Pitch Competition, and about a year later went on to win a WeWork Creator Award worth about $360,000 using a similar pitch strategy.

Figure 6: Robert Olivier, founder and CEO of GrubTubs pitches at the City of Austin's annual [Re]verse Pitch Competition. Learn more about GrubTubs at www.grubtubs.com

3. Emotional pull

"People will forget what you said, people will forget what you did, but people will never forget how you made them feel."

- Maya Angelou

Through my consulting on crowdfunding campaigns, I've seen many campaigns focus too much on the technical features of their product or service and not enough on storytelling. Instead of touting all the features of your product, demonstrate its benefits and show how it helps solve a challenge in someone's life.

One of the best ways to connect with the crowd is by sharing part of your own story – your *story of self*. Why are you pursuing this business? What led you to where you are today? What lessons have you learned along the way? The crowd wants to back more than just a cool product; they want to support you in your entrepreneurial journey.

Above all, you need to emanate passion in your pitch. Campaigns that use phrases like "passion, dream, inspired, believe, and impact" in their pitches are more likely to reach their fundraising goal.[254] In a study of 64 angel investors who evaluated over 200 investment opportunities, Pace University Professor of Management, Dr. Melissa Cardon, found a significant relationship between the level of perceived passion in an entrepreneur's pitch and the likelihood that the angels would invest in their companies.[255] When you practice your pitch in front of a friend, coach or mentor, ask them to rate you on passion.

Carmine Gallo is a renowned communications coach. He's worked with high-profile executives like John Sculley, Tony Hsieh and Howard Shultz, just to name a few. In his bestselling book, *Talk Like TED*, he studied some of the most successful keynotes in the history of TED talks – those that received over a million views online. He found that about two-thirds of the best speakers' content appealed to emotions (pathos) through stories. Data, facts and stats (logos) accounted for about a quarter of the content, and the rest helped establish the speaker's credibility (ethos).[256] As you draft an outline for your pitch, check to see if the content follows this recipe for success.

"When we hear a fact, a few isolated areas of our brain light up, translating words and meanings. When we hear a story, however, our brain lights up like Las Vegas, tracing the chains of cause, effect and meaning. Stories are the best invention ever created for delivering mental models that drive behavior."

-Dan Coyle

Author of *The Culture Code*

---

4. Convincing testimonials

When was the last time you started a new show or went to the movies? There are so many choices that it can be hard to decide by just scrolling through all the options. Now, how often have you seen a movie or started a new show on Netflix because a friend recommended it specifically or because it got great reviews on *Rotten Tomatoes*? We're much more likely to try something if a friend or trusted source calls it *certified fresh*, gives it a thumbs up, or ranks it five stars.

When you're just starting out, you might not have a lot of product/service reviews. So, how do you get those? Think about how you can go from zero reviews to one. First ask a friend or family member to review your product or service. Give your product or service away for free in exchange for an honest testimonial or recommendation.

One of the most effective ways to build trust is to establish credibility. Start working now to obtain reviews and testimonials, and then highlight those in your pitch.

5. Genuine and professional speaker

It's best if you are the one behind the camera as the spokesperson for your business. For those who are a bit camera-shy, it might be intimidating, but keep practicing. When viewers see the founder of a business telling their own story, it feels more authentic. You don't have to be perfect. If you stay true to yourself, your sincerity and passion will outshine any perceived flaws.

It's also okay if you don't want to do the entire pitch yourself. In that case, you might hire a voice-over artist to narrate over visuals or product demonstrations, etc. I cannot stress enough how much more effective crowdfunding videos are when the founder at least introduces themselves and the company and/or makes the closing ask or thanks the audience at the end.

Avoid using cookie-cutter animated explainer video formats. These are typically found as templates or cheap offerings on various freelancing platforms. A cartoon spokesperson is probably not going to create an emotional connection with your audience. More likely, it's going to come off as cheesy, and that's going to reflect negatively on your business.

6. High quality video and background music production

Crowdfunding Capital Advisors (CCA) found that the clear majority of successfully funded campaigns had good or excellent-quality production. If you don't have the capability to produce a high-quality video yourself, consider hiring someone who can. It's an investment worth making. Remember, the quality of the video reflects how much you care about quality. If your video is poor quality, why should the crowd expect anything different from your business?

7. Matching of product/service value proposition to a market need

You need to convince the crowd that you have a business model that makes sense. Use the powerful combination of emotion and data to make your case. Justify the reasons why you believe your business will be successful.

8. Clear conveyance of the investment opportunity and market potential

One of the most common mistakes that I see in crowdfunding videos is the use of recycled company promo videos and/or generic product/service explanations. These types of videos were designed for convincing potential customers to buy from the business. They don't include strategic information about the business or any details about the investment opportunity.

Make sure you're tailoring your video pitch for investors. That means explaining how you plan for investors to make a return on their money. What's your exit strategy? If you don't at least have a few ideas, then you haven't given enough thought as to how investors get a return. Also, be honest about both the upsides and risks involved.

When Jeff Bezos approached his parents as early investors in Amazon.com, he told them that there was a 70 percent chance that they would lose their entire investment.[31] He was upfront and realistic with them about the financial risk, and they invested approximately $100,000 anyway. It's mind-boggling to try and imagine the return on investment they received from that prescient decision. Yet, they made their investment decision understanding the high risk involved – Bezos didn't try to oversell them or exaggerate his chances of succeeding. It's important to be honest and transparent with potential funders.

9. Founding team introductions and confidence in their ability to execute on the proposed business strategy

Who's behind the business? Crowdfunding is inherently transparent. Introduce yourself and share your background. Also introduce the key people on your team who will make this business a success.

The crowd wants to feel confident that your business can successfully execute the strategy you've outlined. So, when you pitch, make sure you show confidence in yourself and your team members.

Back in Chapter 1, we explored the importance of balancing between confidence and overconfidence. It's important to reiterate that advice again in this chapter as we think about our confidence in pitching to potential investors. Lori Greiner, in her bestselling book, *Invent it, Sell it, Bank It*, advises against entrepreneurs letting their "confidence slide into arrogance or rudeness." It might sound like common sense, but Greiner has seen many entrepreneurs "lose lucrative deals because they were so smug, were inflexible, or carried themselves with such a sense of entitlement that no one wanted to do business with them."[257] Be confident, but humble. Be knowledgeable and personable. Find the right balance in your tone when responding to questions from the crowd.

10. Explanation of why you need the funding and how you plan to utilize the funds raised.

Again, crowdfunding is a transparent process, so you must be willing to share your strategy. Be specific about how you plan to use the money raised. Don't just ask for $100,000 for marketing. Explain how you plan to use that $100,000. What's your marketing strategy? How will you acquire customers and work them through your sales funnel? The better you can convey this information, the more confident the crowd will be that you've thought things through and will be a good steward of their money.

Elevator Pitch Scorecard

As you practice and refine your pitch, use the questions and scorecard below to check how you're doing. Practice your pitch in front of a friend or mentor and have them grade you on the questions below and give you feedback about how you might improve. Below is an elevator pitch scorecard,[249] evaluated on a five-point Likert scale:

1. I would pursue a follow-up meeting to learn more about this business opportunity.

Strongly agree	Agree	Neutral	Disagree	Strongly disagree

2. I would be interested in seeing the business plan for this opportunity.

Strongly agree	Agree	Neutral	Disagree	Strongly disagree

3. How likely am I to enthusiastically recommend this opportunity to a friend or colleague?

Very likely	Likely	Neutral	Unlikely	Very unlikely

4. I would be interested in performing due diligence on this opportunity.

Strongly agree	Agree	Neutral	Disagree	Strongly disagree

5. The founder strongly believes in their idea and they are determined to make it work.[258]

Strongly agree	Agree	Neutral	Disagree	Strongly disagree

Summary

Bootstrapping is an ideal way for new entrepreneurs to start their business. Common bootstrapping strategies include:

- Keeping your day job while you get your business off the ground
- Deferring owner salaries for as long as possible
- Borrowing or share equipment or space
- Bartering

- Buying used or leasing instead of purchasing

Bootstrapping has its pros and cons. You will need patience to bootstrap your business because the bootstrapped path is defined by slower growth and more time between major milestones. Yet, bootstrapping creates options where few existed before. For that reason, it's a valuable toolkit for the resilient entrepreneur.

Crowdfunding democratizes startup and growth financing for small businesses. There are relatively few institutional barriers to raising funds from the crowd. Anyone willing to learn the best practices and put in tremendous effort can successfully raise funds.

Perks and rewards-based crowdfunding is a great option for raising approximately $20,000 or less. **Crowdfund investing** is better for businesses that need to raise upwards of ten times that amount. The average successful crowdfund investment campaign is between $165,000 and $245,000.[244]

Confidence in your ability to **pitch** your business concept is a key aspect of entrepreneurship. If you heed the lessons in this chapter, you'll be more confident in pitching to investors, partners, and other stakeholders. As we've learned already, confidence is an integral part of becoming more resilient.

Chapter 6: Giving and Receiving Feedback

"I think it's very important to have a feedback loop, where you're constantly thinking about what you've done and how you could be doing it better."

- Elon Musk

At age 26, John Kennedy Toole began writing a novel called *A Confederacy of Dunces*. About a year later he sent his manuscript to Simon and Schuster, a major publishing company. The text found its way to their senior editor, Robert Gottlieb. After reading the manuscript, Gottlieb offered "sharp criticism" and at one point even went as far as to call the work "meaningless."[259]

Toole set about revising the book, but after nearly two years of back-and-forth, he and Gottlieb reached a stalemate with Toole refusing to concede on certain changes he felt were integral to the story. As a result, Gottlieb refused to publish. Three toiling years of work and rework, and the book remained in the rejection pile. Toole was devastated by Gottlieb's dismissal.

Feeling mortally wounded, Toole plummeted into despair. He became paranoid that although Gottlieb had rejected his manuscript, he surreptitiously stole ideas from it and included them in other works that Simon and Schuster published.[260] These accusations were unfounded, but it didn't matter because that's the story Toole told himself.

In 1969, at only 32 years of age, Toole committed suicide.[261] We will never know if Toole had a diagnosable mental illness or what other factors outside of his work led to his decision to take his own life. A 2015 study conducted by UC Berkley, UC San Francisco and Stanford revealed that as many as 30 percent of entrepreneurs suffer from some form of depression.[262] It's much harder for these entrepreneurs to bounce back from rejection, learn from it and persevere ahead.

Toole's story is tragic, but the greatest tragedy of all was that he died never knowing what might have been, had he just kept trying. If it weren't for Toole's mother, none of us would have ever known. After his death, Mrs. Toole championed her son's manuscript and tried again to get it published. Again, it was rejected, this time by more than one publisher. Yet Mrs. Toole would not be deterred. She kept trying until it was finally published in 1980, eleven years after her son's death. Initially, only 2,500 copies were printed, but strong demand eventually resulted in over 50,000 copies being sold within its first year of publication. A year later, John Kennedy Toole was posthumously awarded the Pulitzer Prize for Fiction. *Confederacy of Dunces* would go on to sell almost 2 million copies in 18 different languages worldwide.[263]

"Reflect and remind yourself that an accurate criticism is the most valuable feedback you can receive."

-Ray Dalio

Founder of Bridgewater Associates and author of *Principles*

How many entrepreneurs give up, not knowing just how close they really were to the next milestone? How many crater at the first, second or even third bite of criticism? What separates them from the resilient entrepreneur? The answer is that resilient entrepreneurs can process and handle constructive, critical and even outright negative feedback. They are self-disciplined in their objective evaluation of feedback about ideas, products, tactics and strategies. They can recognize and discount the voice inside their head that tells them that the feedback is an attack on their personal identity.

As early-stage entrepreneurs, we need validation from time to time. Validation is encouraging feedback. It highlights the effort we've invested and the positive things we've accomplished. For example, hearing a business coach or mentor tell you, "I can see you're putting a lot of thought and effort into this business" shows an acknowledgement of your determination.

Pausing to recognize early milestones can also be validating: "You registered your business entity this past week? Congratulations! That's a big step in a startup's journey!" Validation helps reinforce commitment, which is especially important when we're just starting out. Before long though, a fledgling entrepreneur needs constructive feedback if they are to make noticeable progress.[138] Coaching is a valuable form of constructive feedback for entrepreneurs; We will explore coaching in detail in the next chapter.

In the New York Times bestselling book, *Thanks for the Feedback: The Science and Art of Receiving Feedback Well*, authors Douglas Stone and Sheila Heen recognize that how resilient we are influences how we respond to positive and negative feedback.[264] Resilient entrepreneurs are more likely to process and accept negative, constructive, and even instructive feedback better and faster than entrepreneurs with lower levels of resilience. They're also able to respond to feedback with energy and motivation to improve, as opposed to shutting down. They're able to openly listen to feedback instead of thinking about how they're going to defend their actions.

How you interpret and respond to the feedback you receive says a lot about your ability to transform different types of feedback into learning opportunities. In this chapter, I offer some tips and best practices around asking for and receiving feedback. Feedback is a two-way exchange, so we will highlight roles and responsibilities of both the giver and receiver of feedback.

Ultimately, feedback receivers are their own gatekeepers, controlling which feedback they choose to accept and reject. In fact, they get to choose if and when they are willing to receive any feedback in the first place. A prudent entrepreneur should always be willing to listen to feedback about their business. However, you don't always have to agree with the feedback. If there is something you don't agree with, ask the giver of the feedback for clarification. Exploring their thought process will help you better understand the logic and assumptions they used to form their advice.[303]

There are also certain times and places where you might not be in the best position to receive feedback. It's okay to say, "I'm not in the mindset to objectively receive feedback right now, but I would like to hear what you have to say. Do you mind if we schedule a feedback session for another time?"

In *Thanks for the Feedback*, the authors place an emphasis on how well we listen to and receive feedback. If you're not actively listening or if you're being defensive about the feedback you're receiving, you're unknowingly returning a form of feedback to the other person. When you immediately begin to explain and justify yourself after hearing feedback, you are telling the feedback giver that you're not interested in feedback at all. The person giving feedback probably isn't interested in a debate. You need to assume that they're giving you their honest opinion. If they sense that you don't want to actively listen to what they have to say, they're not going to waste their time.

A good indicator of whether you're doing this is when you're thinking about a response while the other person is speaking. This can often be difficult to avoid, but if you find yourself doing this, then you're not actively listening. You shouldn't feel like you must respond to feedback right away. Listen and acknowledge that the person giving feedback has been heard. Tell the person providing feedback that you're grateful for their time. Be clear that you're willing to listen to the feedback they have to offer, but they should understand that you will not necessarily implement all their advice.

Saying this out loud is as much for your benefit as it is for the person giving the feedback. Don't waste everyone's time trying to convince someone that their perspective is wrong or misinformed. That's not the point. You should view feedback givers as collaborators, not callous critics.

Also, be inviting of constructive and candid feedback. If the person giving feedback seems to be holding back, give them some reassurance that it's okay to be honest. Many people tend to be agreeable and actively avoid controversial topics that they believe might hurt someone's feelings.[138] If the feedback giver is too agreeable and unwilling or unable to be straightforward, then they're at best unhelpful and at worst are causing more harm than good. If you spot this happening, consider looking for feedback elsewhere.

> "No matter how unfair the criticism, your first job is to listen with the intent to understand, not to defend yourself. Reward criticism to get more."
>
> - Kim Scott
> Author of the bestselling book *Radical Candor*

Accepting feedback well is an art that takes practice, patience and self-awareness. It's also a skill you can actively work to improve. One way to get better is to understand that not all feedback is the same. Let's distinguish between what the authors of *Thanks for the Feedback* term as *evaluative feedback* versus *coaching feedback*.

As a business coach, I might ask an entrepreneur, "Have you considered advertising on Facebook or (insert popular social media platform here)?" On the surface, this sounds like a reasonable question for a business coach to ask. I might add that "a lot of small businesses are advertising on Facebook and other social media platforms."

Maybe they tried Facebook advertising once, but weren't convinced it was worth the investment, or maybe they didn't try it because they weren't confident they understood social media well enough to make the investment. In the coaching profession, we call these solution-oriented questions.[265] On the surface, I posed what seemed to be a question, but it was really a very specific suggestion – *"advertise on Facebook"* – disguised as a question.

When I try to make my advice more credible by adding that many other small businesses are advertising on Facebook, I've introduced the feedback as an evaluative statement. I'm comparing the entrepreneur's efforts to an ideal business owner's modern-day advertising tactic. The entrepreneur might have heard my feedback and thought, "Of course I've explored advertising on social media; Does my coach think I'm living under a rock?!" This is a defensive reaction – shields up. In this scenario we might feel that we're being evaluated based on our current knowledge and performance compared to other small business owners.

If the entrepreneur hasn't tried because they're not confident in their knowledge, skills or abilities to do it effectively, they might think, "I'm an awful business owner and an even worse marketer - I don't understand social media advertising as well as other small business owners!" This reaction is about a lack of self-efficacy. They may be misperceiving it as feedback that conflicts with their *story of self* – they thought they were a competent small business owner, but this feedback is making them think otherwise.

Before we conclude that this entrepreneur is being too sensitive or isn't being open-minded, let's open our minds to the fact that these miscommunications happen all the time, both in business and in social settings. We often have a mismatch in how feedback is perceived versus the feedback giver's original intent.

Let's look at how constructive feedback would help the message get across. Some better coaching questions might be delivered in a more open-ended, less suggestive format like, "Tell me about the advertising tactics or strategies you've already tried.

How did those past advertising campaigns perform? How do you measure the success of those strategies? What other advertising methods have you considered, or thought might be effective? Are there any that you'd be interested in learning more about?"

With these questions, the entrepreneur is being coached toward self-discovery. This method helps them reveal new ideas that they come up with on their own. This makes them more likely to embrace and implement those ideas. This scenario illustrates coaching an entrepreneur toward a growth mindset, as opposed to one where they focus on evaluating performance against others. Evaluative feedback is much more threatening to our identity and *story of self* than coaching.[264]

The mental contrasting technique discussed in the goal setting chapter can also help with receiving feedback. As you'll recall, mental contrasting is about embracing our grand aspirations, while also being keen to the nearer-term obstacles standing in the way. Dr. Oettingen's research found that people who received negative or constructive feedback were better able to process and integrate feedback into action plans, especially if they had also used mental contrasting to establish their goals and action plans.[132]

Feedback isn't a zero-sum ultimatum. I have more options than simply accepting or rejecting feedback. If you're not sure if and how feedback should fit into your business plan, you can implement feedback through experimentation. With a growth mindset, we're more likely to try out a piece of feedback before rejecting it outright, and the best way to do that is using lean startup principles.

Lean into feedback

"I think great founders are relentless and stubborn in their vision for how the world should be, but very pragmatic and flexible with their day-to-day or week-to-week tactics."

- Alexis Ohanian
Co-founder of Reddit and startup investor

Experimentation is the foundation of the Lean Startup Methodology, introduced earlier. The lean method is the entrepreneurship equivalent to the scientific method. Its steps involve: questioning the environment, conducting background research, establishing a hypothesis, running real-world experiments, adjusting, retesting, adjusting, retesting... In short, the lean method forces us to challenge our assumptions about new products, services and business processes by soliciting feedback from key stakeholders early and often.

The Lean approach begins with our new idea. A new idea is like having a baby. It is our creation. We brought it into this world. Regardless of what it looks like, we think it's beautiful, and we're ready to love and nurture it unconditionally. That unconditional love is important. It fuels the passion needed to raise and develop our idea into its full potential. We are ready to invest as much time and money in it as is necessary because we believe its potential is extraordinary.

However, before we invest too much time or energy, our idea is whisked away for an initial examination. Through a magnifying glass, our idea's extraordinary potential is questioned with skepticism. Under bright lights, deficiencies are exposed. Those who we assumed would love our idea as much as we do, look at it with a confused expression on their face.

At this juncture, we have a choice. We can embrace the lean approach, or we can discount its value. A common justification for the latter is to compare our business journey to the path taken by successful visionary founders like Steve Jobs or Elon Musk.[267] These visionaries, so the logic goes, didn't listen to the cynics who said it couldn't be done. They were successful in disrupting their industries precisely because they were stubborn trailblazers.

While that is indisputable, broadly speaking, it fails to consider a couple of important nuances. The first is that even though these visionaries never doubted their grand plans, leapfrogging the limits of what was previously believed to be possible, they did incorporate feedback throughout their journey. Jony Ive is the Chief Design Officer at Apple. Recalling his time working alongside Jobs, he noted that "Jobs would pitch wild ideas and expected people to give him open, honest feedback, sometimes called 'fearless feedback.'"[266] For every homerun idea that Jobs brought to market, there were many more that never saw the light of day. Even the most idealistic entrepreneurs solicit and listen to critical feedback.

The second important distinction is that these founders dreamed big, but started small, failing frequently along the way to success. We look at Apple, Tesla, and SpaceX and we see dreams that have come true. What we don't appreciate as much is the tireless iteration that was necessary to fine tune the products, services and business processes that made these businesses iconic.

Receiving feedback, especially critiques we didn't expect or don't agree with can feel threatening. That's because if we decide to accept feedback and change something about our idea, it won't seem the same afterward. It will look different from what we originally had in mind. This can lead to a sense of loss.[267]

This is one reason why entrepreneurs are sometimes susceptible to confirmation bias. Confirmation bias or confirmatory bias is the inclination to search for, acknowledge and/or reinterpret information that reinforces our current beliefs.[268] We desperately want to hear that we're on to something with our idea. So, when one person gives us critical feedback about our idea, product or service and a different person gives only praise, we tend to ignore or discount the critiques in favor of the positive feedback that reaffirms our theories.

Figure 7: Confirmation bias causes us to seek out information that confirms our current beliefs while ignoring or discounting information that challenges it.

It can also be difficult to absorb critical feedback because of how we associate ourselves with our idea. If we feel we've spawned and parented an idea, we can be led to believe that it was created in our own image. Thus, a criticism of the idea, can feel like a direct attack on our personal identity.[269] When doubt is cast upon our sense of self, our natural defense response is to deny or discount such notions.[267]

When on the defensive, we might directly challenge the feedback we receive. We will justify our thought process and decision making. The feedback session turns into a debate. On the other hand, if we're too agreeable, we might not challenge feedback directly. Instead, we might recoil and stop soliciting advice altogether. We stop going to business functions because we're intimidated by feedback we might receive. We begin to isolate ourselves and seek out feedback only from those who we know will be supportive.[267]

When we start to feel threatened by feedback, it's important to call back to our *story of self.* We are not defined by our business idea. We have each taken a unique path to get where we are today. Each of us have unique values, personality traits, and strengths. If we believe our *story of self* and distinct qualities are an asset, they will serve as an unshakable foundation, regardless of the feedback we receive. This perspective helps us distinguish between feedback about the business and feedback we might misperceive as a personal criticism.

It takes discipline to sit and listen openly to someone else's critiques. It requires restraint not to jump in and defend our idea. It necessitates mindfulness to recognize that feedback about our idea is not the same thing as criticism against us personally. When we detach our ideas from our sense of self and listen objectively to feedback, we improve our business' odds of survival. It is the difference between a professional entrepreneur and one who acts purely on emotion.

"Sometimes we are too close to a situation. Entrepreneurs can be blinded by emotion, by our love of what we have built, unable to see it fresh and with the eyes of a more objective outsider."

- Howard Schultz

Former CEO and Chairman of Starbucks

Prospective Sense-making

Entrepreneurs consistently face risk and uncertainty throughout their journey. They are tasked with making important decisions and investments using incomplete information. In many cases, the most rewarding outcomes tend to be the riskiest propositions. The process of prospective sense-making is the capture and analysis of information that will be used to make the best decision possible.[270]

When we solicit and analyze feedback from others, we can increase the amount and quality of information available to us. This is especially true if we are soliciting feedback from people with a diversity of experience, credentials and perspectives. One challenge with diversified feedback is that it might produce conflicting information. How do we make sense of the ambiguity?

One useful strategy is to solicit enough feedback from a variety of sources so that you can begin to recognize patterns. This is best done when you can lay out the feedback visually. Try pulling insights from your notes and write them on sticky notes. Then post the notes on a wall and see if any natural groupings or themes emerge. The best way to do this is with collaborators who can see things from different perspectives. Ask your partner, friend, mentor, or business coach for help making sense of feedback.

Another good strategy is to design an experiment around points of conflicting feedback. Let's imagine we're trying to decide on a brand name and logo for our business. We've created a list of possible names. Now, we can survey or interview people to help us narrow down our list. Here are some questions we might ask:

1. What comes to mind first when you see this brand name? What do you associate this name with?
2. Which name do you think best represents the business we're in?
3. Why do you think so? Why don't these other names represent the business as well?

4. Which names are most memorable? Why?

Hopefully, through this process, a clear choice, or at least a couple of good choices will emerge. Next, we can take our brand name and sketch out some possible logo designs to complement it. They don't have to be perfect. A rough drawing will suffice. Then, we can take these logo prototypes and get additional feedback. Again, here are some questions we might ask:

1. What first comes to mind when you see this logo? What do you associate it with?
2. If this logo represented a person, what qualities or characteristics would you say this person had?
3. Is there anything you dislike about the logo? Please explain.
4. If you were to break apart and rearrange this logo, how might you rearrange it? What would you take away? What would you add?

There are other sense-making techniques, most of which involve collaboration with others. If you find yourself struggling to make sense of ambiguous or conflicting feedback, it's a good idea to get an unbiased, outside perspective. The next chapter will explore how we can do that through coaching and mentoring.

In summary, to execute the lean startup method and prospective sense-making effectively, we must be as passionate about process as we are about our business idea. Adopting these processes and approaching feedback as an objective professional will help us be more resilient to criticism and the cycles of continuous improvement. When all is said and done, feedback helps get us closer to our dreams. We only need to lean in and listen.

Failure is just another form of feedback

"Failure is the only opportunity to begin again, this time more intelligently."[39]

- Henry Ford, Founder of Ford Motor Company

To conclude this chapter, I've included a short section highlighting several quotes and anecdotes about perceived failures along the entrepreneurial path. You will recognize the entrepreneurs behind these stories. You'll be familiar with their products, services and the successes they've achieved. Yet, to reach the milestones they did, they had to fail, fall, bruise and begin again.

"It's fine to celebrate success, but it is more important to heed the lessons of failure." [39]

- Bill Gates

Those with the fixed mindset are measured and defined by the failures they experience, but entrepreneurs with the growth mindset learn from failure and persevere. For them, failure is feedback, and feedback is a gift.

"The unexpected failure demands that you go out, look around and listen. Failure should always be considered a symptom of an innovative opportunity and taken seriously as such."

- Peter Drucker
"The Founder of Modern Management"

When Sara Blakey, the founder of SPANX, was growing up her father used to ask her, "What did you fail at this week? 'The logic seems counterintuitive, but it worked beautifully. He knew that many people become paralyzed by the fear of failure. They're constantly afraid of what others will think if they don't do a great job and, as a result, take no risks.... His question, 'What did you fail at this week?' was a push to stretch.' It was an attempt to normalize failure, to make it part of a casual dinner conversation. Because when you seek out situations where you might fail, failure loses some of its menace. You've been inoculated against it."

- Sara Blakely as told to Chip and Dan Heath
Authors of *The Power of Moments*

This doesn't mean that the failures aren't painful. It just means we can fail and yet maintain the belief that we can do better next time.[154] Failure is feedback and the more feedback we receive, the less uncomfortable it becomes. This is one of the most important characteristics of a resilient entrepreneur.

"Something not many people know is that I was actually rejected by QVC the first time I tried to sell my product there. I sent QVC a sample of my product. They promptly returned it to me with a 'No, thank you.'"

- Lori Greiner, known today as the "Queen of QVC"

Next time you falter, check your mindset. It's natural to feel deflated after a setback, but don't let your dejection stagnate until it turns sour. Take a moment, take a day or two if you need to. Then, lift yourself up, reset your outlook, and get back to work.

Daymond John, co-founder of FUBU clothing line and co-star of ABC's Shark Tank reality show, was denied financing 27 times before finally securing funding.

If you are denied financing a dozen times will you give up? Or will you try a dozen more times if need be? If you're trying to make your first sale and the first 20 doors you knock on turn you away, will you quit? Or, will you knock on another 20 doors until one opens?

Brene Brown is the author of three number one New York Times bestsellers, yet when she was trying to publish her first book, she received over 40 rejections before she decided to self-publish.[6]

When you've put your heart and soul into designing your product and the first person you show it to is unimpressed, how will you respond? Will you abandon it in the corner of the garage? Or will you test it again, reiterate it if necessary, and refine it until you find what works?

Walt Disney's early animations were repeatedly rejected by Life Magazine. Still, Disney sketched on. Some of his initial short films were rejected by MGM Studios because executives there believed that cartoons were a fad that was bound to fade. Besides that, MGM co-founder, Lois Mayer, said that Mickey would never work because "women are terrified of mice, especially a mouse ten feet tall on the motion picture screen."[153]

"For more than a decade, a glass bottle containing a thin brown liquid had sat on my desk. What appeared at first glance to be a stout version of an old-fashioned soda bottle was actually a carbonated coffee drink that, back in the late 1990s, Starbucks had co-invented, marketed and then watched fail miserably. Mazagran. The name was printed across the bottle in white capital letters, but the product's symbolism was also imprinted on my psyche: Celebrate, learn from, and do not hide from mistakes."

- Howard Schultz
Former CEO and Chairman of Starbucks

James Dyson set out to invent a better vacuum cleaner – one without the hassle of bags. During the process, he built "one prototype at a time, making one change at a time. He failed and learned and failed again. It took 5,127 prototypes before he finally built the better vacuum. Today Dyson's personal net worth is estimated to be more than $5.8 billion."

- James Dyson, founder of Dyson Ltd.
(as told to Guy Raz on NPR's podcast, *How I Built This. 12 Feb 2018*)

Each of these entrepreneurs were bumped and bruised along their path to success. Yet, their stories are remarkable because they chose to persevere past hardship. What type of person can face rejection over 5,000 times, and still try again, all the while expecting a better result? It's the resilient entrepreneur who can withstand the relentless failure, lessons learned, pivots and continuous improvement required to become remarkable.

I hope these vignettes have inspired you. In the next chapter, we'll look at how coaching and mentoring are used to help us sustain our passions and keep us focused.

Chapter 7: Coaching and Mentoring

"One of the first things I learned was that there was a relationship between screwing up and learning. The more mistakes I made, the faster I learned. As you can imagine, I was very efficient. I tried to surround myself with smart advisors, and I tried not to make the same mistake twice."

- Michael Dell
Founder of Dell Computers

The idea of mentoring is as old as Homer's Odyssey. In the ancient epic tale, Odysseus, off fighting in the Trojan War, assigns a trusted advisor, Mentor, to oversee his son's education and development while he is away.[271] In modern times, mentoring is commonplace, especially in major corporations and high-tech startup circles. Regardless of industry, mentorship can be of tremendous value.

As you begin this chapter, you might be asking yourself, "Do I need a coach or mentor for my business? Do I have the time, and will it be worth it? I feel like I'm doing fairly well; can a coach or mentor really make that much of a difference in my business?" These are all great questions to have.

As you contemplate these questions, let me ask you one more... Imagine for a moment that you need to have an important medical procedure performed. It's an unpleasant scenario to think about, and one I hope you never have to face, but stay with me. You have a choice between two surgeons, both with the exact same educational credentials – they both graduated in the same year from the same top medical school. Each surgeon received similar high marks on all exams and performed outstandingly in their residency. They also have an equal number of years of experience doing the exact same surgery you need, and both have equivalent success rates.

The only difference between the two surgeons is that one of the surgeons worked with a coach – a retired medical professor - for four months in the past year to improve on a few small things. During that time, the coach offered feedback to the surgeon on how to better use lighting during the procedure and how to better position themselves over the patient when operating to provide more control and stability. This surgeon was pleasantly surprised and grateful for the level of awareness they gained from the coach, and they started to implement a few adjustments to their posture and the lighting in the operating room. The other surgeon passed on the coaching opportunity, believing that they didn't really need coaching. After all, they were already performing quite well and had obtained the most prestigious medical credentials.

Knowing this information, which surgeon would you choose? I think it's safe to assume that almost everyone would lean toward the surgeon who received the coaching. If our lives depend on it, we want the best surgeon available, even if they're just a little bit better than the next best option. We also want the surgeon who is doing everything they can to better themselves, to continuously learn and grow. This isn't a hypothetical anecdote. It's a true story told by Dr. Atul Gawande, a surgeon, Harvard Medical School professor and author of multiple bestselling books. He recounts his coaching experience in a tremendous TED talk given in 2017. For Dr. Gawande, coaching takes someone who is good and makes them great. "A coach provides a more accurate picture of our reality, instills positive habits of thinking, and breaks our actions down and then helps us build them back up again," he says.

"Mentors focus on improvement: Can you push a little bit further? Can you shoulder a little more responsibility? They introduce a productive level of stress."

-Chip and Dan Heath
Authors of *The Power of Moments*

Studies have shown that coaches and mentors can help entrepreneurs in many ways. Below are just a few of the potential benefits:[272]

- Opportunity to think more strategically about your business
- A devoted time to reflect
- Identification of new business opportunities.
- Introduction and access to the contacts and resources in the mentor's network.
- Increased knowledge around marketing, management and finance.
- Development of new skills and adoption of higher-level business techniques and strategies.
- Increased confidence, self-worth and self-efficacy in your entrepreneurial knowledge, skills and abilities.
- Avoidance of common pitfalls.
- Increased focus on attaining goals.
- A sounding board to bounce around ideas and brainstorm.

According to the American Society for Training and Development (ASTD), 75 percent of business executives point to mentorship as having played a significant role in their success.[273] This is especially true if you're a sole proprietor - working with one mentor or coach immediately doubles the size of your team, giving you access to a sounding board, brainstorming partner and confidant. If you've left the corporate world to become an entrepreneur, you go from a team environment to one of isolation.

Everyone is limited in what they can achieve alone. An often-cited African proverb says *if you want to go fast, go alone, but if you want to go far, go together*. Oftentimes it's more challenging to digest and analyze information from our solitary perspective. Having someone to discuss business strategy and challenges with helps reduce the feeling of isolation. Through my experience coaching more than a thousand entrepreneurs, this is the most frequent feedback I hear about the value of coaching or mentorship.

Working with a mentor also encourages small business owners to remain introspective about their business. It's easy to get bogged down and immersed in the day to day business activities. Allowing for time to think longer-term and more strategically is an integral part of being successful. Mentorship gives us permission to step back and reflect on the bigger picture.

Now, I'll ask you again, do you really need a business coach? If you want to continuously strive to improve and be the best entrepreneur you can be, then the answer should be a resounding yes!

This is especially true if you're a new sole-proprietor - finding the right mentor should be one of the first things you do. It can lead to you becoming a more resilient entrepreneur.

Remember, the first couple of years along the entrepreneurial journey are often the most difficult. According to the Small Business Administration, only about 69 percent of new businesses survive beyond the first two years of the startup phase and only 50 percent survive beyond five years.[274]

When mentees are exposed to the lessons learned from a mentor, they can model effective entrepreneurial behavior and avoid common pitfalls. Access to a mentor's best practices and bruises increases the self-efficacy of the mentee – they will more likely believe they're prepared for the entrepreneurial journey, and that belief will be self-fulfilling in providing the additional resiliency an entrepreneur needs to become successful.

Entrepreneurial self-doubt can lead to an entrepreneur quitting the startup early but hearing about the ups and downs of the mentor's journey, can increase an entrepreneur's confidence and self-efficacy. In fact, studies conducted using data provided by the Global Entrepreneurship Monitor show that an entrepreneur's confidence increases, on average, by as much as 10 percent for entrepreneurs who are actively engaged with a mentor.[305]

Psychologists have found that we often suspend logical reasoning during times of intense adversity.[24] We've all made poor choices when under pressure and stress. The startup and growth phases of business are ripe with pressure points but working through these challenges with a mentor can be invaluable. In fact, an active mentoring relationship during a startup's first couple of years can increase the odds of survival by as much as 11 percent, according to MicroMentor.[275]

MicroMentor is a social enterprise created by the global humanitarian nonprofit, Mercy Corps. MicroMentor's mission is to "help burgeoning entrepreneurs and nonprofit founders thrive through mentoring." Since 2013, they've worked to achieve this mission through their global online mentor-matching platform. It's free to sign up and you can look for a mentor across the U.S to work with. SCORE.org is another great resource for mentoring. SCORE is a national nonprofit network of 10,000 volunteer mentors with experience in dozens of different industries.

Locate the nearest SCORE chapter to you (there are more than 300 nationwide) or create an account through MicroMentor and start a mentoring relationship today! Before you do though, let's review some things you should consider when seeking the best mentor match for you.

"If you have enough desire and energy, and follow the guidance of an effective mentor, you will amaze yourself (and the rest of the world) with your accomplishments."

- Robert Herjavec
Entrepreneur and Investor

Finding the Right Mentor or Coach

"Mentors do not seek to create a new person; they simply seek to help a person become a better version of themselves. Mentors are, after all, primarily concerned with teaching, and a teacher is there to inspire."

-John Wooden
Coach, author, mentor and teacher

I will use the terms mentor and coach interchangeably at times, but they're not the same. According to UK Innovation Foundation, NESTA, "mentoring generally differs from coaching in that it involves a greater focus on specific industry experience and relevance... mentoring relationships are less formal and goal-oriented than coaching."[276] Many mentors have either started their own business or worked at the executive level in an established company at some point in their careers.

Mentoring might also be a longer-term relationship compared to coaching, with most mentoring relationships lasting anywhere between six months to five years, and meeting, on average, about once a month.

Some mentoring relationships might last a lifetime, like the one between Polaroid's founder, Edwin Land and his mentor, Julius Silver.[277] Julius was Edwin's summer camp counselor when Edwin was a young teenager. When Edwin started his business in 1932, Julius, a lawyer by trade, became a trusted advisor. Julius would serve as Edwin's mentor for the next 50 years until Edwin retired from Polaroid in 1982.[278]

Coaching relationships might emerge more ad hoc. Some coaches have specialties in certain subject matter areas like finance or marketing. As a business coach, I typically serve as a business generalist – my knowledge might be a mile wide and an inch deep. I don't have all the answers, but I probably know at least a few resources where you can find them. Where I am an expert is on process – the process of helping my client discover their path forward.

Either way, a good mentor or coach is someone who "inspires curiosity, challenges assumptions and expectations (gives feedback), guides us by asking probing questions, is honest and direct about what he/she doesn't know, [and] is eager to learn..."[279] They don't typically provide direct answers to problems, but will facilitate a conversation that helps an entrepreneur think through possibilities and find the answers on their own.

"Coaching is the art of facilitating the performance, learning, and development of another."

- Myles Downey
Author of Effective Modern Coaching

A poor coaching or mentoring relationship has been shown to lower a mentee's learning.[280] Thus, having no mentoring relationship at all is often better than having a poor mentoring experience. For this reason, it's important that we don't just accept any mentoring relationship. We need to find the right mentor for us and build a positive relationship with that person. Studies have also shown that when a mentoring relationship is positive, the mentee is much more likely to pay it forward – one day becoming a mentor to the next wave of entrepreneurs.[306] This is the virtuous cycle that helps develop and pass on resilience from one aspiring entrepreneur to the next. Let's look at some important factors to look for when seeking out a mentor.

Experience

"Mentoring can be described as using one's wisdom (the product of reflection on experience) to help another person build their own wisdom."

- Lancer, Natalie; Clutterbuck, David; Megginson, David
Authors of Techniques for Coaching and Mentoring

Your mentor should have relevant business and/or leadership experience. That experience doesn't necessarily need to be in the exact same industry you're in. If it is, great, but it's not a deal breaker if it isn't. A lot of innovation and creativity can happen at the intersections of seemingly unrelated fields.

An experienced mentor should be able to share transferable lessons learned and advice, even if their background is in a different industry. Keep an open-mind and look for ways you can relate their experience to your own.

Also, beware any biases you might have against mentors with a bit of gray in their hair. Research has shown that experience, measured in years, is directly correlated with higher levels of resilience.[281] We can benefit tremendously from an experienced mentor who has had to overcome their own bouts of adversity.

Some mentees have adopted a creative approach for finding a mentor with the relevant experience they're interested in learning from. Coach Wooden, mentioned earlier in the chapter, credits Abraham Lincoln and Mother Teresa as two of his lifelong mentors. Wooden was born in 1910, 45 years after Lincoln was assassinated. Mother Teresa was also born in 1910, but Wooden never had the opportunity to meet her either. So, how is it possible that he claims these two people, both of whom he never met, as his mentors?

Wooden describes learning from them vicariously by voraciously reading everything he could written by them and about them. Former President of Entertainment for *Telemundo* and successful media entrepreneur, Nely Galán credits Warren Buffet as one of her mentors, even though they've never met.[282] Similarly, Napoleon Hill, author of *Think and Grow Rich,* one of the bestselling self-help books of all time, describes being mentored by many great entrepreneurs and leaders that came before him. Hill closely examined these people's lives and invited them to join his imaginary council of advisers.

Invite inspirational leaders and mentors that you might never get an opportunity to meet in person into your brain-trust of mentors. If you're in real estate, read about Barbara Corcoran, the queen of New York real estate. If you're starting a coffee shop, read books by Howard Shultz, longtime President and CEO of Starbucks. If you're starting a fashion business, read everything you can about Daymond John, co-founder of FUBU. There are so many impressive and accomplished people to choose from.

To be clear, I'm not advocating for surrogate mentors in lieu of real, in-person mentoring. This method is simply a great supplement to your current mentoring relationship. By deeply studying our proxy mentors' lives and careers, we can learn a lot from their failures and best practices. How amazing is it that we have almost instant, affordable access to their knowledge and advice? Who will you include in your council of mentors?

You can also learn passively from the mentors you encounter every day. Billionaire entrepreneur and investor, Mark Cuban, highlights the right growth mindset when it comes to thinking more broadly about mentors. "With every effort, I learned a lot," he says. "With every mistake and failure (not only mine, but also those around me), I learned what not to do. I also got to study the success of those with whom I did business."[79]
So keep your antennae tuned to what you can learn from those you're doing business with.

Style

There is a spectrum of mentoring and coaching styles ranging from instructive ("You should do this") to facilitative, helping the entrepreneur solve their own challenges and realize new opportunities through self-discovery.[283] I adapt my coaching style along that spectrum depending on the situation, but as much as possible, I prefer to act as a collaborative facilitator. In that role, I ask a lot of probing questions and offer various prompts to help an entrepreneur see a challenge or opportunity from a different strategic perspective.

For example, a lot of entrepreneurs ask me what I think about their product or service, and whether I think it might be successful. When I was just starting out as a coach, I'd often give a direct, honest answer. As I became more experienced though, I realized that my opinion is based on a single consumer preference. Whether I like the product or not isn't relevant because one solitary customer or non-customer doesn't validate or invalidate a business model. I'm often not part of the target market and my biased opinion could unfairly skew an important strategic decision.

Instead of telling them whether I personally like the product, I pose some important questions back to them: Who is your target market? Have you tested this product with them? What do your customers tell you? How many repeat customers do you have? How many referrals are you getting through word-of-mouth? If the entrepreneur has a challenging time answering some of these questions, then we've highlighted a potential area for them to focus on.

It's more important to guide an entrepreneur toward a self-discovered solution or a new realization than to simply give what you might think is the right answer because it's quicker or easier to do so.

The guiding technique, often referred to as the maieutic or Socratic Method, is the most effective style for learning, satisfaction and building self-efficacy in entrepreneurs.[283] Be cognizant of which style underscores your mentoring relationship. Is the mentor serving as a guide or are they acting more like a cofounder?

Sometimes it can be helpful to get direct advice in a pinch. "Where a task is clear and well understood" by the entrepreneur, a more directive mentoring approach might be appropriate.[283] Yet, if a more educated or experienced mentor is consistently directing a mentee's next steps it can create dependency, which diminishes an entrepreneur's autonomy and is detrimental to long-term success. Interestingly, research suggests that as much as 1/3 of business mentors slip into this directive role more than might be appropriate.[284] Both parties in the mentoring relationship should be aware of which style works best for a given situation and be upfront if the relationship is sliding into a directive style too frequently.

Alignment

You want a mentor that you can connect with on some level. Share your *collaboration canvas* to look for areas of alignment. Similar demographic characteristics like having the same gender or ethnicity might help with establishing that connection, but they're not the only things to look for. Those factors are superficial compared to the deep insights we gained about ourselves in the chapter on authenticity. Research on entrepreneurial mentoring suggests that demographic characteristics like gender and age have no effect on mentoring outcomes.[279] Furthermore, with so much divisiveness in our society we can and should establish meaningful connections with people of a different gender, age group, religion, race or ethnicity.

Sheila Lirio Marcelo is the founder and CEO of Care.com, an online platform connecting families with caretakers. She was born in the Philippines and later immigrated to the United States when she was six years old.[285] She credits one of her mentors, George Bell, for helping her stay true to herself and gain the confidence she needed to pursue her entrepreneurial passion.[286]

When asked about her mentoring relationship, she said she intentionally sought out a male mentor. She didn't need a Filipino-born or female mentor to benefit from mentoring. When the New York Times asked about her about her decision to work with a male mentor, she explained that, "Closing the gender gap in business is a conversation that women have with other women. We absolutely need to provide a supportive community for each other, but if we're truly going to level the playing field, men have to be part of the equation."[287]

The same should be true for male entrepreneurs seeking out a female mentor. Dick Costolo, during his tenure as CEO of Twitter, was coached by Kim Scott. When Kim worked as a Director at Google, she was coached by a leadership advisor named Fred Kofman.[303]

The three most important mentors in my professional career were all women – Rosa Rios Valdez with Business and Community Lenders of Texas, Dr. Jana Minifie, my business school professor at Texas State University (who would later become my boss when I worked for her as a graduate instructional assistant), and Vicky Valdez with the City of Austin's Small Business Program. In my current role as a coach, I mentor many female entrepreneurs. When mentorship achieves its highest purpose, the mentee becomes the mentor and a virtuous cycle is cast forward, regardless of gender, race or any other surface-level characteristic.

Dr. Brad Johnson, Professor of Psychology at the U.S Naval Academy, is an expert on mentoring. His research reveals that although "cross-gender mentorships tend to form slower than same-gender mentorships, once they lift off, these mentorships are as effective or even more so in producing career-altering outcomes – especially for female mentees."[289]

When seeking a mentor consider exploring similarities that extend beyond demographic characteristics. Discover possible connections based on values, personality, strengths, creative problem-solving preferences, learning styles, interests, and attitudes. If you can find meaningful commonalities and focus on those, you're more likely to have a positive mentorship experience.

A first step toward building trust with your mentor is to discuss how you learn best, how you prefer to receive feedback, the way you approach a new challenge, etc. This is a great way to start a new coaching relationship.[264] There are some example trust-building questions to guide your coaching conversation in the *Coach and Mentor Question Guide*, located in the appendix.

"When a teacher or coach or any kind of mentor is consistent in his or her principles, it creates trust between the mentor and the people he or she is mentoring."

- John Wooden
Author, coach, mentor, and teacher

Make the Most of Mentoring

Kash Bhagwat-Brown is a volunteer business mentor in the U.K. Kash says he mentors simply because he enjoys it, adding that the "diversity of the mentoring opportunities keeps [him] fresh and honest." Kash also enjoys learning about the "business models being used in the companies [he] works with and how they approach their different strategies for growth and success."[288]

Other mentors, like Daymond John, founder of FUBU and co-star of the hit reality TV show, Shark Tank, mentors entrepreneurs for "the chance to see how these young people think, how they interact with a product, how they move about in the marketplace."

The benefits of mentorship can and should be mutually rewarding for both the mentee and the mentor. Volunteer mentors often benefit from the intrinsic rewards of giving back to society. They might also be interested in generativity, which is the positive feeling we get when we feel we're helping to shape future generations.[289] Research has shown that these altruistic actions reinforce the resiliency of the mentor, as well as the mentee.

Like any healthy relationship, there must be give and take from both sides. The same is true for a mentoring relationship. When you first meet with your mentor or coach, ask them what they hope to get out of the relationship.

Some mentors might be interested in investment opportunities. Having this motive isn't necessarily a bad thing, but discussing this up front is critical to an open and honest mentor relationship. If, as a mentee, you're not looking for an investor, say so and set those expectations up front. On the other hand, having smart money (an investor who is also a mentor or adviser) can have a lot of benefits. Whichever way you decide, just make sure it's all out in the open from the beginning and ask the mentor if he or she looks for investment opportunities in the businesses that they mentor.

An effective mentoring relationship will have reciprocal levels of effort from both the mentor and mentee. It's not a one-way intervention and it's not about benefiting just by showing up. As a mentee, the more effort you put into the relationship, the more you will gain from it.

Mentoring isn't a marriage.

Don't "marry" the first mentor you meet. It is okay to try different mentors until you find the one that seems to be the best fit.[306] It's possible that the first potential mentor you meet with won't be the right one for you, but don't give up after one or two mismatches.

Also, be proactive in your search for a mentor. Start looking for the right mentor now. Don't wait until you've stumbled into a difficult situation and you feel like you need coaching right away. When we're in an urgent situation, we feel rushed to choose the first decent option that emerges.

As a coach, I've encountered this scenario often. I'll get a call from an entrepreneur who signed a commercial lease without securing the startup financing they needed. Now, they need help applying for a small business loan. Because the stakes are high, and the deadlines are critical, we don't typically have enough time to establish trust and build rapport before we dive into the crisis.

Finally, when you do find a mentor you like, you can form a long-lasting relationship together, but it doesn't have to be an exclusive relationship. You can utilize several mentors or business coaches at once to get a breadth of knowledge and advice from a team of advisors.

Establishing Trust

"When one person trusts, and another is trustworthy, there is trust."

- Charles. H Green and Andrea P. Howe
Co-authors of the Trusted Advisor Field Book

You cannot have an effective mentoring relationship without first establishing a foundation of trust between the mentor and the mentee. Building trust and rapport is vital to establishing a productive working relationship and efforts should be made to do so before ever delving into technical topics or soliciting any advice. The temptation to jump in and offer solutions too soon is common, but we must resist that impulse to offer what seems to be a quick fix to a problem. Establishing trust is critical before offering advice because it will affect how mentees respond to a mentor's suggestions.[290] So, step back and learn a little about the entrepreneur and their business before you offer specific recommendations.

Lamia Walker is the founder of HouseSitMatch, an online platform connecting travelers with reputable house and pet sitters. Lamia worked with Kash Bhagwat-Brown, the volunteer mentor we mentioned earlier. When asked about establishing her mentoring relatiopnship with Kash, Lamia says, "How you feel on your initial introduction can render the coffee at your first meeting either unpalatable or absolutely stimulating. The chemistry must be right."[291] Introductions represent the first step in establishing trust and unsurprisingly study after study show trust to be one of the most significant variables in predicting an effective coaching or mentoring relationship.[272]

One such study, at Case Western Reserve University in Cleveland, Ohio, showed that positive emotional attractors (PEAs), which accentuate compassion for someone's vision and dreams, can create a sense of social-emotional security and a feeling of social attachment in the person being coached.[292] PEAs are things a coach or mentor can say or do that demonstrate understanding and buy-in for the entrepreneur's *story of self*, as well as their vision, hopes and dreams for the future. An example of a PEA statement from a coach/mentor might be, "I can see what you're trying to accomplish. Your product or service is really going to make a difference in people's lives and you've got a chance to disrupt this industry."

Using functional magnetic resonance imaging (fMRI), the researchers at Case Western monitored brain activity of individuals receiving coaching. When PEAs were used during coaching, they observed increased activity in the medial parietal cortex, which is an area of the brain that has consistently been shown to activate during autobiographical recall (*the story of self*) and visioning (dreaming about the ultimate business goal).[293] This area of the brain has also been shown to link to emotions of admiration, compassion and human connection.[294] This is why asking about an entrepreneur's *story of self* (autobiographical recall) and their business goals is a good way to begin a new mentoring/coaching relationship.

The researchers contrasted these PEAs with negative emotional attractors (NEAs). A NEA, in our context, might resemble the following statement by a coach or mentor, "Nice idea, but you don't have the funding to get it off the ground," or "That's a unique concept, but you're lacking the technical skills and background to implement it."

As you can see, these negative statements identify real obstacles to overcome, but they are presented as evaluative judgements about the entrepreneur's weakness, as opposed to challenges that they might be able to solve. The researchers measured brain activity when NEA statements were made. They found that when someone heard a negative, judgmental statement, the sympathetic nervous system (SNS) was triggered. The SNS is more colloquially referred as the fight-or-flight response.[295]

We normally associate the fight-or-flight response with being under mental or physical threat. In the context of entrepreneurship, negative emotional statements that invoke this reaction aren't necessarily bad. Entrepreneurs need to identify and acknowledge things that threaten their business. If they're having trouble recognizing them, it's the job of mentors and coaches to help them, and to do that we need to have candid conversations about the pitfalls that lie ahead.

At the same time, we obviously want to establish a meaningful human connection as opposed to initiating a fight-or-flight response. To do both, we must separate process from content. The mentoring or coaching process is designed to help us identify challenges and co-create possible solutions together, but before we can trust the process or the content (advice), we need to establish trust on the human level.

Therefore, positive emotional attractors are important when a new relationship is formed. This doesn't mean we build false hope or only look at the entrepreneur and their business through rose colored glasses. The point is to make the entrepreneur feel comfortable and safe so that they will want to open-up and express the salient challenges and vulnerabilities that they're struggling to overcome. It takes time to build trust and rapport. A focus on establishing a foundation of trust early on will allow you to candidly offer prudent, practical advice later.

As I've mentioned previously in this book, mindfulness meditation is a proven technique for the resilient entrepreneur. It's also a technique that coaches, mentors and entrepreneurs can practice together. As little as 5 to 15 minutes of mindfulness meditation before a session begins can help both the coach and the entrepreneur clear their minds, set a positive intention and sharpen their focus. This practice also helps turn down any emotional anxiety we might be bringing into the meeting, so we can think clearly and more logically.[90]

Kash was able to establish trust and rapport with Lamia and the results are paying off. Since working with Kash as her mentor, Lamia has increased HouseSitMatch's revenue by 20 percent.[291]

"People don't care how much you know until they know how much you care."

- Theodore Roosevelt

In my coaching role, I find myself sometimes making the mistake of not taking enough time to appreciate an entrepreneur's broader vision before I start diving into the details about the salient challenge or ripening opportunity. I did this recently with an entrepreneur named Shannon. Shannon is in the jewelry business and her mission is to empower women's individual style and self-discovery through her jewelry designs. Shannon designs and sells jewelry, but she said she says she's really in the business of changing the world by empowering underserved women. She sought out coaching on her elevator pitch in preparation for an upcoming opportunity with a pitch competition.

Shannon only had a couple of weeks to refine her pitch before the competition, so I felt a sense of urgency to get down to business right away. When I advised Shannon to recalibrate her pitch to strike a better balance between the noble mission of changing the world and the business model, I could see her fight-or-flight response kick in. She defended her social mission and explained how it was the core of her business. I could tell she was frustrated with me for seeming too obtuse to understand and appreciate her vision and because I wasn't bought into the bigger picture, she didn't trust me enough to hear the advice I was offering on her pitch.

When advice focuses on knowledge sharing, resources and tools, entrepreneurs are open and receptive. When a coach suggests or recommends the entrepreneur adjust a certain behavior, expect resistance unless trust has been established.[296]

The authors of the *Trusted Advisor*, one of the most authoritative works on building trust in business, help break down trust into four main components: credibility, reliability, intimacy and self-orientation. Things we do to increase our credibility, reliability and intimacy with others help increase trustworthiness. On the other hand, selfish behaviors, those that we do while primarily thinking about how we will benefit ourselves, lead to decreased trustworthiness. When the authors put these into an equation it looks like this:[297]

$$Trust = \frac{Credibility + Reliability + Intimacy}{Self - orientation}$$

Figure 8: The Trust Equation. Source: The Trusted Advisor

Credibility is about believability. Do you really know what you're talking about? Are you up to speed on new developments that are relevant to your area of expertise? Also, when you don't know something do you say so? When you honestly admit that you don't know something you are also building trust.

Reliability is about consistently doing what you say you're going to do. Do you show up on time for our meetings or are you consistently late and cancelling at the last minute? When we finish our meeting with action items do you complete those tasks reliably, or do you instead bring excuses to the next meeting explaining why you didn't get them done?

Intimacy builds trust through a human touch and collaboration. Human touch includes things like listening empathetically, showing a genuine interest in each other's lives beyond business, sharing something personable like a short story about your weekend or recent vacation, etc.

Collaboration might include rolling up your sleeves and working on something together. When I'm working with clients on their financials, I sometimes sit with them for a several hours and we go through each financial statement together, checking their numbers and exploring the formulas behind the spreadsheets.

Self-orientation degrades trust. When you do something for someone else, do you do it to be genuinely helpful, or are you doing it because you have something to gain for yourself? When you contribute something to a project or solution do you yearn for recognition or are you okay with someone else getting credit? When you make a connection for someone or share a resource, lead, etc. with nothing much to gain, it helps build trust. When you do things for others only because it will also benefit you, other people will notice, and it will degrade trust.

To become trustworthy, we must work to increase our credibility, reliability and intimacy while minimizing our self-orientation. One way to decrease self-orientation is to increase self-awareness, something we highlighted earlier in the book. The authors of the Trusted Advisor found that the more self-aware someone is, the lower their self-orientation tended to be.[297]

Brené Brown expands on these four pillars with her anatomy of trust, which she conveniently explains in the acronym, BRAVING: Boundaries, Reliability, Accountability, Vault, Integrity, Nonjudgement, and Generosity.[6] I highly recommend her books if you're interested in learning more. Let's take a closer look at the areas not addressed by the trust equation through the lens of a business mentoring relationship:

Boundaries

It's extremely important to set the mentoring relationship's boundaries and expectations up front. As a mentor or coach, my role is to offer guidance and advice. I'm not a contractor or employee of the business. I don't perform tasks and complete the work on behalf of the entrepreneur – that's their responsibility.

Also, because family is one of my core values, time designated to be with family is sacred. That means I'm not going to have unrestricted availability late into the evenings and on the weekends. What boundaries are important to you?

Reliability – (aforementioned in the trust equation).

Accountability

Accountability is about owning up to our mistakes. Flawlessness is not an expectation. Yet, when we do stumble, we need to be open and acknowledge our errors. By lowering our defenses and showing vulnerability, we build trust.

Vault

The vault means we respect confidentiality of information. If something was shared in confidence, it should remain private. Research conducted on telling secrets shows that people share secrets because they believe it strengthens a relationship.[95] That's true when secrets are shared and then locked away in a confidential vault. On the other hand, when secrets are shared with others outside the circle of confidentiality, trust is broken.

Small businesses need to be able to share sensitive information with their mentor. Sometimes a non-disclosure (NDA) and/or confidentiality agreement can help establish a foundation of trust, but it isn't necessary. I typically offer to sign an NDA that I provide on the entrepreneur's behalf. I'm not in the business of stealing ideas, so I offer the NDA as a sign of good faith.

In my experience though, the entrepreneurs with the most paranoia about the theft of their idea were also the most distracted from executing their business plan. Still, I'm as accommodating as possible, within reason, if it helps establish a foundation of trust.

Integrity

"Real integrity is doing the right thing, knowing that nobody's going to know whether you did it or not."

-Oprah Winfrey

There is no integrity in saying one thing and doing another. How well do you and your business live by your stated values? When the path gets bumpy shortcuts will reveal themselves, but many shortcuts include shortcomings. A virtuous compass will keep you on the right track. Always act with integrity. When in doubt, ask a coach or mentor to help you navigate through any gray areas.

Nonjudgement

When we evaluate others, we do so through the lens of our own personality traits and morals. We're susceptible to unconsciously discounting others whose values differ from ours. We believe they're inferior to us in some way. However, this isn't a productive outlook on the world. It's also exhausting to continuously evaluate others and compare them to ourselves.

When we judge people before they've had a chance to exhibit trustworthiness, we have robbed ourselves of the opportunity to trust. It takes discipline, but withholding judgement allows us to give people a chance to earn our trust. We should be willing to give people the benefit of the doubt, which is a concept in trust related to generosity.

Generosity

"Don't confuse stories with facts... When you generate stories in the blink of an eye, you can get so caught up in the moment that you begin to believe your stories are facts... Earn the right to share your story by starting with your facts. Facts lay the groundwork for all delicate conversations."

- Kerry Patterson, Joseph Grenny, Ron McMillan and Al Switzler
Authors of Crucial Conversations

When someone does something that affects us, we typically don't start with all the facts behind their intentions and motivations. This can lead to us filling in the missing bits of information by coming up with stories that help us make sense of a situation. We do this all the time. The problem, however, is that the stories we come up with a typically filled with fiction.

For example, let's look at a newly formed business partnership. Audrey and Liana are interested in starting up a Montessori school. Both work as Montessori teachers. They've been kicking around the idea of starting their own school and they're anxious to get started.

I coach a lot of new business partners. I like to ask them about each partner's roles and responsibilities. *Who will oversee bringing in new business? Which operational duties will each person oversee? What do your financial management controls look like?* When I asked Audrey and Liana these questions there was an awkward silence.

"We haven't really discussed it, said Audrey. "We can just figure some of these things out as they come up, right?"
"Yeah, sure." Replied Liana. "Audrey is more of the people person, so I just assumed you'd be in charge of new student enrollment and I can manage our staff and finances."
Audrey listened and shook her head in agreement, but then she clarified. "Well, yeah, I can take the lead on enrollment, but it's not all on me to bring in new business, right? I'm going to need you to help make some phone calls and attend some parent networking events too."
Liana paused before responding. It was obvious she hadn't envisioned herself in that role before.

Within about two minutes of discussing their roles and responsibilities, we were able to uncover where some expectations weren't aligned. Liana thought Audrey would do all the new student enrollment. Audrey agreed she should take the lead, but she expects some help from Liana, especially as the business is just getting off the ground. They each had expectations for themselves and their new partner. Yet, they hadn't voiced or written them down because their excitement and optimism created a blind spot.

Let's imagine Audrey and Liana didn't have this conversation and six months after opening they only had half as many students as they expected they would. Now they're having a disagreement about their marketing and sales strategy. Liana wants to brainstorm with Audrey, but Audrey is finding it difficult to be receptive to Liana's ideas. Audrey feels like she does everything when it comes to sales and marketing while Liana hasn't put any effort into bringing in new students. They're both starting to feel resentment toward each other.

In this scenario, Audrey and Liana hadn't discussed expectations. Because they weren't working with all the facts, they started to fill in the blanks with stories they told themselves about one another. As the authors of *Crucial Conversations: Tools for Talking when Stakes are High* remind us, "Stories don't get better with time – they ferment. Then, when we eventually can't take it anymore, we say something we regret."[298]

Audrey told herself that Liana wasn't taking the business seriously because she didn't want to help with enrollment. Liana thought sales and marketing was Audrey's turf and she had been hesitant to step in to try and help. Now she's telling herself that Audrey isn't carrying her weight in the business and she's starting to question the partnership.

In creating trust, we must show generosity, kindness and respect toward the other person. That means when we don't have all the facts, we presume the other person is acting in good faith with a mutually beneficial outcome in mind. It wasn't that Liana didn't care about the business or that she didn't want to help with sales and marketing. She had just assumed that it was Audrey's role.

When we default to generosity, we ask clarifying questions to learn the facts before we start telling ourselves a false story. Four or five months into the business, when student enrollment seemed stalled, Audrey might have said, "Liana, I know I'm primarily responsible for new enrollment, but would you mind following up on a few new leads I'm pursuing. I could really use your help until we get enough students to break even."

Communication and the Power of Inquiry

"Coaching enables people to tap into their own wisdom to help them achieve their goals, improve their performance, gain clarity, become more self-aware and aware of others, and to develop self-responsibility. It is a developmental dialogue typically involving the coach asking the client skillful questions."

- Liz Hall
Author of Mindful Coaching

An effective mentor or coach should also demonstrate effective communication. As a rule of thumb, our coaches should be listening and asking thoughtful, probing questions about twice as much as they will be giving specific pieces of advice. Studies of group communication show that although questions account for only 6 percent of dialogue, they're the catalyst for 60 percent of discussion.[258] It's especially important to listen and ask questions when a new relationship is first being established. The initial mentoring session, or even the first several sessions, should be about understanding, as opposed to advice-giving, brainstorming or problem-solving.[264]

Remember, it's not the coach's role to make decisions for the business owner. The coach's role is to guide the entrepreneur. A good coach will avoid the impulse to jump in too quickly to give what they believe is the right answer all the time. This is done best when coaches help keep us focused on adhering to a fundamental business process, as opposed to only focusing on a desired outcome. A byproduct of focusing on the process will be that the entrepreneur is accomplishing tasks and objectives that get them closer to achieving their end goal.[138] Don't let you and your coach get too caught up in the dream state we discussed in the goal setting chapter.

The best coaching and mentoring focuses us on achieving our goals. Some nascent entrepreneurs might seek mentorship to help them turn a hobby or lifestyle business into a more formalized operation with increased revenues. Mentors can help guide the entrepreneur through this transition by ensuring the entrepreneur has the right performance goals to formalize their business. It's also important for mentors to help hold the mentee accountable to their mastery goals. As outlined in the chapter on goal setting, mastery goals are about obtaining new knowledge and improving our current skillsets and abilities.

Mentorship is most common in a one-on-one format, but mentors can also be a positive influence through keynotes, panel discussions and small group mentoring.

The success of the mentor-mentee relationship will depend on a wide range of factors including personality traits, decision-making style and the business' lifecycle stage.[299]

During introductions and pleasantries, it's helpful for mentors and mentees to learn whether they're engaging or reserved, introverted or extroverted. If the mentee is reserved, it might mean that more time needs to be spent building trust and rapport, and that's okay. The best mentoring relationships are built over time. Remember, aspiring entrepreneurs come from all kinds of backgrounds and their demeanor has been shaped over the years through the experiences they've had in their lives and the people they have encountered along the way.

One of the first things you can do to break the ice is to talk about yourself a little. I have both education and experience related to small business advising and entrepreneurship, which I highlight in a brief one or two-minute bio with the person I'm meeting with. After I've discussed a little about myself, I ask the client to tell me a little bit about themselves. This is usually enough to open a dialogue with the client, but if he or she needs a little extra coaxing I'll ask what brought them in and what can I do to help them. If you don't feel comfortable talking about yourself, you can talk about the organization you represent. The goal here is to build credibility, trust, and rapport- we want the both parties to feel comfortable enough to engage in a productive coaching session.

On the other hand, some entrepreneurs might be more engaging from the start and the rapport building process will begin organically and develop more comfortably. Some entrepreneurs aren't shy about sharing their goals and aspirations from the get-go. Be sure not to let the conversation stray too far from the business-related issues though. If you find that someone is rambling on about a superfluous topic bring them back by asking them what specifically brought them to you and where exactly they see you being able to help them. This question leads to an important next step, which is to set realistic expectations.

Set Realistic Expectations

"The mentor nourishes a dream in the mentee and sets the mentee into creative flight, tempering idealism with the wisdom of experience."

- Lori Davis, Marc Little, William Thornton
The Art and Angst of the Mentoring Relationship

We've all heard the success stories of aspiring entrepreneurs growing their business from nothing into a cash cow venture, but that's far from the experience of most small business owners. This is especially true if we're pursuing more of a *Main Street* or *mom and pop shop* type business, as opposed to the high growth ventures often found in the tech sector.

Research has shown that aspiring entrepreneurs who are motivated by non-financial outcomes are more likely to achieve success, and those who are overly focused on purely financial rewards are more likely to abandon the business in pursuit of more financially consistent employment opportunities[300]. Most of financial projections I've seen in business plans include wildly overestimated sales and net profit figures. In addition, the owner's salary projections, especially in the first years of the startup, seem misaligned with the financial slog that often accompanies the first twelve months of a new business.

Mentors will spot a "get rich quick" business idea. They will help unveil more realistic financial expectations, and ways that the entrepreneur might test their idea in the marketplace to gain valuable customer feedback. Helping set realistic expectations from the beginning can help mitigate disappointment later. It's important to clarify that mentors aren't trying to dissuade people from embarking on an entrepreneurial endeavor, we're simply ensuring that they have realistic expectations about what's ahead.

John Wooden was a legendary college basketball coach. In fact, he was named the best coach of all-time by ESPN.[301] The designation encompasses the best coach among all sports, not just basketball. In Wooden's book, *A Game Plan for Life: The Power of Mentoring*, he reminds us that "while mentoring is usually about building someone up, it can occasionally be about taking someone down a notch or two, too—provided the dressing down is done with that person's best interest at heart and that it stems from love."[302]

Some studies show that people with clear expectations about entrepreneurship are more likely to start the business they set out to create.[305] This is because they have the information they need to make a clear and informed decision and will be far less likely to be surprised by the demanding work and tribulations of the startup journey.

Sheryl Sandberg has had a stellar career leading and coaching people at the Treasury Department, Google and now at Facebook where she is the COO. One of Sheryl's mentees at Google was Kim Scott. In Scott's bestselling book, *Radical Candor*, she describes a memorable coaching conversation she and Sheryl had. It was after Kim gave an important presentation at Google. Sheryl offered Kim both praise and constructive criticism. Her candid feedback pointed out Kim's overuse of "um" as a filler-word when presenting. Sheryl suggested Kim consider working with a speech coach. Kim shrugged off Sheryl's advice, discounting the "ums" as "just a verbal tic."

Instead of dropping the issue, Sheryl pressed Kim more directly. "I feel like you're ignoring what I'm telling you," she said. "I can see I am going to have to be really, really direct to get through to you. You are one of the smartest people I know, but saying 'um' so much makes you sound stupid. The good news is a speaking coach can really help with the 'um' thing. I know somebody who would be great. You can definitely fix this."[303] Kim took Sheryl's advice and went to see the speech coach.

Kim could have reacted differently to Sheryl's advice. She could have ignored it or shut down and told herself that Sheryl had called her stupid. She didn't though. Also, Sheryl never said Kim was stupid. She said, "You sound stupid when..."
It's a subtle difference, but Sheryl's criticism, albeit curt, was focused on a correctable behavior. To get Kim's attention, Sheryl felt she had to be, what Kim calls, *radically candid*. Being this direct with a mentee requires we have an established relationship built on trust and genuine regard for the mentee.

Even though Sheryl's feedback was forceful, her motivations kept Kim's best interests in focus. Sheryl envisioned a more confident and credible Kim giving a better presentation in the future. The point of the feedback was to help Kim see what was needed to make that better future a reality.

It would have been a disservice to Kim to let the issue slide. Too often we withhold radical candor because we're afraid we might hurt another person's feelings. We might save someone a fleeting moment of discomfort by sugarcoating criticism, but in the long-term we're impeding someone from reaching their full potential.

We might also be worried that if we're too direct, we'll be labeled as prickly and people might not like us. Yet, excellent mentors are less concerned with themselves and how agreeable they appear to be. Instead, they're relentlessly focused on developing their mentee. They don't settle for second-rate performance. Good mentors will often expect more of the mentee than the mentee expects of themselves.[289] This is how our expectations get stretched. This is how we grow and excel to surprisingly higher levels of success.

I'll share one more example from my own coaching experience. I was participating in a roundtable discussion with several aspiring entrepreneurs and mentors. Alice and her husband were at my table. They were interested in opening a 12,000 ft^2 fitness center, complete with a juice and smoothie bar. They estimated the project would cost upwards of $1 million, but they didn't have near enough money to finance the project themselves. They wanted to learn about funding options.

As they shared their dream, one of the other mentors at the table got excited about the concept. Even though the couple had less than 20 percent of the funds required to start the business, he advised them not to worry about the financing. He assured them that they had a great idea and would be able to raise enough money through crowdfund investing.

My advice was more tempered. After asking a few probing questions, I learned that, although they were physically fit, neither one of them had any experience in the fitness or food service industries. I admitted that their lack of experience would make it difficult to establish credibility with financiers, especially considering the relatively large amount of money they needed to raise. I encouraged them to think about a scaled down version of the business. Perhaps they might start with a 2,000 ft^2 – 3,000 ft^2 instead of 12,000 ft^2 and hold off on the juice bar until year two or three. Perhaps they could find a partner with direct industry experience. This would be a leaner startup strategy.

As soon as I began to offer a vision that differed from their ambitious dream, I saw their energy deflate. The other mentor vehemently disagreed with my assessment. "You have to go for your dream," he encouraged. "Don't settle for anything less." The mentor offered to help them with their fundraising campaign, and of course, they began to gravitate more toward him. His validation was too attractive and passionate to ignore. I stayed engaged in the discussion for another half hour and offered the candid advice I thought they needed to hear.

As our time finished up, the other mentor and I gave the couple our business cards. As I left the table, I could hear them and the other mentor planning a follow-up meeting. I didn't hear from Alice or husband until five months later when Alice emailed me. She wanted to meet to continue discussing financing options. She had applied for a business loan, but it was denied. The lender recommended they bring in additional private investment or scale down the project.

She didn't mention anything about the other mentor or a crowdfunding campaign. I presume they received similar feedback when they pitched their idea to one of the equity crowdfunding platforms.

The lesson is to watch out for mentors and coaches who only offer validating encouragement. Anyone can pump you full of platitudes like "Go for your dreams!" The paradox of this example is that I cared more about this couple's dream because I presented them with a viable way to reach them. Yes, it was a longer, slower (and leaner) startup option, but that's the path that many of the successful businesses you see have had to take. The other mentor's advice, although pleasant to hear, misdirected them down an unrealistic path. They unfortunately wasted five months of time and effort spinning in place.

Although we need direct feedback to set us straight, we also need praise, especially praise that recognizes our growth mindset. We might not achieve every performance goal we set for ourselves, but if we're working hard toward those goals and learning from missteps, our coaches and mentors should acknowledge our efforts with affirmation. Positive feedback and encouragement reinforce resiliency in an entrepreneur. It lets us know that we're moving in the right direction and motivates us to keep learning.

Summary

Searching for and selecting a business coach or mentor to meet with should be one of the first things you do as you set out on your entrepreneurial journey. A coach/mentor can support you in many ways:

- Opportunity to think more strategically about your business
- Identification of new business opportunities.
- Introduction and access to the contacts and resources in the mentor's network.
- Increased knowledge around marketing, management and finance.
- Development of new skills and adoption of higher-level business techniques and strategies.
- Increased confidence, self-worth and self-efficacy in your entrepreneurial knowledge, skills and abilities.
- Avoidance of common pitfalls.
- Increased focus on attaining goals.
- A sounding board to bounce around ideas and brainstorm.

Use this chapter to find the right mentor for you. Look for alignment of values. Learn about your mentor's experience. Let him or her know how you learn best and the best way to give you feedback.

Focus on establishing trust before jumping into problem solving too soon. Encourage the right set of questions to help establish trust.

Conclusion

We began this book by looking at the *story of self*. If you didn't stop to reflect on your own story as you read through that chapter, I encourage you to do so now. Look at the events of your life that got you to where you are today. Most people start reflecting on the events that made a big impact on them between the ages of 15 and 25, but wherever you are in life, take a moment to find your entrepreneurial origin story. As you write your *story of self*, ask yourself some of the following questions:[39]

1. When was your first exposure to the idea of entrepreneurship? It doesn't have to be a business endeavor in the traditional sense, it could have been that time you participated in fundraising for a school activity or sport. What did you like about that experience? What didn't you like? What did you learn? How does that experience relate to the entrepreneurial journey you're on today?
2. Think of a difficult situation you encountered when you were younger. How did you deal with that challenge? What did you learn from it?
3. Was there a special person in your life that taught you something new (A parent, a grandparent, an aunt, an uncle, a coach, a teacher a friend, etc.)? Was that person there for you during a challenging time? How did they help you? What did you learn?
4. Reflect on a time when you were given a new responsibility that you might not have felt ready for at the time. How did you respond? Did it make you more self-reliant?
5. Remember a time when you worked really hard for something. How was it that you were able to persevere

when you might have wanted to quit instead? Did the hard work pay off? What did you learn from this experience?

Your entrepreneurial journey will often begin with the recognition of a challenge or opportunity followed by an idea about how to solve it. The idea emerges in your mind and you begin to pursue an implementation plan. You initially set off on this quest alone – one person with a grand vision.

The challenge is this journey is new to you and the outcome is unpredictable. That novelty and unpredictability, according to Dr. Sonia Lupien, Director of the Center for Studies on Human Stress, are two prominent drivers that can lead to toxic stress.[304] Higher levels of resiliency are required to cope with the stress of starting a new venture.

Entrepreneurs are more likely to be successful when they've built up resiliency to face the obstacles and adversity that comes with starting a business. It's those entrepreneurs that are more quickly and frequently able to access supportive resources and implement the techniques laid out in this book that will be more resilient.

Be inspired by other people's stories of trial and triumph. Read voraciously about entrepreneurs and business leaders that you admire. Learn vicariously through their experiences. Find a coach or mentor that you can learn from and who can help keep you on track. This should be one of the very first things you do as you embark on your entrepreneurial journey.

When you do find the right mentor, work with them on setting and refining your goals. Ask them to help keep you accountable to your goals. Remember that mastery or learning goals are just as important as performance goals.

Invest in knowing yourself better. What are your guiding values? How do those values affect the vision and mission of the business? Embrace your personality traits, but beware that they might sometimes create blind spots. Also, embrace your strengths and talents and recognize the strengths and talents of your collaborators. As much as possible put yourself in a position where you can work from your strengths. You cannot do everything by yourself. Eventually you will need to delegate. Effective leaders will put people in positions where they can leverage their strengths too. Are you doing this with your team? The Collaboration Canvas is a useful tool to help you better understand yourself and others. Use the canvas when onboarding new collaborators and building teams around new projects.

When financing a new business, remember that there are viable alternatives to traditional lending and venture capital. Bootstrapping has proven to be a worn path for many resilient entrepreneurs as they struggled well in their endeavor. Are there bootstrapping strategies that you can incorporate now? Crowdfunding has emerged as another feasible financing option for aspiring entrepreneurs and small business owners. Bootstrapping and crowdfunding require a lot of patience and hard work. Yet, they put you in the driver's seat. There aren't institutional barriers holding you back. If you put the time and effort into these financing strategies, and adopt the best practices outlined in this book, you will find the funds you need.

Resilient entrepreneurs know how to receive feedback. They passionately seek out critiques that will help them improve their business. Are you actively seeking out feedback on your products and services? Are you consistently receiving coaching, so you can achieve your goals?

These chapters have outlined the methods and mindset you need to be successful. Remember, true failure only happens when you throw in the towel and give up on your dream. The rest of the time, you're learning new knowledge, skills and abilities that will help you reach your goal. If you've read this book and believe that statement to be true, then you've already become more resilient. I will not end this book by wishing you the best of luck in business. Instead, I will wish you the resilience you need to succeed.

Appendix

The Role of Entrepreneurial Development Organizations

"Resilience is something that may be very hard to see, unless you exceed its limits, overwhelm and damage the balancing loops, and the system structure breaks down."

- Donella H. Meadows
Author of Thinking in Systems: A Primer

Entrepreneurial development organizations (EDOs) can utilize the information presented in this book to engage and ignite the latent entrepreneurial spirit in their community. The Global Entrepreneurship Monitor found that approximately 56 percent of people believe they have the necessary knowledge, skills and abilities to start a successful business, but only 16.6 percent have the intention to start a business.[305] This number should be much higher because entrepreneurship is a leading indicator of our country's ingenuity and competitiveness.

We can start to increase interest in entrepreneurship by providing the capacity building resources to help entrepreneurs successfully navigate the difficult startup and growth phases of business. The study of resilience as it relates to entrepreneurship and economic development is important because businesses are started and grown by people with varying motivations, backgrounds, and personalities.

Because resilience is something that can be learned, it's the responsibility of EDOs and academia to ensure that the principles of resilient entrepreneurship are integrated into their curricula and development programs. If you're a business mentor/coach, teacher or economic development policy-maker, you can integrate the ideas and insights from this book into your programs, services and policies. It will help you develop more resilient entrepreneurs so that you can encourage and sustain more entrepreneurship in your community.

Research has shown that nascent entrepreneurs who recognize they have access to supportive resources in their community's economic development ecosystem are more likely to successfully grow their business beyond the startup stage.[300] This is because the resources provided by an entrepreneurial or economic development ecosystem contribute toward resilience. Resilient entrepreneurs are more likely to create new revenue-generating businesses and are thus more likely to create new jobs. Here are some thoughts on policies and programs EDOs can adopt to increase resilience among their community of entrepreneurs:

1. Increase the frequency and variety of entrepreneurial success stories, especially stories among female and minority-owned entrepreneurs.
2. Ensure that resilient goal-setting is an integral part of your capacity building programs and curricula.
3. Support entrepreneurial self-awareness and mastery through education programs. Help entrepreneurs develop new KSAs, and as part of their mastery goals, help them celebrate learning achievements.
4. Incorporate entrepreneurial resilience into your performance measures. Use the Entrepreneurial Resilience Assessment (ERA) described in Chapter 1 to establish a

baseline and measure improvement in resilience as entrepreneurs successfully complete your programs.

5. Instead of offering traditional financial incentives or loans to small businesses, educate them on the value of bootstrapping and crowdfunding their business. Host pitch competitions for nascent entrepreneurs so they can practice their pitch and use the momentum of winning a competition to attract other funding sources.
6. Support entrepreneurial mentorship and coaching programs. A report by U.K Innovation Foundation, NESTA, found that entrepreneurs who receive mentoring show increased job creation and after-tax profits.[276] While a positive mentoring relationship can result in significant benefits, a poor mentoring experience can have a negative effect on a mentee's entrepreneurial intentions, self-efficacy and resilience.[306] For this reason, it's important to provide potential mentors with pre-mentoring training.

   It's best if you allow prospective mentees to choose their own mentors, as opposed to onerously dictating the relationship through your own match-making process. No matter how you structure your match-making method, it's unlikely to outperform mentees selecting mentors for themselves based on their own perceived needs. I recommend only pairing if the mentee asks for a recommendation.

   It's okay to charge a nominal fee to mentees for accessing your mentors. The fee shouldn't be prohibitive but should be enough to give the mentee a feeling of ownership in taking the mentor relationship seriously and working to achieve positive outcomes. If you're worried about a fee being prohibitive for certain low-income entrepreneurs, you can structure a scholarship application and waive the fee for those who are unable to afford it.

Collaboration Canvas Template

Resilience and Disaster Preparedness Strategies

In addition to these recommendations for proactively building resilience at the individual level, there are other broader policies and programs you can put in place to prepare for the worst when disaster strikes.

While writing this book I had the opportunity to visit the Southeastern region of North Carolina. In early October of 2016 Hurricane Matthew hit this region, dumping about 15 inches of rain over a period of two days. 28 people were killed.[307] Beyond the tragic loss of life, the economic impact was estimated at $4.8 billion.[308]

This devastation would be enough to put any area into distress for years. Then, in September of 2018, Hurricane Florence made landfall in the same region, pouring nearly 36 inches of rain in some places.[309] 40 people lost their lives and damage was estimated at $13 billion.[308] While many communities have been hit by disaster, few have had to reel from back-to-back hurricanes with the destructive force of Matthew and Florence.

During my visit, I spoke with about a dozen economic developers throughout the region. One individual told me that he believed he lost approximately 50 percent of the small mom and pop shop businesses in his county. He didn't expect many of them to reopen. Imagine losing 50 percent of the small businesses in your community. How would you respond? Do you think you'd be capable of bouncing back?

I learned a lot during my brief time in North Carolina, but my biggest take-away was the question my counterparts continued to focus on: *what assets do we still have?* Focusing on the strengths of the assets that remain, we encourage a growth mindset throughout the ecosystem. The rate at which you can transition from asking, *what have we lost?* to *what do we still have that we can rebuild from?* is a great indicator of resilience. This is an important question for every economic development ecosystem to answer. What assets do you have that might help small businesses start, grow and get back in business after a disaster? Where is that inventory of resources located? Is it transparent and accessible?

Besides asking what the ecosystem can do to support small businesses, also be willing to ask what small businesses can do to support the community during and after a disaster. In October of 2018 Austin experienced torrential flooding. The flood waters overwhelmed our water treatment capacity and the entire city was on a boil water notice for about a week. During that week some businesses, including several coffee shops, were forced to close their doors because of their limited capacity to boil or otherwise provide potable water.

As local government acted to try and return clean drinking water, our local breweries volunteered to turn their operations into water boiling facilities. Their capacity to boil water at scale was an asset that wasn't identified prior to the flooding. So often we see individuals and businesses reach out to help during a crisis, but we don't know what that capacity to assist looks like. Ecosystems have an opportunity to inventory these assets, so that in times of crisis they can be quickly called upon to help a community in need. When we begin to ask *what resources and strengths do we have*, we open ourselves up to more options and improve our resiliency.

Coach and Mentor Question Guide

Inquiry is the engine that drives a successful coaching or mentoring relationship. Here are some of the go-to questions that I use in my coaching/mentoring sessions. I don't ask them verbatim, but they're good guiding discussion points:

Trust building questions (start here):

1. Before we begin, tell me a bit about your expectations for coaching. Have you worked with a coach before? What do you hope to gain from coaching?
2. Now that I've introduced myself and shared a little bit about my background, what questions do you have about me, or about mentoring/coaching in general?
3. Imagine we're riding together in an elevator. How would you describe your business in the short time it takes before we reach our destination? We'll take time to get into the details of your business, but first I want to capture the big picture.
4. Tell me a bit about your background. Where are you from? What path led you to entrepreneurship?
5. Before we discuss specific challenges or opportunities that you have on the forefront of your mind, first help me better understand the vision you have for your business? What does ultimate success look like for you?

Better Understanding the Challenge or Opportunity:

1. How do you feel things are going with the business? When you think about working toward your vision, what obstacles do you see standing in the way? What might help you achieve your longer-term goals?
2. What research have you conducted on the challenge or opportunity? What feedback have you received from

customers, partners, collaborators, etc.? What have you learned from this research and feedback?

3. What have you already done to address these challenges/opportunities? Which strategies or tactics have worked better than others? Why do you think they worked? Why do you think the others didn't work?
4. What other ways might we solve this challenge or seize this opportunity?

Focusing on Goals and Action Items:

1. Now that I know more about your ultimate dream, what do you need to do now to make that dream a little more of a reality tomorrow?
2. If you were coaching yourself, what focus areas would you tell yourself are most important right now and why?[310]
3. Now that we've identified a strategy going forward, how do you put that strategy into practice? What's one thing you need to do to achieve your goal? What's another thing you need to do? How will doing those things help you make progress?
4. How well do you feel your goals align with your values? Are you pursuing the right things based on what you've identified is important to you?
5. Beyond performance goals, have we also identified relevant mastery goals to help you develop as an entrepreneur? If not, what are some learning goals that can help you grow to become a more effective business owner?
6. Who can help you achieve this goal? Who else can help? How will you connect with these helpful people? Who might be able to make an introduction?
7. What tools or resources do you need to use to achieve your goal? How might you get access to this tool or resource?

8. When will you complete these tasks? Can you commit to completing them by a specific date? How might you hold yourself accountable to these deadlines? How can I help hold you accountable?
9. Looking at the tasks that take up the majority of your time, how well would you say those tasks are aligned with helping you achieve your goals? If they're not well-aligned, what might you do to delegate or simply let go of some of those tasks that are distracting you from progressing toward your goals?

Giving and Receiving Feedback:

1. How do you prefer to receive feedback? Are you familiar with the difference between coaching feedback and validation? Is it okay if I give you coaching feedback that I believe will help you reach your goals?
2. How comfortable are you with me (your coach) challenging your assumptions, some of which might be derived from deeply held beliefs?[310]
3. Who else might give you feedback on this idea, product, service, etc.?
4. How will you solicit feedback? Through a survey, an interview, observation, etc.?
5. Are there anyways you can obtain feedback more quickly and/or less expensively?
6. How might you evaluate the feedback you receive? How might you design an experiment to test different ideas and iterations? How will you conduct the experiment? How might you capture and analyze the data you receive? How can I help in this process?

Questions for a Growing Business:

1. Do you aspire to grow your business? If so, tell me about the reasons leading to your decision to grow the business. What does that growth look like?
2. What concerns do you have about growing your business?
3. What new/additional resources will you need to grow?
4. How might you finance that growth?
5. What processes and standard operating procedures would help you better organize and scale your business?
6. As the founder and chief executive officer of this business, what additional jobs are you doing on top of the duties associated with those job titles? Which duties do you feel are least relevant to your primary role as founder and CEO?
7. What might you delegate to other people so that you can free up more time for you to work on the business, as opposed to working in the business?

Recommended Reading

Introduction – The Story of Self

Brown, Brené. *Rising Strong: How the Ability to Reset Transforms the Way we Live, Love, Parent, and Lead.* Random House. 25 Aug. 2015.

Nadella, Satya. *Hit Refresh: The Quest to Rediscover Microsoft's Soul and Imagine a Better Future for Everyone.* Harper Business. 26 Sept. 2017.

Chapter 1: Entrepreneurship and Resilience

Cuban, Mark. *How to Win at the Sport of Business*. Diversion Books. 21 Nov. 2013.

Thiel, Peter; Masters, Blake. *Zero to One: Notes on Startups, or How to Build the Future.* Random House, LLC. 16 Sep. 2014.

Gaddis, Gay. *Cowgirl Power: How to Kick Ass in Business and Life.* Center Street Publishing. 23 Jan. 2018.

Jay, Meg. *Supernormal: The Untold Story of Adversity and Resilience.* Twelve Publishing. 14 Nov. 2017.

Hirshberg, Meg. For Better or For Work: A Survival Guide for Entrepreneurs and Their Families. An Inc. Original. 4 March. 2012.

Markman, Art. Smart Change: Five Tools to Create New and Sustainable Habits in Yourself and Others. TarcherPerigee Publishing. 7 Jan. 2014.

Greiner, Lori. Invent it, Sell it, Bank it!: Make you Million-Dollar Idea into a Reality. Ballantine Books. 11 March. 2014

Maxwell, John C. Sometimes You Win – Sometimes You Learn: Life's Greatest Lessons Are Gained from Our Losses. Center Street Publishing. 8 Oct. 2013.

Chapter 2: Stories of Entrepreneurial Resilience

Haidt, Jonathan. The Happiness Hypothesis: Finding Modern Truth in Ancient Wisdom. Hachette Book Group. 26 Dec. 2006.

Ricard, Matthieu. Happiness: A Guide to Developing Life's Most Important Skill. Hachette Book Group. 14 Dec. 2008.

Chapter 3: Goal Setting

Dalio, Ray. Principles: Life and Work. Simon & Schuster. 19 Sep. 2017.

Hsieh, Tony. Delivering Happiness: A Path to Profits, Passion and Purpose. Grand Central Publishing. 20 May. 2010.

Oettingen, Gabriele. Rethinking Positive Thinking: Inside the New Science of Motivation. Current Publishing. 16 Oct. 2014.

Holiday, Ryan. The Obstacle is the Way: The Timeless Art of Turning Trials into Triumph. 1 May. 2014.

Danko, William D. The Millionaire Next Door. RosettaBooks. 30 Nov. 2010.

John, Daymond; Paisner, Daniel. Rise and Grind: Outperform, Outwork and Outhustle Your Way to a More Successful and Rewarding Life. Currency Publishing. 23 Jan. 2018.

Doerr, John. Measure What Matters: How Google, Bono, and the Gates Foundation Rock the World with OKRs. Portfolio Publishing. 24 April. 2018.

Dweck, Carol S. Mindset: The New Psychology of Success. Random House. 28 Feb. 2006.

Holiday, Ryan. Ego is the Enemy. Portfolio Publishing. 14 June. 2016.

Gabler, Neal. Walt Disney. Vintage Publishing. 31 Oct. 2006.

Chapter 4: The Authentic Entrepreneur

Eurich, Tasha. Insight: The Surprising Truth About How Others See Us, How We See Ourselves, and Why the Answers Matter More Than We Think. Random House. 2 May. 2017.

Thacker, Karissa. The Art of Authenticity: Tools to Become an Authentic Leader and Your Best Self. Wiley Publishing. 8 Feb. 2016.

Dell, Michael. Direct from Dell: Strategies that Revolutionized an Industry. HarperCollins. 21 Sep. 2010.

Peterson, Kay; Kolb, David A. How You Learn is How You Live: Using Nine Ways of Learning to Transform Your Life. Barrett-Koehler Publishers. 17 April. 2017.

Chapter 5: Funding

John, Daymon; Paisner, Daniel. The Power of Broke: How Empty Pockets, a Tight Budget, and a Hunger for Success Can Become Your Greatest Competitive Advantage. Currency Publishing. 19 Jan. 2016.

Sivers, Derek. Anything You Want: 40 Lessons for a New Kind of Entrepreneur. Portfolio Publishing. 15 Sep. 2015.

Corcoran, Barbara. Shark Tales: How I Turned $1,000 into a Billion Dollar Business. Portfolio Publishing. 9 Feb. 2011.

Gibson, Marcus; Gianforte, Greg. Bootstrapping Your Business: Start and Grow a Successful Company with Almost No Money. CreateSpace. 16 Jan. 2013.

Gallo, Carmine. Talk Like TED: The 9 Public-speaking Secrets of the World's Top Minds. St. Martin's Press. 4 March. 2014.

Chapter 6: Giving and Receiving Feedback

Stone, Douglas; Heen, Sheila. Thanks for the Feedback: The Science and Art of Receiving Feedback Well. 4 March. 2014.

Scott, Kim. Radical Candor: Be a Kick-ass Boss Without Losing Your Humanity. St. Martin's Press. 14 Mar. 2017.

Ries, Eric. The Lean Startup: How Today's Entrepreneurs Use Continuous Innovation to Create Radically Successful Businesses. Currency Publishing. 13 Sep. 2011.

Chapter 7: Coaching and Mentoring

Gawande, Atul. The Checklist Manifesto: How to Get Things Right. Metropolitan Books. 1 April. 2010.

Wooden, John; Yeager, Don. A Game Plan for Life: The Power of Mentoring. Bloomsbury Publishing. 14 Oct. 2009.

Galán, Nely. Self Made: Becoming Empowered, Self-reliant, and Rich in Every Way. Spiegel & Grau Publishing. 31 May. 2016.

Johnson, W. Brad; Ridley, Charles R. The Elements of Mentoring. St. Martin's Press. 2 June. 2015.

Hall, Liz. Mindful Coaching: How Mindfulness can Transform Coaching Practice. Kogan Page Publishing. 3 Apr. 2013.

Green, Charles H; Howe, Andrea P. The Trusted Advisor Fieldbook: A Comprehensive Toolkit for Leading with Trust. Wiley. 22 Nov. 2011.

Brown, Brené. Braving the Wilderness: The Quest for True Belonging and the Courage to Stand Alone. Random House. 12 Sep. 2017.

Patterson, Kerry; Grenny, Joseph; McMillan, Ron; Switzer, Al. Crucial Conversations: Tools for Talking When Stake are High. McGraw-Hill Education. 16 Sep. 2011.

Berger, Warren. A More Beautiful Question: The Power of Inquiry to Spark Breakthrough Ideas. Bloomsbury Publishing. 4 Mar. 2014.

Acknowledgements

My loving wife and editor extraordinaire, Christie. Thank you for the many hours you spent going through this book with a fine-tooth comb. You often had our baby in one arm and this book in the other. You are truly amazing, and I am so grateful for you.

My lifelong friend, Michael Moore. Michael, I especially appreciate your timely and consistent feedback. This book would not have been possible without a trusted friend like you to help keep it progressing.

Dr. Jana Minifie, who helped set me on the path I'm on today. I remember the first time I took her entrepreneurship class as an undergraduate at Texas State University, I was surprised by the candid feedback she gave our team. We were working on a group project and our first deliverable wasn't up to standard. Jana set us straight with some stern direction. I can't say that I was as appreciative of the candor then, but I am so grateful for it today. The higher standards she demanded of me have carried over in what I expect of myself, my colleagues and the clients I coach. Thank you for your guidance and mentorship – you are truly one of the greatest teachers I will ever know.

My dear friend Jason Allen, thank you for your vision and guidance. You helped me see the bigger picture and opened my eyes to new connections among the concepts in this book.

Dr. Miha Vindis. Thank you for taking the time to review my book. I highly value your feedback, and your endorsement means a lot to me. I look forward to reading your first book once it's published.

Maura Newell, Sarah Sharif, Lucas Martin, Natalie Betts, DeAnne Pearson, Daniel Gallagher and Janice Omadeke – thank you for the early feedback and edits as beta readers. You may never truly know how valuable your input was as I stumbled along trying to find the right voice and flow. Thank you all.

To design the book cover, I ran a crowdsourcing contest on 99designs.com. 56 designers from around the world submitted over 500 different design concepts. Thank you to all the designers who participated and working hard making numerous tweaks and iterations.

Notes

[1] Shapero, Albert, and Lisa Sokol. "The social dimensions of entrepreneurship." (1982).

[2] Trapnell, P.D. & Campbell, J.D.. (1999). Private Self-Consciousness and the Five-Factor Model of Personality: Distinguishing Rumination from Reflection. Journal of Personality and Social Psychology. 76. 284-304. 10.1037/0022-3514.76.2.284.

[3] https://www.spanx.com/about-us/

[4] Raz, Guy. Spanx: Sara Blakely. How I Built This. NPR. 12 Sep. 2016. <http://www.npr.org/podcasts/510313/how-i-built-this>

[5] Moalem, Sharon. Inheritance: How Our Genes Change Our Lives – and Our Lives Change Our Genes. Grand Central Publishing. 15 Apr. 2014.

[6] Brown, Brené. Rising Strong: How the Ability to Reset Transforms the Way we Live, Love, Parent, and Lead. Random House. 25 Aug. 2015.

[7] D'Argembeau, A., Cassol, H., Phillips, C., Balteau, E., Salmon, E., & Van der Linden, M. (2014). Brains creating stories of selves: the neural basis of autobiographical reasoning. *Social Cognitive & Affective Neuroscience*, *9*(5), 646-652.

[8] Lilgendahl, J. P., & McAdams, D. P. (2011). Constructing Stories of Self-Growth: How Individual Differences in Patterns of Autobiographical Reasoning Relate to Well-Being in Midlife. *Journal Of Personality*, *79*(2), 391-428.

[9] Nadella, Satya. Hit Refresh: The Quest to Rediscover Microsoft's Soul and Imagine a Better Future for Everyone. Harper Business. 26 Sept. 2017.

[10] Choueke, R. W. E., and R. K. Armstrong. "Management development for the entrepreneur?." *16th Small Business Policy and Research Conference, Nottingham*. 1992.

[11] Janoff-Bulman, R. (2006). Schema-change perspectives on posttraumatic growth. *Handbook of posttraumatic growth: Research and practice*, 81-99.

[12] Miller, D., & Le Breton-Miller, I. (2017, January). Underdog Entrepreneurs: A Model of Challenge-Based Entrepreneurship. *Entrepreneurship: Theory & Practice*. pp. 7-17. doi:10.1111/etap.12253.

[13] Kosoff, Maya. Report: Ousted Tinder Cofounder Settled Her Sexual Harassment Lawsuit Against the Company for 'Just Over $1 Million'. Business Insider. 4 Nov. 2014. < http://www.businessinsider.com/whitney-wolfe-settles-sexual-harassment-tinder-lawsuit-1-million-2014-11>

[14] O'Connor, Clare. Billion-dollar Bumble: How Whitney Wolfe Herd Built America's Fastest-growing Dating App. Forbes Magazine. 12 Dec. 2017 https://www.forbes.com/sites/clareoconnor/2017/11/14/billion-dollar-bumble-how-whitney-wolfe-herd-built-americas-fastest-growing-dating-app/#535f0674248b

[15] Tait, Amelia. Swipe Right for Equality: How Bumble is taking on Sexism. Wired Magazine. 30 Aug. 2017. <http://www.wired.co.uk/article/bumble-whitney-wolfe-sexism-tinder-app>

[16] Garcia, Ahiza. Bumble Founder Created the App after Experiencing Online Harassment. CNN Money. 19 Sep. 2017. <http://money.cnn.com/2017/09/14/technology/business/bumble-whitney-wolfe-fresh-money/index.html>

[17] www.bumble.com

[18] Zipkin, Nina. The Founder of Bumble Reveals How the 'Question of Nine' can help you Stay Focused. Entrepreneur.com Jun. 2017 <https://www.entrepreneur.com/article/295185>

[19] GEM. (n.d.). Percentage of population involved in setting up a new business in North America in 2016, by country. In Statista - The Statistics Portal. Retrieved August 24, 2017, from https://www.statista.com.lsproxy.austincc.edu/statistics/315402/nascent-entrepreneurship-rate-in-north-america/.

[20] Reynolds, PD. *Entrepreneurship in the United States: The Future is Now*. New York. Springer. 2007.

[21] Maxwell, John. C; Wooden, John. Sometimes You Win - - Sometimes you Learn: Life's Greatest Lessons Are Gained from Our Losses. Center Street. 1 Sep. 2015.

[22] Gage, Deborah. "The venture capital secret: 3 out of 4 start-ups fail." *Wall Street Journal* 20 (2012).

[23] CBInsights. Top 20 Reasons Why Startups Fail. https://www.cbinsights.com/reports/The-20-Reasons-Startups-Fail.pdf?utm_campaign=Report%20-%20Content%20Emails&utm_medium=email&_hsenc=p2ANqtz-_UAWhs4peZ1801pJOxPYX6MnCm0A7FO-jTZtpoVeMAY1za7xPTN1NzFFOlaJZ89K9ZNJWHj9xLZr-a__j3r8yNhYZgD9pOjOFplpFa6MgcZYDXCKc&_hsmi=24695183&utm_content=24695183&utm_source=hs_automation&hsCtaTracking=61ab122e-019b-4f59-8699-c9c960ead242%7Cfed300a8-9488-4239-92b3-bb641191e0d0

[24] Holland, Daniel V., and Dean A. Shepherd. "Deciding to persist: Adversity, values, and entrepreneurs' decision policies." *Entrepreneurship Theory and Practice* 37.2 (2013): 331-358.

[25] https://www.entrepreneur.com/slideshow/300234#22

[26] Lee, Jin, et al. "Developing entrepreneurial resilience: implications for human resource development." *European Journal of Training and Development* 41.6 (2017): 519-539.

[27] Bygrave, William D. "The entrepreneurship paradigm (I)." *Entrepreneurship: Critical Perspectives on Business and Management* 3.1 (2002): 415.

[28] Bullough, A., Renko, M., & Myatt, T. (2014). Danger zone entrepreneurs: The importance of resilience and Self-Efficacy for entrepreneurial intentions. *Entrepreneurship Theory and Practice, 38*(3), 473-499. doi:10.1111/etap.12006
[29] Stanley, Thomas J; Danko, William D. The Millionaire Next Door. RosettaBooks. 30 Nov. 2010
[30] Drucker, Peter F. Innovation and Entrepreneurship. Harper Collins. 17 Mar. 2009.
[31] Stone, Brad. The Everything Store: Jeff Bezos and the Age of Amazon. Little, Brown and Company. New York. 2013
[32] Inc. Magazine. The CEO Survey: Turning Entrepreneurial Dreams into Reality. Pg. 64. Sep. 2017.

[33] Barbara-Sanchez, Virginia; Atienza-Sahuquillo, Carlos. Entreprenuerial Motivation and Self-employment: Evidence from Expectancy Theory. Springer. 16 March. 2017. Springerlink.com
[34] McNaughton, Rod B., and Brendan Gray. "Entrepreneurship and resilient communities–introduction to the special issue." *Journal of Enterprising Communities: People and Places in the Global Economy* 11.1 (2017): 2-19.

[35] Corner, Patricia Doyle, Smita Singh, and Kathryn Pavlovich. "Entrepreneurial resilience and venture failure." *International Small Business Journal* 35.6 (2017): 687-708.

[36] Taylor, Shelley E. "Asymmetrical effects of positive and negative events: the mobilization-minimization hypothesis." *Psychological bulletin* 110.1 (1991): 67.
[37] Buang, Nor Aishah. "Entrepreneurs' Resilience Measurement." *Entrepreneurship-Born, Made and Educated*. InTech, 2012.
[38] Moenkemeyer, Gisa, Martin Hoegl, and Matthias Weiss. "Innovator resilience potential: A process perspective of individual resilience as influenced by innovation project termination." *Human Relations* 65.5 (2012): 627-655.
[39] Duchek, Stephanie. "Entrepreneurial resilience: a biographical analysis of successful entrepreneurs." *International Entrepreneurship and Management Journal* (2016): 1-27.
[40] Markman, Gideon D., Robert A. Baron, and David B. Balkin. "Are perseverance and self-efficacy costless? Assessing entrepreneurs' regretful thinking." *Journal of Organizational Behavior* 26.1 (2005): 1-19.
[41] Fisher, Rosemary, Alex Maritz, and Antonio Lobo. "Does individual resilience influence entrepreneurial success?." *Academy of Entrepreneurship Journal* 22.2 (2016): 39.

[42] Logan, Julie. "Dyslexic entrepreneurs: the incidence; their coping strategies and their business skills." *Dyslexia* 15.4 (2009): 328-346.

[43] Shaywitz, Sally. What is Dyslexia? The Yale Center for Dyslexia and Creativity. Yale University. 2017 http://dyslexia.yale.edu/dyslexia/what-is-dyslexia/
[44] Bernard, M. J., & Barbosa, S. D. (2016). Resilience and entrepreneurship: A dynamic and biographical approach to the entrepreneurial act. *M@ n@ gement*, *19*(2), 89.
[45] Charreire-Petit, Sandra, and Julien Cusin. "Whistleblowing et résilience: Analyse d'une trajectoire individuelle." *M@ n@ gement* 16.2 (2013): 142-175.
[46] Fredrickson, Barbara L. "The value of positive emotions." *American scientist* 91.4 (2003): 330-335.
[47] Stixrud, William; Johnson, Ned. The Self-driven Child: The Science and Sense of Giving Your Kids More Control Over Their Lives. Penguin Books. 2018.
[48] http://ppc.sas.upenn.edu/people/martin-ep-seligman

[49] Seligman, Martin E.P. Learned Optimism: How to Change Your Mind and Your Life. Vintage. 3 Jan. 2006.
[50] Brown, Roger, and Sibin Wu. "Does entrepreneurs'optimism pass on to the employees?: the impact of entrepreneurial optimism on employees in small and medium sized businesses." *United States Association for Small Business and Entrepreneurship. Conference Proceedings*. United States Association for Small Business and Entrepreneurship, 2016.
[51] Bandura, Albert. *Self-efficacy: The exercise of control*. Macmillan, 1997.
[52] Gervais, Simon, J. B. Heaton, and Terrance Odean. "Overconfidence, investment policy, and executive stock options." (2003).
[53] Cooper, Arnold C., Carolyn Y. Woo, and William C. Dunkelberg. "Entrepreneurs' perceived chances for success." *Journal of business venturing* 3.2 (1988): 97-108.
[54] Simon, Mark, and John Kim. "Two sources of overconfidence: Incorporating disconfirming feedback in an entrepreneurial context." *Journal of Small Business Strategy* 27.3 (2017): 9-24.
[55] https://www.umflint.edu/som/mark-simon
[56] Hayward, Mathew LA, et al. "Beyond hubris: How highly confident entrepreneurs rebound to venture again." *Journal of Business Venturing* 25.6 (2010): 569-578.
[57] Simon, Mark, and Rodney C. Shrader. "Entrepreneurial actions and optimistic overconfidence: The role of motivated reasoning in new product introductions." *Journal of Business Venturing* 27.3 (2012): 291-309.
[58] Griffin, Dale W., and Carol A. Varey. "Towards a consensus on overconfidence." (1996): 227-231.
[59] Project Implicit. About Us. < https://implicit.harvard.edu/implicit/aboutus.html>
[60] U.S Bureau of Labor Statistics. Women in the Labor Force: A Databook. Report 1049. BLS Reports. May 2014. <https://www.bls.gov/cps/wlf-databook-2013.pdf>

[61] Banaszak, Shannon. Women in the Workforce Before 1900. Oswego State University of New York. Dec 12. 2012. <http://www.oswego.edu/Documents/wac/Dens%27%20Awards,%202013/Banaszak,%20Shannon.pdf>

[62] National Science Foundation. National Center for Science and Engineering Statistics (NCSES). Women, Minorities, and Persons with Disabilities in Science and Engineering. Arlington, VA. NSF 17-310. Jan 2017. <https://nsf.gov/statistics/2017/nsf17310/digest/about-this-report/>

[63] Gupta, Vishal K; Turban, Daniel B; Wasti, S. Arzu; Sikdar, Arijit. "The Role of Gender Stereotypes in Perceptions of Entrepreneurs and Intentions to Become an Entrepreneur". Entrepreneurship Theory and Practice. Page 397-417. Mar 2009.

[64] Rashotte, Lisa S. and Murray Webster, Jr. 2005. "Gender Status Beliefs." Social Science Research. 34: 618-633.

[65] Freeland, Robert E., and Lisa A. Keister. "How does race and ethnicity affect persistence in immature ventures?" *Journal of Small Business Management* 54.1 (2016): 210-228.

[66] Coleman and Robb. "A Comparison of New Firm Financing by Gender: Evidence from the Kauffman Firm Survey".

[67] Miller, C. C. (2017, June 11). Why Don't More Women Start Businesses? *New York Times*, p. 6(L). Retrieved from https://lsproxy.austincc.edu/login?url=http://link.galegroup.com/apps/doc/A495169555/OVIC?u=txshracd2487&xid=06f9eb93

[68] Coleman, Susan; Robb, Alicia. Empowering Equality: 5 Challenges Faced by Women Entreprenuers. Third Way Next. 26 Apr. 2017. <http://www.thirdway.org/report/empowering-equality-5-challenges-faced-by-women-entrepreneurs>

[69] Lugo, Maria V., and Lois Shelton. "The Interface of Ethnicity and Gender in the Resilience of Minority and Women Entrepreneurs." *Academy of Management Proceedings*. Vol. 2017. No. 1. Academy of Management, 2017.

[70] American Express Open. The 2016 State of Women-owned Business Report. Womenable. Apr. 2016. http://www.womenable.com/content/userfiles/2016_State_of_Women-Owned_Businesses_Executive_Report.pdf

[71] https://www.blackline.com/about

[72] http://www.marketwatch.com/investing/Stock/BL

[73] Aspan, Maria. Meet the Woman Who Broke Silicon Valley's Gender Barrier – and Built a $1.5 Billion Tech Company. Inc. Magazine. Sep. 2017. <https://www.inc.com/magazine/201710/maria-aspan/blackline-therese-tucker.html>

[74] Bort, Julie. This 55-year-old Woman Made History and $140 Million by Taking Her Tech Company Public on Friday. 28 Oct. 2016. < http://www.businessinsider.com/blackline-therese-tucker-makes-history-millions-ipo-2016-10>

[75] Burns, Hilary. How Hiring Impatient – Even Crazy – Employees Helped this Business Gain 900 Clients. 28 Aug. 2014. BizWomen – The Business Journals. <https://www.bizjournals.com/bizwomen/news/profiles-strategies/2014/08/when-nobody-in-their-right-mind-is-just-what-you.html?page=all>
[76] Mitra, Sramana. 257th 1Mby1M Entrepreneurship Podcast with Therese Tucker, BlackLine. One Million by One Million Blog. 8 Jun. 2017. <http://www.sramanamitra.com/2017/06/08/257th-1mby1m-entrepreneurship-podcast-with-therese-tucker-blackline/>
[77] St. Jean, Etienne; Audet, Josee. "The Role of Mentoring in the Learning Development of the Novice Entrepreneur". International Entrepreneurship and Management Journal. 8 (1). Pages 119-140. 2012

[78] Canal, Emily. Rising and Grinding with Daymond John: The Entrepreneur and TV Star Explains the Value of Goals and Grit – and Shark Tank Idiots. Inc. Magazine. Pgs. 24-28. March. 2018.
[79] Cuban, Mark. How to Win at the Sport of Business. Diversion Books. 21 Nov. 2013.
[80] Kantor, Jodi; Streitfeld, David. Inside Amazon: Wrestling Big Ideas in a Bruising Workplace. The New York Times. Aug. 15. 2015. <https://www.nytimes.com/2015/08/16/technology/inside-amazon-wrestling-big-ideas-in-a-bruising-workplace.html>
[81] Thiel, Peter; Masters, Blake. Zero to One: Notes on Startups, or How to Build the Future. Random House, LLC. 16 Sep. 2014.
[82]https://factfinder.census.gov/faces/tableservices/jsf/pages/productview.xhtml?src=bkmk
[83] Cardon, Melissa S., and Pankaj C. Patel. "Is stress worth it? Stress-related health and wealth trade-offs for entrepreneurs." *Applied Psychology* 64.2 (2015): 379-420.
[84] Jekot, Hunger. Alumna Runs Successful Austin-based Advertising Firm. The Daily Texan. 5 Nov. 2014. http://www.dailytexanonline.com/2014/11/04/alumna-runs-successful-austin-based-advertising-firm
[85] Gaddis, Gay. Cowgirl Power: How to Kick Ass in Business and Life. Center Street Publishing. 23 Jan. 2018.
[86] Seppala, Emma. "How meditation benefits CEOs." *Harvard Business Review* (2015).
[87] Baer, Ruth A. "Mindfulness training as a clinical intervention: A conceptual and empirical review." *Clinical psychology: Science and practice* 10.2 (2003): 125-143.
[88] Torres, Nicole. Mindfulness Mitigates Biases You May Not Know You Have. Harvard Business Review. 24 Dec. 2014.
[89] Hougaard, Rasmus; Carter, Jacqueline; Dybkjaer, Gitte. Spending 10 minutes a Day on Mindfulness Subtly Changes the Way You React to Everything. Harvard Business Review. 18 Jan. 2017.

[90] Passmore, Jonathan. "Mindfulness in Coaching: A Model for Coaching Practice." *Coaching Psychologist*, vol. 13, no. 1, June 2017, pp. 27-30. EBSCO*host*, lsproxy.austincc.edu/login?url=http://search.ebscohost.com.lsproxy.austincc.edu/login.aspx?direct=true&db=pbh&AN=123686423&site=eds-live&scope=site.
[91] Garrison, Laura Turner. A Man and His Monster. Fast Company Magazine. May 2012. Pgs 44-46.
[92] Gardner, Jasmine. Moshi Masters: Mind Candy Bosses Michael Acton Smith and Divinia Knowles Talk Futures, Floating and Families. Evening Standard. 13 Aug. 2014. https://www.standard.co.uk/lifestyle/london-life/moshi-masters-mind-candy-bosses-michael-acton-smith-and-divinia-knowles-talk-futures-floating-and-9665848.html

[93] Tucker, Ian. Michael Acton Smith: 'We Want to Show Meditation is Common Sense'. The Guardian. 8 Oct. 2017. https://www.theguardian.com/technology/2017/oct/08/michael-acton-smith-meditation-common-sense-moshi-monsters-calm-app
[94] Levy, Ari. This Meditation App is Now Worth $250 million and has Trump-related Stress to Thank. CNBC. 26 Mar. 2018. https://www.cnbc.com/2018/03/26/calm-raising-over-25-million-from-insight-at-250-million-valuation.html
[95] Jay, Meg. Supernormal: The Untold Story of Adversity and Resilience. Twelve Publishing. 14 Nov. 2017.
[96] Rosales, Rocio. "Survival, economic mobility and community among Los Angeles fruit vendors." *Journal of Ethnic and Migration Studies* 39.5 (2013): 697-717.
[97] Kuhn, Kristine M., and Tera L. Galloway. "With a little help from my competitors: Peer networking among artisan entrepreneurs." *Entrepreneurship Theory and Practice* 39.3 (2015): 571-600.
[98] Yang, Yunxi; Danes, Sharon. M. Resiliency and Resilience Process of Entrepreneurs in New Venture Creation. Entrepreneurship Research Journal. 2015.
[99] Inc. Magazine. The CEO Survey: Turning Entrepreneurial Dreams into Reality. Pg. 40. Sep. 2017

[100] Dr. Henry Jones has a Ph.D. in Aeronautics and Astronautics from Stanford University. He is a co-founder at Kopis Mobile, which made Inc. Magazine's 2017 list of the 500 fastest growing companies in the United States. He also teaches at the University of Southern Mississippi where is research interests include advanced security techniques for the Internet of Things and rapid development of integrated hardware, firmware and software Products.

1. **What have been the most difficult challenges for Kopis Mobile and how have you and your team overcome those challenges?**

The biggest challenge was company cash flow and salaries for founders. We almost needed to be working another job while were launching this new business. We were working at a company that imploded and that was the instigation that led to the formation of this company. I went completely without pay the first year and that was a financial hardship. That financial insecurity is difficult for a spouse that isn't familiar with entrepreneurship. Going to work at a job all day and not get paid doesn't make sense to some people.

I bought a book by Meg Hershberg on spouses of entrepreneurs and tried to discuss some of the content, but it didn't work. I could have got my spouse more involved from the beginning.

2. **Have any support networks, community resources, economic development programs/services helped along the way?**

The State of Mississippi has Grow MS and helps grow small businesses with a collection of angel investors throughout the state. We only have a population of 2 million total and we're all spread out. They created an angel network and organized pitch meeting and competitions. They helped with vetting before. We raised a little over $1 million in seed funding from this angel network.

In addition, our congressional delegation has been very helpful in opening some doors into our market with the department of defense. They help make connections with the Department of Defense. We partnered with the University of Southern Mississippi to help commercialize our technology.

3. **How do you achieve a work-life balance with a fast-growing company?**

I think the key to work life balance is having really good partners to begin with. This way you can rely on your partners when you need to focus on family. I trust my partners and we help each other out when we need to focus on family. There are higher costs associated with partners, but it resulted in a much healthier situation for all of us.

We started out with 5 founders and had to let one go because they weren't trustworthy. I had to fire a co-founder in a different company before. You're not always going to get it right when it comes to partnerships – structure the paperwork to account for these scenarios. Take the relationship cultivation seriously because you're basically creating a baby with these people. The business is its own entity, just like a child. You have to be willing to be vulnerable, be committed to one another and fight for one another. Looking into our personal network was key.

The last piece of advice is the rule of three – if you don't know at least 3 people who wake up thinking they want to get their hands on your product/service, you're not ready to start a business. It's really easy to love your own ideas, but you need to identify 3 specific people at least who also love your idea to get it started.

4. What advice would you give to a nascent entrepreneur about work-life balance?

I advise other companies to get their spouses on board from the beginning.

[101] Hirshberg, Meg. For Better or for Work: A Survival Guide for Entrepreneurs and Their Families. An Inc. Original. 4 Mar. 2012.
[102] Vannucci, Marla J., and Sharon M. Weinstein. "The nurse entrepreneur&58; empowerment needs, challenges, and self-care practices." *Nursing &58; Research and Reviews* 55.1 (2016): 57-66.
[103] USA Today. "Most Expensive Natural Disasters in The United States as of September 2017 (in Billion U.S. Dollars)." Statista - The Statistics Portal, Statista, www.statista.com/statistics/744015/most-expensive-natural-disasters-usa/, Accessed 19 Dec 2017

[104] Tales from the Memorial Day flood: Readers relive the danger, loss and heroism of 30 years ago. Austin American Statesman. 28 May. 2011. < http://www.statesman.com/news/local/tales-from-the-memorial-day-flood-readers-relive-the-danger-loss-and-heroism-years-ago/fon8Y0HVwOVRUaAucOpdqK/>

[105] Michelle Breyer, R. (1998, Oct 20). Lamar stores take a chance, - Store owners in flood plain gamble between high traffic and high water. *Austin American-Statesman (TX)*, p. D1.. Retrieved from http://infoweb.newsbank.com/resources/doc/nb/news/0EA0777BB1F58ABE?p=NewsBank
[106] Raz, Guy. Whole Foods Market: John Mackey. How I Built This. NPR. 15 May. 2017.
<http://www.npr.org/series/490248027/how-i-built-this>
[107] Dinges and Claudia Grisales, G. (2015, May 27). Waterlogged N. Lamar merchants dig in, clean up, say they're staying. *Austin American-Statesman (TX)*, p. A1.. Retrieved from http://infoweb.newsbank.com/resources/doc/nb/news/1559843F9C924CF0?p=NewsBank
[108] Stevens, Laura; Gasparra, Annie. Amazon to Buy Whole Foods for $13.7 Billion. Wall Street Journal. 16 June. 2017.
<https://www.wsj.com/articles/amazon-to-buy-whole-foods-for-13-7-billion-1497618446>
[109] Hoffman, K. (2014, Sep 2). Commentary - 'Mattress Mack' slows down, but still works harder than most. *Houston Chronicle (TX)*, p. 1.. Retrieved from http://infoweb.newsbank.com/resources/doc/nb/news/1501EE34DFEB6AD0?p=NewsBank
[110] Larry A. Weinrauch, MD, Assistant Professor of Medicine, Harvard Medical School, Cardiovascular Disease and Clinical Outcomes Research, Watertown,

MA. Review provided by VeriMed Healthcare Network. Also reviewed by David Zieve, MD, MHA, Isla Ogilvie, PhD, and the A.D.A.M. Editorial team.
[111] Zucker, Shaina. Heart Condition Puts 'Mattress Mack' Back in the Hospital. Houston Business Journal. 27 Sep. 2013.
[112] Hall, Christine. Face to Face with...Jim "Mattress Mack" Mclngvale. Houston Business Journal. 26 Apr. 2009.
<https://www.austinlibrary.com:2373/houston/stories/2009/04/27/story14.html>
[113] 'Mattress Mack' Ready to Rebuild. Houston Business Journal. 5 Jun. 2009.
[114] STEFFY, L. (2006, Nov 10). Mattress Mack: One man, one store, one of a kind. *Houston Chronicle (TX)*, p. 1.. Retrieved from
http://infoweb.newsbank.com/resources/doc/nb/news/1155499F0FC18220?p=NewsBank
[115] Rogers, Brian. Gallery Fire Suspect Likely to Never Face Trial. Houston Chronicle. 13 March. 2013. http://www.chron.com/news/houston-texas/houston/article/Gallery-fire-suspect-likely-to-never-face-trial-4351976.php
[116] CLAUDIA FELDMAN, B. (2010, May 23). A boy who gives this time receives Civic spirit touches even life of Mattress Mack DONATE: Young man selected as Jefferson Award winner. *Houston Chronicle (TX)*, p. 1.. Retrieved from
http://infoweb.newsbank.com/resources/doc/nb/news/12FF1B90C5B62C68?p=NewsBank
[117] Pulsinelli, Olivia. Mattress Mack to Receive Award from Bush Family. Houston Business Journal. 23 Dec. 2013.
[118] McCarthy, Kelly. Petition to Honor Houston's 'Mattress Mack' Gets Support. ABC News. 1 Sep. 2017. < http://abcnews.go.com/US/petition-honor-mattress-store-owner-opened-doors-harvey/story?id=49565176>
[119] Strunk, Delaney. A Furniture Store Owner Opened His Shops to Flood Victims and Hundreds Poured In. BuzzFeed. 29 Aug. 2017.
<https://www.buzzfeed.com/delaneystrunk/houstons-mattress-mack-opens-furniture-store-to-house?utm_term=.fgLJx3Wg9p#.tegVY5EOMk>
[120] Summer, J. (2016, Nov 23). 'Mattress Mack' touts the importance of small businesses at Kingwood luncheon. *Houston Chronicle (TX)*, p. A003.. Retrieved from
http://infoweb.newsbank.com/resources/doc/nb/news/160FF4FF1B51C258?p=NewsBank
[121] Sammond, Mike; Krumins, Tiffany. Tiffany Krumins Show: 2018 Kickoff Show. 3 Feb. 2018. http://businessradiox.com/podcast/tiffany-krumins-show/tiffany-krumins-show-19/
[122] Chun, Janean. Tiffany Krumins, AVA the Elephant: The Shocking News She Got After 'Shark Tank". Huffington Post. 12 Mar. 2012.
https://www.huffingtonpost.com/2012/03/12/tiffany-krumins-ava-the-elephant_n_1327716.html

[123] Chapman, Samantha; Genet, Danielle; Valiente, Alexa. 'Shark Tank': Where Are They Now. ABC News. 2 May. 2014. http://abcnews.go.com/Entertainment/shark-tank-now/story?id=23421719#2
[124] https://www.tiffanykrumins.com/about
[125] Seale, Shelly. Building Blocks: Stitch Texas Co-founder Vesta Garcia talks about the business of growing a business. Austin Woman Magazine. 28 Feb. 2017. https://issuu.com/austinwoman/docs/aw_mar_2017
[126] http://www.alsa.org/about-als/facts-you-should-know.html
[127] DeCarlo, Jonathan. Women's, Girls' and Infants' Apparel Manufacturing in the U.S. IBIS World. Dec. 2017
[128] Greene, Francis J., and Christian Hopp. "Are Formal Planners More Likely To Achieve New Venture Viability? A Counterfactual Model And Analysis." *Strategic Entrepreneurship Journal* 11.1 (2017): 36-60.
[129] Locke, Edwin A., and Gary P. Latham. "Building a practically useful theory of goal setting and task motivation: A 35-year odyssey." *American psychologist* 57.9 (2002): 705.

[130] Boyd, Brian K. "Strategic planning and financial performance: a meta-analytic review." *Journal of management studies* 28.4 (1991): 353-374.
[131] Hsieh, Tony. Delivering Happiness: A Path to Profits, Passion and Purpose. Grand Central Publishing. 2010.
[132] Oettingen, Gabriele. Rethinking Positive Thinking: Inside the New Science of Motivation. Current. 16 Oct. 2014.
[133] Curry, L. A., Snyder, C. R., Cook, D. L., Ruby, B. C., & Rehm, M. (1997). Role of hope in academic and sport achievement. *Journal of Personality and Social Psychology, 73*(6), 1257-1267. http://dx.doi.org/10.1037/0022-3514.73.6.1257

[134] http://psych.nyu.edu/oettingen/index.html
[135] Csikszentmihalyi, Mihaly. *Flow and the psychology of discovery and invention*. New York: Harper Collins, 1996.
[136] Tikkamäki, Kati, Päivi Heikkilä, and Mari Ainasoja. "Positive stress and reflective practice among entrepreneurs." *Journal of Entrepreneurship, Management and Innovation (JEMI)* 12.1 New Topics in Entrepreneurship and Innovations Management (2016): 35-56.
[137] Holiday, Ryan. The Obstacle is the Way: The Timeless Art of Turning Trials into Triumph. Portfolio. 1 May. 2014.
[138] Markman, Art. Smart Change: Five Tools to Create New and Sustainable Habits in Yourself and Others. TarcherPerigee Publishing. 6 Jan. 2015.
[139] Halvorson, Heidi Grant. Succeed: How We Can Reach Our Goals. Plume. Page 26. 23 Dec. 2010.
[140] Burka, J., & Yuen, L. (2008). Procrastination. Cambridge, MA.: Da Capo Press.

[141] Van Gelder, J.-L., de Vries, R. E., Frese, M., & Goutbeek, J.-P. (2007). Differences in psychological strategies of failed and operational business owners in the Fiji Islands. Journal of Small Business Management, 45(3), 388.
[142] Farooqi, Rahela and Amaara Rehmaan. "A Comparison of Loyalty Programs of Two Lifestyle Retail Stores Using the Net-Promoter Score Method." *Pranjana: The Journal of Management Awareness*, vol. 13, no. 2, Jul-Dec2010, pp. 38-46. EBSCO*host*. lsproxy.austincc.edu/login?url=http://search.ebscohost.com.lsproxy.austincc.edu/login.aspx?direct=true&db=bth&AN=60949322&site=eds-live&scope=site.
[143] Hechavarria, Diana M; Renko, Maija; Matthews, Charles. The Nascent Entrepreneurship Hub: Goals, Entrepreneurial Self-efficacy and Startup Outcomes. Springer Science + Business Media, LLC. 14 Aug. 2011.
[144] Zhao, Haifeng, and Sibin Wu. "The Power of Motivation–Goal Fit in Predicting Entrepreneurial Persistence." *Social Behavior and Personality: an international journal* 42.8 (2014): 1345-1352.

[145] Aarts, Henk; Chartrand, T.L; Custers, R; Danner, U; Dik, G; Jefferis, V; Cheng, C.M. Automatic Goal Adoption and Social Stereotypes. 2003.
[146] Pink, Daniel. When: The Scientific Secrets of Perfect Timing. Riverhead Books. 9 Jan. 2018.
[147] https://www.entrepreneur.com/slideshow/300234#28
[148] Simons, Joke, Siegfried Dewitte, and Willy Lens. "The role of different types of instrumentality in motivation, study strategies, and performance: Know why you learn, so you'll know what you learn!." *British Journal of Educational Psychology* 74.3 (2004): 343-360.
[149] Harackiewicz, Judith M., and Andrew J. Elliot. "Achievement goals and intrinsic motivation." *Journal of personality and social psychology* 65.5 (1993): 904.
[150] Lamine, Wadid, Sarfraz Mian, and Alain Fayolle. "How do social skills enable nascent entrepreneurs to enact perseverance strategies in the face of challenges? A comparative case study of success and failure." *International Journal of Entrepreneurial Behavior & Research* 20.6 (2014): 517-541
[151] https://arubaaloe.com/pages/our-story
[152] Serra, Karen Lizzette Orengo. "Perseverance Practices in Small and Medium Enterprises: An Entrepreneurial Perspective for Business Growth and Internationalization." *Neumann Business Review* 3.1 (2017): 96-120.
[153] Gabler, Neal. Walt Disney: The Triumph of the American Imagination. Vintage. 9 Oct. 2007
[154] Dweck, Carol. Mindset: The New Psychology of Success. Random House Publishing. 28 Feb. 2006
[155] Cerasoli, Christopher P., and Michael T. Ford. "Intrinsic motivation, performance, and the mediating role of mastery goal orientation: A test of self-determination theory." *The Journal of psychology* 148.3 (2014): 267-286.

[156] Keith, Nina, et al. "Informal learning and entrepreneurial success: a longitudinal study of deliberate practice among small business owners." *Applied Psychology* 65.3 (2016): 515-540.
[157] Stambaugh, Jeff, and Ronald Mitchell. "The fight is the coach: creating expertise during the fight to avoid entrepreneurial failure." *International Journal of Entrepreneurial Behavior & Research* (2017).

[158] Renko, Maija and Freeman, Michael J., How Motivation Matters: Conceptual Alignment of Individual and Opportunity As a Predictor of Starting Up (July 13, 2017). Journal of Business Venturing Insights, Volume 8, November 2017, Pages 56-63. Available at SSRN: https://ssrn.com/abstract=3002041

[159] Thomsen, D. K., Tønnesvang, J., Schnieber, A., & Olesen, M. H. (2011). Do people ruminate because they haven't digested their goals? The relations of rumination and reflection to goal internalization and ambivalence. *Motivation and Emotion*, *35*(2), 105-117.
[160] Lazarus, Richard S. "Psychological stress and the coping process." (1966).
[161] http://www.paultrapnell.com/
[162] Przepiorka, A. M. (2017). Psychological determinants of entrepreneurial success and life-satisfaction. *Current Psychology, 36*(2), 304. doi:10.1007/s12144-016-9419-1
[163] Grote, Dick. 3 Popular Goal-setting Techniques Managers Should Avoid. Harvard Business Review. 2 Jan. 2017.
[164] Aarts, Henk; Gollwitzer, Peter M. Goal; Hassin, Ran R. Contation: Perceiving is for Pursuing. Journal of Personality and Social Psychology. Volume 87. 1. Pp. 23-37. 2004 <https://pdfs.semanticscholar.org/47cd/75cb6b1765c736d44e73d296e30516aa9818.pdf>
[165] Chris Loersch, Henk Aarts, B. Keith Payne, Valerie E. Jefferis, The influence of social groups on goal contagion, In Journal of Experimental Social Psychology, Volume 44, Issue 6, 2008, Pages 1555-1558, ISSN 0022-1031, https://doi.org/10.1016/j.jesp.2008.07.009. (http://www.sciencedirect.com/science/article/pii/S0022103108001170)
[166] Manzano-García, Guadalupe, and Juan Carlos Ayala Calvo. "Psychometric properties of Connor-Davidson Resilience Scale in a Spanish sample of entrepreneurs." *Psicothema* 25.2 (2013).
[167] Seligman, Martin EP. *Authentic happiness: Using the new positive psychology to realize your potential for lasting fulfillment*. Simon and Schuster, 2004.

[168] Dalio, Ray. Principles: Life and Work. Simon and Schuster. 19 Sep. 2017.
[169] Jensen, Susan M. and Fred Luthans. "Relationship between Entrepreneurs' Psychological Capital and Their Authentic Leadership. (Undetermined)."

Journal of Managerial Issues, vol. 18, no. 2, 15 July 2006, pp. 254-273. EBSCO*host*, www.austinlibrary.com:8443/login?url=https://search.ebscohost.com/login.aspx?direct=true&db=bft&AN=510613605&site=ehost-live&scope=site.

[170] Hmieleski, Keith M., Michael S. Cole, and Robert A. Baron. "Shared authentic leadership and new venture performance." *Journal of Management* 38.5 (2012): 1476-1499.

[171] Kruse, Kevin. The 80/20 Rule and How it Can Change Your Life. Forbes. 7 Mar. 2016. https://www.forbes.com/sites/kevinkruse/2016/03/07/80-20-rule/#38e84aa33814

[172] Herjavec, Robert. You Don't Have to Be a Shark: Creating Your Own Success. St. Martin's Press. 17 May. 2016.

[173] Cho, Young Sik, and Joo Y. Jung. "The relationship between metacognition, entrepreneurial orientation, and firm performance: an empirical investigation." *Academy of Entrepreneurship Journal* 20.2 (2014): 71.

[174] Eurich, Tasha. Insight: How Small Gains in Self-Awareness Can Help You Win Big at Work and in Life. Random House. 02 May. 2017.

[175] Murphy, Mark. The Dunning-Kruger Effect Shows Why Some People Think They're Great Even When Their Work is Terrible. Forbes. 24, Jan. 2017. https://www.forbes.com/sites/markmurphy/2017/01/24/the-dunning-kruger-effect-shows-why-some-people-think-theyre-great-even-when-their-work-is-terrible/#18cbdf685d7c

[176] S. Howard, Christopher, and Justin A. Irving. "The impact of obstacles defined by developmental antecedents on resilience in leadership formation." *Management Research Review* 37.5 (2014): 466-478.

[177] Cooper, Arnold C., and Kendall W. Artz. "Determinants of satisfaction for entrepreneurs." *Journal of Business Venturing* 10.6 (1995): 439-457.

[178] George, Bill, et al. "Discovering your authentic leadership." *Harvard business review* 85.2 (2007): 129.

[179] Srivastava, S. *2018. Measuring the Big Five Personality Factors.* University of Oregon. Accessed *25 Jun. 2018.* http://psdlab.uoregon.edu/bigfive.html.

[180] Grant, Adam. Goodbye to the MBTI, the Fad That Won't Die. Psychology Today. 18 Sep. 2013. https://www.psychologytoday.com/us/blog/give-and-take/201309/goodbye-mbti-the-fad-won-t-die

[181] Pappas, Stephanie. Personality Traits and Personality Types: What is Personality? Live Science. 7 Sep. 2017. https://www.livescience.com/41313-personality-traits.html

[182] Baer, Drake. This Personality Trait Predicts Success. Business Insider. 30 Apr. 2014. http://www.businessinsider.com/conscientiousness-predicts-success-2014-4

[183] Obschonka, Martin, Christian Fisch, and Ryan Boyd. "Using digital footprints in entrepreneurship research: A Twitter-based personality analysis of superstar entrepreneurs and managers." *Journal of Business Venturing Insights* 8 (2017): 13-23.

[184] Lebowitz, Shana. Scientists say your personality can be deconstructed into 5 basic traits. Business Insider. 27 Dec. 2016. http://www.businessinsider.com/big-five-personality-traits-2016-12

[185] Zhao, Hao, Scott E. Seibert, and G. Thomas Lumpkin. "The relationship of personality to entrepreneurial intentions and performance: A meta-analytic review." *Journal of management* 36.2 (2010): 381-40.

[186] Baer, Drake. Malcolm Gladwell Says IKEA Built a Multibillion-Dollar Brand Because Its Founder Had this Disagreeable Personality Trait. Business Insider. 14 Oct. 2014. http://www.businessinsider.com/malcolm-gladwell-on-ikea-founder-personality-trait-2014-10

[187] Shontell, Alyson. Why 'Arrogant Jerks' Become Rich and Successful in Silicon Valley. Business Insider. 22 Nov. 2014. http://www.businessinsider.com/asshole-ceos-startup-founders-and-success-2014-11

[188] Schultz, Howard; Gordon, Joanne. Onward: How Starbucks Fought for Its Life without Losing Its Soul. Rodale Books. 27 Mar. 2012.

[189] https://www.ancestry.com/corporate/about-ancestry/company-facts

[190] Heifetz, Justin. "Ancestry.Com Co-Founder's Lessons in Entrepreneurship." *Gallup Business Journal*, Oct. 2014, p. 1. EBSCO*host*, www.austinlibrary.com:8443/login?url=https://search.ebscohost.com/login.aspx?direct=true&db=bth&AN=99659066&site=ehost-live&scope=site.

[191] Bates, Daniel. From Selling Floppy Disks from Their Car to Record Breaking Website: Ancestry.com Agrees to $1.6 Billion Buyout, Making Multi-millionaires of its Execs. DailyMail.com. 22 Oct. 2012. http://www.dailymail.co.uk/news/article-2221451/Ancestry-com-agrees-1-6-billion-buyout-making-multi-millionaires-execs.html

[192] https://www.gallupstrengthscenter.com/home/en-us/cliftonstrengths-themes-domains

[193] The Team Coaching Zone. Episode #074: Paul Allen: Coaching the Hidden Potential of Individuals and Teams. http://www.teamcoachingzone.com/paul-allen/

[194] https://www.linkedin.com/in/paulballen/

[195] DeLeon, Mariah. What Really Happens When You Hire the Wrong Candidate? 9 Apr. 2015. Entrepreneur.com. https://www.entrepreneur.com/article/244730

[196] Pettigrew, Ian. "Bounce Back! Coaching Resilience Through Strengths. Gallup. 7 Apr. 2014. http://coaching.gallup.com/2014/04/bounce-back-coaching-resilience-through.html

[197] Badal, Sangeeta Bharadwaj; Ott, Bryant. Delegating: A Huge Management Challenge for Entrepreneurs. Gallup. 14 Apr. 2015. http://news.gallup.com/businessjournal/182414/delegating-huge-management-challenge-entrepreneurs.aspx?g_source=&g_medium=&g_campaign=tiles

[198] Gemmell, Robert M. "Learning styles of entrepreneurs in knowledge-intensive industries." *International Journal of Entrepreneurial Behavior & Research* 23.3 (2017): 446-464.

[199] Peterson, Kay; Kolb, David. A. How You Learn is How You Live: Using Nine Ways of Learning to Transform Your Life. Berrett-Koehler Publishers. 17 Apr. 2017.

[200] https://www.bridgewater.com/

[201] Sivers, Derek. Anything you want: 40 Lessons for a New Kind of Entrepreneur. Portfolio. 15 Sep. 2015.

[202] Corcoran, Barbara; Littlefield, Bruce. Shark Tales: How I Turned $1,000 into a Billion Dollar Business. Penguin Group. 9 Feb. 2011.

[203] Elkins, Kathleen. Barbara Corcoran worked 22 jobs before age 23 – here's the one she learned most from. CNBC Money. 26 March. 2018. https://www.cnbc.com/2018/03/26/barbara-corcoran-says-waiting-tables-teaches-you-to-succeed.html

[204] Dell, Michael; Fredman, Catherine. Direct from Dell: Strategies that Revolutionized an Industry. HarperCollins e-books. 21 Sep. 2010.

[205] Ries, Eric. The Startup Way: How Modern Companies Use Entrepreneurial Management to Transform Culture and Drive Long-term Growth. Currency. 17 Oct. 2017

[206] Griswold, Alison; Love, Dylan. 17 Business Titans Who Overcame Dyslexia. Business Insider. 25 Oct. 2013. http://www.businessinsider.com/business-titans-who-overcame-dyslexia-2013-10

[207] Blanchflower, David G., Phillip B. Levine, and David J. Zimmerman. "Discrimination in the small-business credit market." *The Review of Economics and Statistics* 85.4 (2003): 930-943.

[208] Parker, Simon C., and Yacine Belghitar. "What happens to nascent entrepreneurs? An econometric analysis of the PSED." *Small Business Economics* 27.1 (2006): 81-101.

[209] Bryant Howroyd, Janice. Forbes Profile. 05 May. 2017. https://www.forbes.com/profile/janice-bryant-howroyd/

[210] Gibson, Marcus; Gianforte, Greg. Bootstrapping Your Business: Start and Grow a Successful Company with Almost No Money. CreateSpace. 16 Jan. 2013.

[211] Malmström, Malin. "Typologies of bootstrap financing behavior in small ventures." *Venture Capital* 16.1 (2014): 27-50.

[212] Staw, Barry M. "The escalation of commitment to a course of action." *Academy of management Review* 6.4 (1981): 577-587.

[213] VERMEULEN, FREEK and NIRO SIVANATHAN. "Stop Doubling Down on Your Failing Strategy: How to Spot (And Escape) One Before It's Too Late." *Harvard Business Review*, vol. 95, no. 6, Nov/Dec2017, pp. 110-117. EBSCO*host*, lsproxy.austincc.edu/login?url=http://search.ebscohost.com.lsproxy.austincc.edu/login.aspx?direct=true&db=bth&AN=125760157&site=eds-live&scope=site.

[214] Roche, Maree, Jarrod M. Haar, and Fred Luthans. "The role of mindfulness and psychological capital on the well-being of leaders." *Journal of occupational health psychology* 19.4 (2014): 476.

[215] Hafenbrack, Andrew C., Zoe Kinias, and Sigal G. Barsade. "Debiasing the mind through meditation: Mindfulness and the sunk-cost bias." *Psychological Science* 25.2 (2014): 369-376.

[216] Ricard, Matthieu; Goleman, Daniel. Happiness: A Guide to Developing Life's Most Important Skill. Little, Brown and Company Publishing. 14 Dec. 2008.

[217] Klein, Gary. Performing a Project Premortem. Harvard Business Review. Sep. 2007 https://hbr.org/2007/09/performing-a-project-premortem

[218] Kaikati, Andrew M., and Jack G. Kaikati. "Doing business without exchanging money: The scale and creativity of modern barter." *California management review* 55.2 (2013): 46-71.

[219] "Entrepreneurs Say Managing Through Recession Makes them Sharper Business Owners." American Express Open Small Business Monitor. 15 April. 2009.

[220] Fleming, Lee, and Olav Sorenson. "Financing by and for the Masses: An Introduction to the Special Issue on Crowdfunding." *California Management Review* 58.2 (2016): 5-19.

[221] Mollick, Ethan, and Alicia Robb. "Democratizing innovation and capital access: The role of crowdfunding." *California management review* 58.2 (2016): 72-87.

[222] Cantwell, Maria. 21st Century Barriers to Women's Entrepreneurship. 23 July. 2014. Majority Report of the U.S Senate Committee on Small Business and Entrepreneurship. https://www.sbc.senate.gov/public/_cache/files/3/f/3f954386-f16b-48d2-86ad-698a75e33cc4/F74C2CA266014842F8A3D86C3AB619BA.21st-century-barriers-to-women-s-entrepreneurship-revised-ed.-v.1.pdf

[223] Younkin, Peter, and Keyvan Kashkooli. "What problems does crowdfunding solve?." *California Management Review* 58.2 (2016): 20-43.

[224] Eakin, Rory. When Raising Capital Online, The Gender Gap is shrinking. 3 June. 2015. CircleUp. https://circleup.com/blog/2015/06/03/when-raising-capital-online-the-gender-gap-is-shrinking/

[225] Greenberg, Amanda. Equity Crowdfunding is Changing the Landscape for Underrepresented Founders. Forbes. 18 May. 2018 https://www.forbes.com/sites/amandagreenberg/2018/05/18/equity-crowdfunding-is-changing-the-funding-landscape-for-underrepresented-founders/#4ca556a27fba

[226] Statista. Crowdfunding. 2018

[227] The Crowdfunding Center. Leading Crowdfunding Platforms Worldwide in 2016, by number of campaigns. Aug. 2017. Statista. www.thecrowdfundingcenter.com

[228] Rubin, Slava. Slava Rubin: How I Started Indiegogo. NextShark. 10 Sep. 2015. https://nextshark.com/indiegogo-ceo-slava-rubin-on-the-three-keys-for-a-successful-crowdfunding-campaign/

[229] https://www.kickstarter.com/projects/ryangrepper/coolest-cooler-21st-century-cooler-thats-actually

[230] Statista; Kickstarter. Most Successfully Completed Kickstarter Projects as of January 2018, based on amount of total funds raised (in million U.S. dollars).

[231] Fiegerman, Seth. The New King of Kickstarter. Mashable. 26 Aug. 2014. https://mashable.com/2014/08/26/kickstarter-coolest-cooler/#7CZm90QkngqJ

[232] Clifford, Catherine. 7 Secrets From the Man Who Turned a Kickstarter Flop Into the Most Successful Campaign Ever. Entrepreneur.com 27 Aug. 2014. https://www.entrepreneur.com/article/236882

[233] https://www.arrow.com/en/indiegogo/program-overview

[234] Rogoway, Mike. Coolest Cooler Settles with Oregon Department of Justice. The Oregonian. 26 Jun. 2017. http://www.oregonlive.com/business/index.ssf/2017/06/coolest_cooler_settles_with_or.html

[235] Schlosser, Kurt. Thousands of Kickstarter Backers Still Waiting on Coolest Cooler May Have to Wait Another 3 Years. GeekWire. 24 June. 2017. https://www.geekwire.com/2017/thousands-kickstarter-backers-still-waiting-coolest-cooler-may-wait-another-3-years/

[236] Mollick, Ethan. Crowdfunding. Coursera.org. https://www.coursera.org/learn/wharton-crowdfunding/home/info

[237] Barnett, Chance. SEC Approves Title III of JOBA Act, Equity Crowdfunding with Non-Accrediteds. Forbes Magazine. 30 Oct. 2015. https://www.forbes.com/sites/chancebarnett/2015/10/30/sec-approves-title-iii-of-jobs-act-equity-crowdfunding-with-non-accredited/2/

[238] Alois, JD. Prominent Group of Fintech Leaders Send Letter to SEC Chair Jay Clayton Demanding an Increase in Regulation Crowdfunding to $20 Million. Crowdfund Insider. 23 Jul. 2018. https://www.crowdfundinsider.com/2018/07/136823-prominent-group-of-fintech-leaders-send-letter-to-sec-chair-jay-clayton-demanding-an-increase-in-regulation-crowdfunding-to-20-million/?utm_source=CCA+Master+List&utm_campaign=64677645ab-

EMAIL_CAMPAIGN_2018_08_08_01_31&utm_medium=email&utm_term=0_b3d336fbcf-64677645ab-712237721

[239] McCarney, Patrick. "False Start: Carving a Niche for Established Small Business Participation in Regulation Crowdfunding Rules Designed for Startups." *Ind. L. Rev.* 51 (2018): 277.

[240] Data Proves Regulation Crowdfunding is a Revenue, Net Income Generator AND a Jobs Engine – What else is our Government and Media Waiting for? Crowdfund Capital Advisers. 31 Jul. 2017. http://crowdfundcapitaladvisors.com/data-proves-regulation-crowdfunding-revenue-net-income-generator-jobs-engine-else-government-media-waiting/

[241] Neiss, Sherwood. Industry tells Securities and Exchange Commission why they should Raise the Regulation Crowdfunding Cap to US$20M. 19 Jul. 2018

[242] Nitani, Miwako, and Allan Riding. "On Crowdfunding Success: Firm and Owner Attributes and Social Networking." (2017).

[243] https://wefunder.com/raise_funding

[244] Statista. Crowdinvesting. May. 2018.

[245] Brown, Ross1, Ross.Brown@st-andrews.ac.uk, et al. "Working the Crowd: Improvisational Entrepreneurship and Equity Crowdfunding in Nascent Entrepreneurial Ventures." *International Small Business Journal: Researching Entrepreneurship*, vol. 36, no. 2, Mar. 2018, pp. 169-193. EBSCO*host*, doi:10.1177/0266242617729743.

[246] Mamonov, Stanislav, and Ross Malaga. "Success factors in Title III equity crowdfunding in the United States." *Electronic Commerce Research and Applications* 27 (2018): 65-73.

[247] Crowdfund Capital Advisors. 4 Aug. 2017 http://crowdfundcapitaladvisors.com/revenue-share-regulation-crowdfunding-profitable-investment-alternative/

[248] Neiss, Sherwood. How Much Does a Regulation Crowdfunding Campaign Actually Cost? Venture Beat. 26 Aug. 2018. https://venturebeat.com/2018/08/26/how-much-does-a-regulation-crowdfunding-campaign-actually-cost/?utm_source=CCLEAR&utm_campaign=3212e538c7-EMAIL_CAMPAIGN_2018_08_21_04_12_COPY_02&utm_medium=email&utm_term=0_3cdffa6ca9-3212e538c7-712237513

[249] clingingsmith, d., & shane, s. (2017). Training aspiring entrepreneurs to pitch experienced investors: evidence from a field experiment in the United States.

[250] John, Daymond. Rise and Grind: Outperform, Outwork, and Outhustle Your Way to a More Successful and Rewarding Life. Random House, LLC. 23 Jan. 2018.

[251] McCollough, Michael A; Devezer, Berna; Tanner, George. An Alternative Format to the Elevator Pitch. The International Journal of Entrepreneurship and Innovation. 1 Feb. 2016. https://doi.org/10.5367/ijei.2016.0211
[252] Your Crowdfunding Video Could be Hurting Your Campaign. Crowdfund Capital Advisers. 9 Jul. 2017.
http://crowdfundcapitaladvisors.com/crowdfunding-video-hurting-campaign/
[253] McSpadden, Kevin. You Now Have a Shorter Attention Span Than a Goldfish. Time Magazine. 14 May. 2015. http://time.com/3858309/attention-spans-goldfish/
[254] Desai, Nihit, Raghav Gupta, and Karen Truong. "Plead or pitch? The role of language in kickstarter project success." (2015).

[255] Mitteness, Cheryl, Richard Sudek, and Melissa S. Cardon. "Angel investor characteristics that determine whether perceived passion leads to higher evaluations of funding potential." *Journal of Business Venturing* 27.5 (2012): 592-606.

[256] Gallo, Carmine. Talk Like TED: The 9 Public-Speaking Secrets of the World's Top Minds. St. Martin's Press. 4 March. 2014.
[257] Greiner, Lori. Invent It, Sell It, Bank It!: Make Your Million-Dollar Idea Into a Reality. Ballantine Books. 11 Mar. 2014
[258] Coyle, Dan. The Culture Code: The Secrets of Highly Successful Groups. Bantam Publishing. 30 Jan. 2018.
[259] Maclauchlin, Cory. Butterfly in the Typewriter: The Tragic Life of John Kennedy Tool and the Remarkable Story of A Confederacy of Dunces. Da Capo Press. Perseus Books Group. 27 Mar. 2012.
[260] Jordison, Sam. A Confederacy of Dunces: A Pulitzer Winner's Struggle to Find a Publisher. The Guardian. 13 Jun. 2017.
https://www.theguardian.com/books/booksblog/2017/jun/13/a-confederacy-of-dunces-a-pulitzer-winners-struggle-to-find-a-publisher
[261] Mother of Author Toole Dies... New York Times. Obituaries. 19 Aug. 1984.
http://www.nytimes.com/1984/08/19/obituaries/mother-author-toole-dies-thelma-ducoing-toole-whose-unflagging-belief-her-son-s.html
[262] Freeman, Michael A.; Johnson, Sheri L.; Staudenmaier, Paige J.; Zisser, Mackenzie R. Are Entrepreneurs 'Touched with Fire'? 17 Apr. 2015.
http://www.michaelafreemanmd.com/Research_files/Are%20Entrepreneurs%20Touched%20with%20Fire%20(pre-pub%20n)%204-17-15.pdf
[263] A Confederacy of Dunces. National Endowment for the Arts.
https://www.arts.gov/article/confederacy-dunces
[264] Stone, Douglas; Heen, Sheila. Thanks for the Feedback: The Science and Art of Receiving Feedback Well. Penguin Book. 4 Mar. 2014.

[265] Stoltzfus, Tony. Coaching Questions: A Coach's Guide to Powerful Asking Skills. Coach 22 Bookstore, LLC. 8 Dec. 2013.
[266] Gallo, Carmine. Steve Jobs Demanded Fearless Feedback and So Should You. Inc. Magazine. 14 June. 2017. https://www.inc.com/carmine-gallo/steve-jobs-demanded-fearless-feedback-and-so-should-you.html
[267] Grimes, Matthew. "The pivot: how founders respond to feedback through idea and identity work." *Academy of Management Journal* ja (2017).

[268] *Plous, Scott (1993), The Psychology of Judgment and Decision Making, p. 233*
[269] Baer, Markus, and Graham Brown. "Blind in one eye: How psychological ownership of ideas affects the types of suggestions people adopt." *Organizational Behavior and Human Decision Processes* 118.1 (2012): 60-71.

[270] Soh, Pek-Hooi, and Elicia Maine. "How Do Entrepreneurs Effectuate in Decision Making? A Prospective Sensemaking Response to Uncertainty." *Paper to be presented at the 35th DRUID Celebration Conference*. 2013.

[271] *Shea, Gordon F. (1997) Mentoring (Rev. Ed.). Menlo Park, CA: Crisp Publications*
[272] EL HALLAM, HORIA & St-Jean, Etienne. (2016). NURTURING ENTREPRENEURIAL LEARNING THROUGH MENTORING. Journal of Developmental Entrepreneurship. 1650012. 10.1142/S1084946716500126.
[273] Woodward, Woody. Why you Need a Mentor and How to Find One. FoxBusiness. 24 Sept. 2012 http://www.foxbusiness.com/features/2012/09/24/why-need-mentor-and-how-to-find-one.html
[274] Small Business Administration. Frequently Asked Questions. https://www.sba.gov/sites/default/files/sbfaq.pdf
[275] MicroMentor. Impact Report 2017. Mercy Corps. 2016 http://solutions.micromentor.org/wp-content/uploads/2017/01/MicroMentor-Impact-Report.pdf
[276] NESTA. A Review of Mentoring Literature and Best Practices. SQW Consulting. Oct. 2009. https://www.nesta.org.uk/publications/review-mentoring-literature-and-best-practice
[277] Bonanos, Christopher. Instant: The Story of Polaroid. Princeton Architectural Press. 10 Aug. 2012.
[278] Arenson, Karen W. N.Y.U Gets $150 Million Gift to Help Lure Top Professors. New York Times. 5 Feb. 2002. https://www.nytimes.com/2002/02/05/nyregion/nyu-gets-150-million-gift-to-help-lure-top-professors.html
[279] Sanchez-Burks, Jeffrey, et al. "Mentoring in Startup Ecosystems." (2017).

[280] Eby, LT; Butts, M; Lockwood, A; Simon, S. Proteges Negative Mentoring Experiences: Construct Development and Nomological Validation. Personnel Psychology, 57(2), 411-447. 2004.
[281] Hallak, Rob, et al. "Firm performance in the upscale restaurant sector: The effects of resilience, creative self-efficacy, innovation and industry experience." *Journal of Retailing and Consumer Services* 40 (2018): 229-240.

[282] Galán, Nely; Garcia, Guy. Self Made: Becoming Empowered, Self-Reliant and Rich in Every Way. Spiegel & Guru Publishing. 31 May. 2016.
[283] St-Jean, Etienne, and Josée Audet. "The effect of mentor intervention style in novice entrepreneur mentoring relationships." *Mentoring & tutoring: partnership in learning* 21.1 (2013): 96-119.

[284] Johansson, Anders W. "How can consultants advise SMEs." *Images of entrepreneurship and small business: emergent swedish contributions to academic research. Lund: Studentlitteratur* (1999): 141-164.

[285] Farrell, Michael B. Care.com, the Big Business of Babysitting: How CEO Sheila Lirio Marcelo persuade Wall Street to bet $91 million on Care.com. 14 Aug. 2014. https://www.bostonglobe.com/magazine/2014/08/14/care-com-big-business-babysitting/4FjpfSq3YUSw3rMn9GraOM/story.html
[286] Sheila Lirio Marcelo.
http://www.toryburchfoundation.org/resources/growth/sheila-lirio-marcelo/
[287] Miller, Claire Cain. Why Women Don't See Themselves as Entrepreneurs. New York Times. 9 Jun. 2017.
https://www.nytimes.com/2017/06/09/upshot/why-women-dont-see-themselves-as-entrepreneurs.html
[288] Bhagwat-Brown, Kash. What's in it for me? The Benefits of Mentoring for the Mentor. 2016. http://www.thefsegroup.com/whats-in-it-for-me-the-benefits-of-mentoring-for-the-mentor/
[289] Johnson, W. Brad; Ridley, Charles R. The Elements of Mentoring. St. Martin's Press. 2 June. 2015
[290] Bennett, Robert J., and Paul JA Robson. "The use of external business advice by SMEs in Britain." *Entrepreneurship & Regional Development* 11.2 (1999): 155-180.
[291] Walker, Lamia. Mentoring for Confidence and Growth. Mentorsme.co.uk. < http://www.mentorsme.co.uk/useful-resources/mentee-case-studies/mentoring-for-confidence-and-growth>
[292] Jack, A. I., Boyatzis, R. E., Khawaja, M. S., Passarelli, A. M., & Leckie, R. L. (2013). Visioning in the brain: An fMRI study of inspirational coaching and mentoring. *Social Neuroscience*, *8*(4), 369-384. DOI: 10.1080/17470919.2013.808259

[293] Buckner, R. L., Andrews-Hanna, J. R. and Schacter, D. L. (2008), *The Brain's Default Network*. Annals of the New York Academy of Sciences, 1124: 1–38. doi:10.1196/annals.1440.011
[294] Immordino-Yang, Mary & McColl, Andrea & Damasio, Hanna & Damasio, Antonio. (2009). Neural Correlates of Admiration and Compassion. Proceedings of the National Academy of Sciences of the United States of America. 106. 8021-6. 10.1073/pnas.0810363106.
[295] Critchley, H. D; Neural Mechanisms of Automatic, Affective and Cognitive Integration. Journal of Comparative Neurology, 493(1), 154-166. 2005. DOI: 10.1002/cne.20749

[296] Audet, Josée, and Paul Couteret. "Coaching the entrepreneur: features and success factors." *Journal of Small Business and Enterprise Development* 19.3 (2012): 515-531.

[297] Maister, David. A; Green, Charles; Galford, Robert. The Trusted Advisor. Free Press Publisher. 25 Sep. 2001.
[298] Patterson, Kerry; Grenny, Joseph, McMillan, Ron; Switzler, Al. Crucial Conversations: Tools for Talking when Stakes are High. McGraw-Hill. 9 Sep. 2011.
[299] Memon, J., Rozan, M. Z. A., Ismail, K., Uddin, M., & Daud, D. (2015). Mentoring an entrepreneur: Guide for a mentor. *SAGE Open, 5*(1) doi:10.1177/2158244015569666
[300] ZANAKIS, S. H., RENKO, M., & BULLOUGH, A. (2012). Nascent entrepreneurs and the transition to entrepreneurship: Why do people start new businesses? *Journal of Developmental Entrepreneurship, 17*(1), 1. doi:10.1142/S108494671250001X
[301] https://www.espn.com/page2/s/list/topcoaches/010518.html
[302] Wooden, John. A Game Plan for Life: The Power of Mentoring. Bloomsbury USA Publishing. 14 Oct. 2009.
[303] Scott, Kim. Radical Candor: Be a Kick-ass Boss without Losing your Humanity. St. Martin's Press. 14 Mar. 2017.
[304] Lupien, Sonia. Well Stressed: Manage Stress Before it Turns Toxic. Wiley Publishing. 2012.
[305] Farashah, Ali Dehghanpour. The Effects of Demographic, Cognitive and Institutional Factors on Development of Entrepreneurial Intention: Toward a Socio-cognitive model of Entrepreneurial Career. Umea School of Business and Economics. Sweden. Springer. 10 Mar. 2015
[306] Brodie, J., Van Saane, S. & Osowska, R. (2017). Help Wanted! Exploring the Value of Entrepreneurial Mentoring at Start-Up. *Industry and Higher Education*. *31*(2), 122-131. doi:10.1177/0950422217691666. ISSN 0950-4222
[307]https://www.newsobserver.com/news/weather/article110917747.html
[308]https://files.nc.gov/ncosbm/documents/files/Florence_Report_Full.pdf

[309] https://ktvq.com/news/trending/2018/09/20/major-preliminary-rainfall-totals-for-hurricane-florence/
[310] Lancer, Natalie; Clutterbuck, David; Megginson, David. Techniques for Coaching and Mentoring. Second Edition. Routledge Publishing. 15 July. 2016

CPSIA information can be obtained
at www.ICGtesting.com
Printed in the USA
BVHW041500120819
555663BV00016B/868/P

9 780578 539775